ECONOMICS IN THE LONG VIEW

Volume 2   Applications and Cases, Part I

Other volumes of this work

ECONOMICS IN THE LONG VIEW

Essays in Honour of W. W. Rostow

Volume 2 APPLICATIONS AND CASES, PART I

Edited by
Charles P. Kindleberger
and
Guido di Tella

First published 1982 by
THE MACMILLAN PRESS LTD
London and Basingstoke
Companies and representatives
throughout the world

ISBN 0 333 32831 0 (volume 2)

ISBN 0 333 32830 2 (volume 1)
ISBN 0 333 32832 9 (volume 3)
ISBN 0 333 33033 1 (the set)

Printed in Hong Kong

Contents

VOLUME 1   MODELS AND METHODOLOGY

VOLUME 2   APPLICATIONS AND CASES, PART I

Note on the Editors

Charles P. Kindleberger, taught at the Massachusetts Institute of Technology from 1948 to 1980, retiring as Ford International Professor of Economics Emeritus; Fellow at the Center for Advanced Study in Behavioral Sciences at Stanford, California. His latest book is *International Money*.

Guido di Tella, Associate Fellow, St Antony's College, Oxford; Professor of Economics, Catholic University, Buenos Aires. Author of, among other books, *Etapas del Desarrollo Económico Argentino* and *Argentina under Perón, 1973–76*.

List of the Contributors

T. C. Barker, Professor of Economic History, University of London.

Sir Alec Cairncross, formerly Master of St Peter's College, University of Oxford.

R. Cameron, William Rand Kenan University Professor of Economics, Emory University.

S. G. Checkland, Professor of Economic History, University of Glasgow; Visiting Fellow, Australian National University, Canberra.

R. Cortés Conde, Senior Research Fellow, Centre for Economic Research, and President of the Instituto Torcuato Di Tella, Buenos Aires.

F. Crouzet, Professor of History, University of Paris–Sorbonne.

E. Dahmén, Professor of Economics and Economic and Social History, Stockholm School of Economics.

C. H. Feinstein, Professor of Economic and Social History, University of York.

R. Findlay, Ragnar Nurkse Professor of Economics, Columbia University, New York.

W. P. Glade, Director, Institute of Latin American Studies and Professor of Economics, University of Texas at Austin.

R. Hall (Lord Roberthall), formerly Economic Adviser to HM Government, United Kingdom.

R. M. Hartwell, Fellow of Nuffield College, University of Oxford.

D. Kendrick, Professor of Economics, University of Texas at Austin.

D. S. Landes, Robert Walton Goelet Professor of French History, Harvard University.

W. A. Lewis, James Madison Professor of Political Economy, Princeton University.

J. Marczewski, Honorary Professor, University of Paris I Panthéon-Sorbonne.

R. M. Marshall, Professor of Economics, University of Texas at Austin, and Secretary of Labour, US Government, 1976–81.

E. S. Mason, University Professor, Emeritus, Harvard University.

R. C. O. Matthews, Master of Clare College and Professor of Political Economy, University of Cambridge.

D. C. North, Professor of Economics, University of Washington.

J. C. Odling-Smee, Senior Economist, International Monetary Fund.

R. de Oliveira Campos, Ambassador of Brazil.

W. N. Parker, Professor of Economics, Yale University.

Sir Michael Postan, sometime Professor of Economic History, University of Cambridge.

C. W. Reynolds, Professor of Economics, Food Research Institute, Stanford University.

Sir Austin Robinson, Professor of Economics, Emeritus, University of Cambridge.

S. B. Saul, Vice-Chancellor, University of York.

P. Temin, Professor of Economics, Massachusetts Institute of Technology.

G. N. von Tunzelmann, Lecturer in Economic History, University of Cambridge and Fellow of St John's College, Cambridge.

Preface

This collection of essays in economic history is intended to honour W. W. Rostow for his outstanding contribution to this discipline over more than forty years. The editors are a former colleague in the Office of Strategic Services, the Department of State, the Massachusetts Institute of Technology and, for one term, at the University of Texas at Austin: Charles P. Kindleberger; and Guido di Tella, a former student of Rostow's at MIT who wrote his first book under his aegis.

Most leading economic historians have come across Rostow's imaginative ideas and opinions, and quite significantly have considered it necessary to come into the discussion, either to support, complement or contradict them. Few have been able to ignore them. As the chapters in the three volumes will show, the contributors from all over the world do not necessarily agree with Professor Rostow's views on economic history, or for that matter on anything else, as they pay tribute to his originality, significance and productivity which have stimulated enormously the historiography on business cycles, economic growth and long-term trends.

This compilation is divided, roughly and arbitrarily, into a first volume on Models and Methodology, and another two on Applications and Cases. A chronological order has been attempted in dividing Volume 2 (pre-First World War) and Volume 3 (post-First World War).

The editors were distressed to learn of Sir Michael Postan's death in December 1981 as the proofs of Volume 1 were being read; they feel a special debt of gratitude to him for his contribution of an appreciation of Rostow's intellectual background and personal development, as well as an evaluation of his main and most important production as an economic historian. From this essay we get a clear picture of Rostow the man and of Rostow the economic historian and social scientist: a personal and indeed welcome introduction to this *Festschrift*, based on information supplied by Dean Elspeth Rostow.

The next three chapters in Volume 1 are by D. C. North,

R. Cameron and S. G. Checkland. They point out the need for economic historians to make use of a broader set of theoretical tools beyond those provided by neo-classical economics. D. C. North stresses the significance of current research in demography, ideology, technological and institutional change, and the way it is transforming economic history, shifting it away from the biases built in the previously narrower approach. This new approach carries over from cliometrics the quantitative method and the rigorous use and testing of hypothesis: by broadening the framework it makes economic history more congenial to the traditional historian, and offers the potential of explaining a vast range of historical observations that could not be accounted for within the compass of neo-classical theory.

In the same vein R. Cameron emphasises the need to expand the scope of our analysis if we are to understand the inter-relationship of population, resources and technology in the process of economic growth, stressing the fact that the economy is conditioned by social institutions, embodying values and attitudes. In the past institutional innovation has been at least as responsible as technological change for the economic transformation of Europe, and can still – hopefully – face the challenges posed by the present demographic upsurge in the world and by the energy shortage.

S. G. Checkland's essay is an attempt to analyse the role of the state in the long-term theory of growth, a subject that brings him to delve in the intimate but not necessarily direct relationship between the state and the stage of growth attained. Three different levels of analysis are explored: universalism based upon the nation-state, an insistence on the degree of national uniqueness, and finally a view rising above the nation-states to some kind of structure of world interaction. If brought together in a new synthesis these can throw light on the intricate problem of the role of the state in the process of growth.

While economic historians may benefit from an extended approach, P. Temin underlines the changes that have taken place within the realm of economic analysis. The economic depression in the first place, the post-World War expansion in the second instance and, more recently, the worldwide inflationary process (accounting for the revival of the more orthodox monetary theories) have had a tremendous bearing on economic theory. While this is generally acknowledged, a different strand is pointed out, of a less orthodox flavour, stemming from some of Keynes's psychological insights and from the behaviourist assumptions of Duesenberry and Simon which throw light on some peculiar but relevant aspects of human conduct. The *homo economicus*, free of restrictions, may not, after all, be the best and most relevant paradigm.

R. M. Hartwell, W. A. Lewis, E. S. Mason and R. de Oliveira Campos move on to the problem that has concerned many economic historians, W. W. Rostow in particular, i.e. the nature, constraints and characteristics of the long-term process of growth. R. M. Hartwell discusses parallelism and divergence in 'historical perspective', by which he means the very long run. For some economic historians the long run is the twenty years of the Kuznets cycle, for others the fifty years of the Kondratieff cycle. Hartwell seeks to push beyond these limits to explore the rise, fall, and occasional failures to move of civilisation, which give the result progress and dissimilarity.

W. A. Lewis in turn analyses the major constraints to growth in mature economies, questioning some of the standard answers (the low savings ratio, the inelasticities in the supply of labour, the lack of natural resources or the scarcity of foreign exchange, entrepreneurship and technology) forcefully arguing that the ultimate constraint is the ability of the institutional system to absorb change in an orderly fashion.

Most fittingly, E. S. Mason and R. de Oliveira Campos deal with the stages approach. Mason stresses the insights into the process of growth contributed by Rostow, both in his *Stages of Economic Growth* and in *The World Economy*, but questions whether the historical examples in the latter provide enough evidence to support the sharp demarcations suggested in the first book, and reveals a more continuous, persistent and cumulative process of growth than the stages theory would lead us to believe.

R. de Oliveira Campos's essay appraises the take-off approach from the point of view of the developing countries, for which purpose he deems it necessary to study the interaction between economics and politics. Rapid growth increases social mobilisation, increasing political demands, thus putting strains on the political system. Instead of being rectilinear, the process appears as an adventure threatened by deadlocks. This author's views are a remarkable example of the new wave of scepticism about growth promoting in a straightforward manner democracy and political stability, at least during the course of the crucial transformation from a developing to a fully developed society.

The chapter by Sir Austin Robinson reflects in turn the increasing scepticism regarding the benefits of rapid industrialisation programmes for new countries, while it puts forward the alternative of an agriculture-led strategy. This alternative is not problem-free, mainly because of the danger of accumulating food surpluses, the risk of benefits failing to filter down and a possible increase in the rate of population growth. Such a strategy, being the more decentralised, is prone to greater administrative problems than the more centralised industrial alternative. Still, in Robinson's view it is an appealing path that many new countries may find worth while exploring.

The first volume is closed by chapters by R. Findlay, C. W. Reynolds, and Guido di Tella, all former students of Rostow. They deal with the connection between trade, rents and growth. Findlay's analysis of the trade–growth nexus in the formative period of the Industrial Revolution points out that the causal arrow must run from growth – in the form of technological change in the manufacturing sector – to trade, rather than the other way round assumed by most of the literature on the subject. But even if the 'manna from heaven' nature of technological progress has to be supplemented, the least that can be said is that trade and growth are inextricably intertwined during the first take-off process known to the world.

Reynolds recalls the Prebisch–Singer terms of trade argument of the 1950s, and remarks the drastic change brought about by the post-1973 rises in the price of oil which resulted in an equally drastic change in the pattern and allocation of the world's economic rent. An attempt is made to measure not only the natural resources-based rent but the other two as well, i.e. the one emerging from market imperfections, source of 'protection' rents, and the one stemming from entrepreneurship, source of the so-called 'innovation' rent. Di Tella ends the first volume with an analysis of the impact of the discovery of new resources on the expansion of the world economy, particularly in the nineteenth century. He distinguishes two different kinds of economic frontier expansions, a less dynamic equilibrium version, and a more dynamic, more equilibrium version, allegedly more relevant to the cases in question. As in the previous contributions, these resources-based rents are put into a more ample perspective, where accumulation and growth are consequences of the strive for non-normal profits by Schumpeterian-styled entrepreneurs.

The second volume deals mainly with specific cases and applications, embracing several centuries and diverse countries in different continents, mostly ordered in a chronological sequence up to the First World War. The volume is relevantly opened by W. N. Parker's views on the European process of development from the standpoint of what he calls a millennial perspective. He selects three different, stylised relationships: the traditional, near subsistence, Malthusian society; the commercial, trade-oriented, expansive Smithian society, free from the limits imposed by the national market on the division of labour; and the capitalist, Schumpeterian society, engaged in a process of creative destruction. The three dominate four particular stages, but are present throughout, their interaction throwing light on the process of growth.

W. P. Glade digs into the roots of the industrialisation process in Latin America, going back to colonial times. Despite the emphasis placed on trade, there is no doubt that the bulk of the goods consumed in the American colonies were produced on the west of the Atlantic. He traces the spread and original organisation of colonial industry, analysing the various reasons which impeded their becoming the springboard to nineteenth-century industrialisation, i.e. the effective insulation from competition and foreign technical knowledge, an insulation that took them further and further away from the European type of evolution.

F. Crouzet's essay explores some aspects of the triangular relationship between the United States, Britain and France between 1793 and 1814, pointing out how, as a consequence of the European War, the United States, a relatively small and new country – by European standards – found itself propelled as a sea-trading power to be reckoned with. This new role was reversed after 1814 when the United States turned away from high-sea ventures and towards 'internal improvements', something not too different from what took place in some European cases: France, Prussia and Belgium. Its power was still to be reckoned with, but its international role receded at least until the middle of the century.

D. S. Landes's detailed account of the French liberation loan of 1871 illuminates the financial conditions prevailing in Europe at the time, showing the limitations that even triumphant powers have in exacting compensation from the vanquished, an experience repeated to some extent the other way round after the First World War. It also shows how the business and financial sectors of both countries vied to take advantage of the loan that had to be issued, with a substantially independent attitude from their respective governments.

S. B. Saul explores in his chapter the peculiarities of a group of small European countries in the nineteenth century. Some special traits are found among such apparently diverse countries as Belgium, Denmark, the Netherlands, Norway, Sweden and Switzerland. They exhibited a greater homogeneity which allowed them to make more easily the necessary social adjustments to take advantage of the new technologies and the changing patterns of trade. Fewer interests had to be reconciled and a more rational economic policy resulted out of this. They were forced, because of their small home markets, to specialise and explore the foreign ones, where they did not find much resistance because of their small significance. These countries had indeed many limitations which are the ones usually pointed out, but in being small they had as well many advantages: as Saul says, 'the importance of being unimportant'.

R. Cortés Conde's analysis of Italian migration from 1880 to 1913 notes the economic determinants of this very intense process and finds a high correlation between the higher level of income in the new American countries, north and south, the result of their higher productivity. The lagged total and average level of remittances are taken as an effective measure of the immigrant's capacity to earn, save and remit. Economic reasons were not the only ones behind these human waves, but they certainly played a crucial and quantifiable role.

T. C. Barker deals with a subject quite in line with Rostow's chief preoccupations, i.e. the role of the new methods of transportation during the nineteenth and early twentieth centuries. While many historians have written extensively about railways, surprisingly few have done so on the spread of motor vehicles, arguably a process which has had an even greater impact not only in transportation, but also in the way of living. The chapter by Barker fills this void, focusing especially on the situation attained before the First World War, more significant than at times is conceded.

The chapter by C. H. Feinstein, R. C. O. Matthews and J. C. Odling-Smee, which closes the second volume, deals with a subject already studied by Rostow in *The British Economy in the Nineteenth Century*. The authors make a new and up-to-date appraisal of the available figures for the 1873–1914 period, both in global and in sectoral terms, which tend to indicate that the alleged retardation of the British economy did not start around 1873, but that it took place only after 1899. An analysis of the productivities of the various factors and sectors is made, where labour and capital productivity can be seen to move in such a way as not to affect total factor productivity, while agriculture and mining can be seen as the main factors influencing the fall in total productivity, joined by manufacturing after 1899.

G. N. von Tunzelmann opens the third volume, which deals with applications and cases for the post-First World War period, with an analysis of the structural change and the role of leading sectors in British manufacturing from 1907 to 1968, questioning the reasons given for the sluggishness of the British inter-war performance, attributed by Rostow to the delay to move from steel, chemicals, and electricity to the typical mass consumption industries: automobiles, plastics, electronics and aeronautics. Von Tunzelmann concludes that the 'shift effect' of resource allocation among sectors was much less important in explaining productivity growth than the internal effect within sectors. Moreover the belief that a structural shift towards the new industries explains the coexistence of high, economy-wide growth rates and high unemployment in the 1930s does not seem to be substantiated.

E. Dahmén's analysis of Sweden's recent industrial development crisis endeavours to merge the conventional macro approach with historical research, utilising a conceptual frame of reference of a neo-Schumpeterian and Austrian type. A sketch of the general economic developments is made, including an account of what most analysts made of macromodelling with broad aggregates, and what this leads them to believe. This kind of analysis disguised some of the major changes that took place particularly in the mid-1960s, a crucial break in the development process, something which would have been detected through a more detailed and disaggregated analysis and a more adequate and broader frame of reference.

D. Kendrick studies the shift in emphasis which is occurring in the macroeconomic paradigm in the US: a shift from the demand to the supply side. This shift is causing a change from aggregative economics, to analysis of the problems in certain sectors and certain regions. This shift calls for a new organisation of the data for the US economy as the ones presently available are organised in aggregative terms for similarly organised econometric models. Insufficient attention is paid to sectors, to the location of economic activity, and to the relationships between economic data. The main purpose of the paper is to explore a new method of organising US economic data, the so-called 'relational database approach'.

R. M. Marshall's concerns refer to the slowing down in productivity growth already detected in the US economy during the 1970s. While recent studies have attempted to find the reasons for this evolution – the shift towards a service economy, the demographic changes in the labour force, the slower growth of investment, the sharp rise in energy prices, the increase in government regulations, and the reduced spending on research – much remains unexplained. One reason is that conventional quantitative techniques fail to capture important behavioural and dynamic forces underlying the productivity process, i.e. individual and national values, relations between workers and management, systems within which workers and enterprises function, and institutional and governmental behaviour. An understanding of these factors must be integrated with traditional resource availability analysis to explain changes in productivity, a statement quite in line with some of the statements made in the first chapters of Volume 1.

We have made one exception in our chronological ordering with Charles P. Kindleberger's contribution, since his subject is very much akin to the one studied by Sir Alec Cairncross. Kindleberger's paper comparing the resumption of gold payments in Britain in 1819 with the restoration of the pound to par in 1925 follows in his tradition of comparative economic history, and is addressed especially to Professor Rostow's expressed view that monetary questions, and the level of sophistication in dealing with them, were less significant before the First World War than after it.

The last three contributions by Sir Alec Cairncross, Lord Roberthall and J. Marczewski deal with shorter-term problems in relatively recent times. Cairncross analyses the traumatic devaluation of sterling in 1949, indeed a turning-point in British economic policy. A detailed narrative of events is made, so as to help the understanding of the conditions and expectations prevailing at the time. This squarely leads to the issue of whether the pressures that led to devaluation were ephemeral, reversible and resistible, or how far they were enduring and likely to be cumulative. An appraisal of the effects of devaluation is obscured by the outbreak of the Korean war, which set the world economy out of balance. However, the wisdom of the decision has to be measured not just in terms of its effectiveness, but also in terms of its appropriateness given the circumstances, and how correctly these were appreciated.

In his chapter Lord Roberthall analyses the British economic performance since the Second World War. The high hopes of overcoming the depression and unemployment in the pre-war years were reasonably successful until the early 1970s, despite an increasing and ominous pressure on the price level. Since 1973, developments in the world and in the UK have been quite different: the outside world has been less benign and the ability of the British economy to adapt has indeed been diminished, while the power and the willingness of the trades unions to exercise it has augmented. The consequences have been felt in increases in the rate of inflation and in the rate of unemployment, reaching figures comparable to all but the worst years of the Depression.

J. Marczewski's paper closes Volume 3, making a comparative analysis of stagflation in France and Germany over the last decade: 1971–9. The analysis is made in quantitative terms starting with the inflationary gap in total resources, followed by that of the structure and evolution of the inflationary gap of costs in France and Germany, which shows a striking similarity. Labour costs, income from property and entrepreneurship, taxes on production (less subsidies), and imports are assessed as contributing to the inflationary gap in costs. A similar analysis is made of the inflationary gap on expenditures, household's consumption and capital formation, enterprises' capital formation, public expenditures and exports. These analyses allow an evaluation of the causes which lie behind the stagflation of these countries and of the world at large.

Volume 3 ends with a bibliography of W. W. Rostow's major works, which unfortunately had to leave aside the long list of articles and addresses, some of them extracurricular, extremely indicative of the evolution of Rostow's thinking.

The editors would like to thank the contributors for their warm response and for their patience in face of the insistence in meeting deadlines. They would also like to thank Lois Nivens for her help in the compilation of the bibliography, and Celia Szusterman for her help in the editing of the three volumes.

1981   C. P. K.
                                                                 G. di T.

1 European Development in Millennial Perspective

W. N. PARKER

All history-writing, whether Ranke's or Rostow's, is a stylisation of the infinity of facts, and all theorising on history is a stylisation of the infinity of relationships among them. Over the past twenty-five years, in teaching the economic history of Europe to graduate students in economics, I have selected three stylised relationships as the core around which to assemble the record. (It is well known that three, being the number of observable dimensions in our human world, is the largest number which people can hold simultaneously in their minds; a science which rests on three factors of production should appreciate the point.)

The groups of relations around which I assemble each year the facts of European economic history bear each the name of a notable economic theorist: Malthus, Smith, and Schumpeter. Malthus is taken to symbolise the evident truth: that a population, reproducing biologically, has the potential of outrunning its food supply. Smith symbolises the notion that the extent of the market limits the division of labour, and that over history the extension of the market raises the limits on the division of labour, producing through scale economies and specialisation higher levels of productivity. Schumpeter is a name for capitalist expansion, deriving from continuous – though fluctuating – technological change and innovation, financed by the extension of credit.

It should be noted at once that these three expansionary processes are not conceived wholly as stages, and do not follow each other in linear sequence over the historical record. All three are tendencies, continuously active. Nevertheless, it is apparent that in the period before 1750, the Malthusian tendency is very strong – before 1500, probably dominant. Between 1500 and 1900, it is overlaid by the

Smithian tendency, yielding productivity growth with growth of trade. And after 1770, or thereabouts, Schumpeter's cast step forward on the stages and the ceaseless transformation of production functions, with its accompanying 'creative destruction', takes over the leading role. The three processes then are themes of the complex opera of history, each dominating a successive Act, but on stage throughout, swelling up together in a happy nineteenth-century trio, and moving together in the world today into – who knows what grand finale.

A sketch of the operation of these processes over history, then, demands not only a simple statement of their essential character, but also an analysis of:

(1) how each came to dominate history in certain periods and to be subordinate in others;
(2) how the transitions from a Malthusian to a Smithian to a Schumpeterian dominance occurred;
(3) what exogenous forces, or processes from political or intellectual history – not readily interpreted in economic or even social terms – impinged to release or to restrict their movement;
(4) what feed-backs occurred from the later Smithian and Schumpeterian processes to the Malthusian population phenomena, and from the Schumpeterian technological change to Smithian trade expansion and market growth.

This paper can offer no more than the merest sketch of the history conceived in these terms. Rostow may see in my three-process schema three of his five-stage schema – the Malthusian traditional society, the Smithian preconditions and the Schumpeterian drive to maturity. But perhaps none of us in European economic history does much more than warm over the three revolutions, agricultural, commercial, industrial – as Lillian Knowles (1926) and Paul Mantoux (1961) present them – but with a little modern spicing.[1] But my schema moves into the present and future, I think, in a rather different direction from the others' and the present paper, moving sketchily over the terrain, tries to follow it there.

MALTHUSIAN PROCESSES IN HISTORY[2]

Malthus and his poor we have always with us. Human society, like that of every other species, runs continuously the danger of excessive population growth, and a history, if not a social policy, can be organised around 'escapes' from it. In Western Europe, there is some historical evidence that widespread population growth occurred, initially stimulating and ultimately dangerous, in the thirteenth and early fourteenth centuries and again in the sixteenth, with the modern rise beginning in the mid- to late-eighteenth century. As a mnemonic, one might accept a rough dating of every third century – the thirteenth, the sixteenth and the nineteenth – as periods of general population rise and the intervening centuries as periods either of disaster (the fourteenth and in Germany the early seventeenth) or of stagnation or merely localised rise (the fifteenth, seventeenth and parts of the eighteenth and twentieth).

There are two problems in such a dating, or in using population trends as a basis of much economic change in these periods. One is that the data on the periods of growth are not very good. The estimates still rest – I believe – largely on the work of Beloch (Beloch, 1900) for 1600 as the centrepoint, on Russell's researches (Russell, 1948) based on the English poll tax of 1377, on Levasseur's collection of contemporary French estimates (Levasseur, 1898, p. 288), and on the early nineteenth century census benchmarks (Reinhard, 1968, Ch. 7–13). Recently local studies of parish records back into the seventeenth century and archaeological evidence of the extent of city walls and margins of cultivation have given the tale some local colour.[3] To use the evidence of rising relative prices of food as evidence for population growth in the thirteenth and sixteenth centuries, and then to attribute that price behaviour solely to population growth is too immediately circular a mode of reasoning to be persuasive. But surely it is fair to feel – as Postan has – that those price movements help to confirm other evidence of a rising trend.

The second problem is whether the limit – if there is one – in the intervening centuries is indeed 'Malthusian'. Is it over-population in some meaningful sense which produces the catastrophe of the fourteenth century and the stagnation (or worse) of the seventeenth, and is it an agricultural restraint which northwest Europe bursts through, or wriggles out of, after 1750? Unquestionably there is short-run sensitivity to local harvest failures. And it does seem inherently plausible that a thicker population is weakened as it presses on food supplies, and is carried off disproportionately more readily by communicable disease and military depradations. But one must admit that it is far from totally clear that the checks that appear are a result of excessive human fecundity rather than wars, climate changes or the random incidence of disease. Perhaps that is all we know and all we need to know.[4]

A MECHANISM FOR THE TRANSITION

An interpretation of economic change from 1300 to 1700 need not rest in any case strongly on strictly Malthusian assumptions. If the mere rough dating of the population rises is accepted, some interesting questions form: that is, why the difference in the population's economic and social behaviour in the three periods? Why did not the expansion of the sixteenth century follow on the thirteenth century peak of medieval expansion? Why was Europe condemned to 150 years of plagues and wars before the Renaissance and the Discoveries? And why then did the industrial and agrarian changes of the post 1770 years not come at once, without the intervening wretchedness, ferment and wars of the seventeenth and early eighteenth centuries? The answer to all such questions is of course that history takes time. In a world of instantaneous adjustment, the modern world – indeed the future itself – would have sprung full blown from the Garden of Eden. Time is required for the parts of the total historical process to unfold, to follow their separate paths and to come together in just the concatenation that produces a particular historical event.

A population on the land can increase at increasing returns, even without trade and specialisation or more intensive cultivation techniques, if movement is into better new areas rather than on to poorer land, as Ricardo had assumed. But it is fairly clear that such a spread of an agricultural population in Europe, which occurred after about 5000 B.C. had come to an end by A.D. 1200. In western Europe there were no surprises in store – only the cutting down of more woodland, movement into highlands, and the draining of marshes. The evidence of pollen samples, dated from soundings in marginal areas, as interpreted by Slicher van Bath (1963, p. 117), seems to show periods when the margin of cultivation of the grains moved back and forth over the poorer land – presumably in response to changing population pressure. It is sufficient, moreover, for a transition from a Malthusian to a Smithian dynamic that the population growth be accompanied by an increase in the total volume of agricultural production above subsistence, that is in the absolute, if not the per capita size of the real, or potential agricultural 'surplus'.[5] If this increase occurs without any pressure on agricultural producers to create and give up – in rents, taxes, or trade – their surplus above subsistence, then the population growth increases the absolute amount of idle rural labour, that is a surplus not exploited either by lords or by the market, but potentially available nonetheless to be worked either in more intensive cultivation on the land, or to move into employment off the land, depending on the returns and opportunities for employment.

Now if a political or economic mechanism for extracting agricultural goods and labour is available, the supplies added or realisable by a growing population above its subsistence are available to enter into trade or production outside agriculture and so to increase the absolute volume of trade and non-agricultural output. Or if the agricultural population retains title to and control over its labour and the fruits thereof, this 'surplus' is available as a broadly based market for non-farm output. Population growth under conditions of not too sharply diminishing returns, that is with marginal product in excess of subsistence greater than zero, increases the total incomes of the class of receivers of rents, tithes, taxes and the like (though individual incomes in their class depend upon its rate of increase as well – since the Malthusian principle knows no class boundaries) and with it, the market for their 'luxuries', as well as the potential market for the cruder goods consumed in peasant households. Whether this latter market demand is realised and becomes effective depends on how hard the lords and tax-gatherers press on the peasantry and on whether merchants can penetrate into the countryside to bring to life latent patterns of peasant demand.

If then trade and non-agricultural production can occur in this situation under conditions of increasing returns (the Smithian dynamic) or in some sort of built-in sequence of endogenous technological change (the Schumpeterian dynamic) population growth induces productivity growth and possibly, depending on the net result of the movements in agricultural and non-agricultural productivity, higher total per capita incomes in the economy as a whole. And if the growth of trade and the availability of industrial or imported products occurs in products and places that can call out the 'potential surplus', that is tempt peasants to work harder, then a mechanism to produce a rising output is operative, to be checked only as the effects of diminishing returns in agriculture (or of some exogenous factor) slows down or reverses the population growth.

INCREASING RETURNS IN TRADE

Is it possible that the expansion of local and overseas trade in the sixteenth and seventeenth centuries, and the industrial growth accompanying this expansion, met with increasing returns? Why should this occur?

It is possible to conceive of several sources. First, there is the standard source of increasing returns: the spreading of fixed costs. River ports and harbours, docks and ships, warehouses and the knowledge of sea lanes – are large items of fixed capital. As their use expanded in Italy in the sixteenth century, in the United Provinces in the seventeenth century and in England in the late seventeenth and eighteenth centuries, per unit costs presumably fell. D. C. North (1958), and R. Davis (1962), well detailed the fall in shipping costs that accompanied the expansion of shipping in the eighteenth and early nineteenth centuries, the elimination of over-capacity and empty back-hauls that accompanied the increased complexity of shipping routes and the greater variety of products to be shipped. The advent of navies, the elimination of piracy, the greater capacity of merchant vessels which could forego the need for armament – these effects of the larger scale of mercantile activity were all present in the expansion of the late eighteenth and early- to mid-nineteenth centuries. May they not also to a degree have been present in the sixteenth? Still it must be admitted that the whole scale of trade in the sixteenth and seventeenth centuries relative to the mass of local agricultural production was minuscule, except for the shipment of eastern European grain through the Sound to the Netherlands and beyond. It seems likely that these shipments furnished the bulk of the Dutch urban grain requirements (de Vries, 1976, p. 161) – not as much as the world furnished England after 1850, but still a lot. Apart from grain, textiles, and timber, the trade – to Spain, France and England, the East – was a trade in 'luxuries'.

Nevertheless, such a trade is not to be despised by the historian infected though he may be by the sensitivity of a democratic and egalitarian age. It is through the trade in luxuries that capitalism enters European agrarian society. The ferment that began with the Crusades and was checked by the crises of the fourteenth and fifteenth centuries bubbles up again in the Renaissance (Postan, 1952; Lopez, 1952). The commodities available through trade – fine textiles, spices, precious metals and metal wares – fitted well the structure of demand in a Europe where, despite gains made by the French peasantry through the labour shortage of the fifteenth century, the rate of exploitation by lords, church and royal courts was high.

Before the growth of 'plantations', and the sugar, tobacco and slave trade of the late seventeenth and eighteenth centuries, the discoveries and overseas trade produced increasing returns in European trade more through their effect in establishing capitalist institutions and practices and supporting centralised state power than directly through the cheapening of luxury goods. Here the scale of state demand may have brought Adam Smith's celebrated principles of organisation into play. The luxury demand, the demand of courts and states was hardly a standardised demand for mass manufactures; a large part of it was a demand for rather simple labour – soldiers, seamen, servants, and construction workers – and above these for 'officials' – tax-gatherers, estate managers, overseers and military officers. But a demand for artisan labour in fairly standard categories accompanied this – for cloth workers, masons, carpenters, tool makers, metal workers, clock-makers, mint masters, book makers, and copiers. And there was a demand for services more properly labelled 'bourgeois', that is the skilled trades – entertainers, academics, artists, actors, doctors, lawyers, and at last businessmen (or at least men of business), bankers, notaries, money changers, enterprisers of all sorts, merchants.[6] None of these trades was new. Trevor-Roper (1967, p. 74) emphasised the growth of a market in courts and administrative centres as well as in the medieval cities – now somewhat eclipsed. The important fact was the new scale on which they all functioned and were demanded. That scale brought division of labour in trades and business services, and it made the provision of overhead capital and institutions – universities, law courts, a civil bureaucracy, and Army – worthwhile. Centralisation made governments stronger – in Philip II's Spain, Henry VIII's England, the France of Richelieu and Mazarin, even in the 'United' Provinces. Did it make them all richer? Did it make for a more efficient utilisation of the surplus extracted from a growing population on the land?[7] In addition to economies of scale in the spreading of fixed physical and insti-tutional (or transactional) costs, the phenomenon of diffusion also occurs – the spreading of arts and knowledge, the imitation at one point of what has always been done and known at another. A third source of growth is regional specialisation on a pan-European scale. Outside of agriculture, can this have been important? Wallerstein (1974, Ch. 4) at least emphasises the economies of centralisation and localisation in financial markets.[8]

The price movements of the late sixteenth and early seventeenth centuries are the salient feature in this history. Once again as in the fourteenth century, the terms of trade turned against industry – and in the midst of a general price inflation. There is indicated here both a growing population pressure and a relatively rapid growth in productivity outside of agriculture. The shift is usually interpreted as rising agricultural prices; but it is also a case of relatively falling industrial prices. And indeed if the surplus from the land is being extracted and commercialised more effectively, peasants might go hungry, but why should supplies on commercial markets be short? And how could the vast new demand for non-agricultural products be satisfied at falling prices, except by appreciable productivity improvements?[9]

This brings us to the final question of technological change in Nef's Industrial Revolution of the sixteenth century (Nef, 1932, 1934).[10] It is evident that some stirrings of technical change were felt – in mining, in metallurgy, and these were responding to a growing demand for metals, and in England for coal. The water wheel was put to more intensive use in milling, fulling and iron working, and with the ribbon loom and the stocking frame, even textile operations were touched at two very specialised points (Usher, 1954, pp. 277–84).

The increase in minting, with royal coinages, utilised the stamping and pressing operations on which Gutenberg drew. So industrial techniques – in ships, firearms, clocks, scientific instruments – improved, but the body of improvement, lacking a new power source or any immense cheapening in raw materials, did not create a wholly new technology or set in motion a self-propelling sequence of technical change.

AGRICULTURAL IMPROVEMENT

To produce a sustained dynamic, it is not enough that the Smithian process of trade expansion should produce growing productivity in trade and industry, a growing middle class demand for large-scale industrial products, or laws and behaviour patterns that facilitate business activity. The Malthusian demon is not yet laid to rest; it requires either 'moral restraint', or increases in agricultural supplies, or both in some combination. I indicated above how some increases in agricultural productivity could occur simply via the expansion of distant trade. Surely the major effect was by regional specialisation such that agricultural regions best suited to grow a crop were put in touch with its markets. The trouble with this is that in times of high transport costs, and uneven distribution of factors, the natural cost differentials of different regions due to natural causes are smothered under transport cost differentials and inter-regional differences in factor proportions. This effect of trade carried on into the nineteenth century, when the world's agricultural regions took their current shape. It increased the world's food supplies after land and ocean transport costs had fallen and capital and labour had spread into new areas, which could outcompete the old. The second effect of trade on agriculture was the diffusion of seeds, stock and techniques. Here the New World's corn and potatoes come into play after the mid-eighteenth century, but in the earlier centuries, nothing of importance is evident.

Trade and urbanisation in the seventeenth and eighteenth centuries do appear to have made inroads on rural underemployment by fostering the growth of rural industries, inducing peasants to work harder and farm more intensively, giving incentive for improvement and specialisation of livestock breeds, and stimulating some steps in the so-called agricultural revolution, that is the conversion of the 3-field system rotation to a system of continuous cropping with sowing or planting of the fallow in cover or root crops. This increased the productivity of land both directly and by the additional fertiliser supplies provided, and the latter at least increased the productivity of the labour in tasks which are fixed per acre. Slicher van Bath shows that in England and the Netherlands yield-seed ratios rose, and on the Continent, a technique of immense reserve capacity was made known and readied for use in the real population expansion of the nineteenth century (van Bath, 1963, p. 280; Jones, 1974, Ch. 2, p. 34).

More important still, the improvements – at least those related to livestock – seem not to have been forced out of the system by population pressure from below – as Boserup's model suggests (Boserup, 1965) – but to have been pulled out by an urban and middle-class demand of high income elasticity. Here then is the 'breather' which population growth may have given at least to England in the decades around 1700 to have allowed incomes and living standards to rise to levels sufficient to form a broader demand for the industrial goods of the Industrial Revolution (John, 1965; Jones, 1974, Ch. 4).

A last element that distinguished the trade and overseas markets of the eighteenth century from their medieval composition in the age of the Discoveries is of course the slave trade, the products of colonial 'plantations', the early exploitation of the surplus, supplies and vast peasant demand of India, and the reproduction of a whole new urban trading society in the west of England ports, Southampton, Bristol and finally Liverpool as sugar, tobacco and colonial cotton enter as the staples, along with New England's fish and timber. I have not seen the weighting of this in England's total trade before 1800, but from 1720 on it is clearly important in its own right as market as well as a source of movable merchandise and liquid wealth for a mercantile class.[11]

THE TRANSITION TO ECO-TECHNIC CHANGE

At this point, that is about 1750, a truly new element enters the scene. It must appear if we are to furnish an answer to the question: why did the collection of iron, machinery, and power inventions that we call the Industrial Revolution not come into existence in the upswing of the sixteenth and early seventeenth centuries at the time of Nef's Industrial Revolution? The answer, I think, is in two parts and both go deeply into the attitudes and organisation that underlie economic change. The first is signified, though much too simply, by what historians call the growth of science; the second, again, by economies of scale and communication. Let me elaborate each a little more fully to indicate the point at which they fused into the single phenomenon, the Industrial Revolution.

Every freshman survey of European history identifies the late sixteenth and the seventeenth centuries with the real beginnings of experimental science and that joint development of both empiricism and rationalism that together have provided western man's understanding of nature and his ephemeral illusion of control over nature which made possible nineteenth and twentieth century expansion and destruction. The rationalism, model-building, exact reasoning from assumed premises has been present as an element in western thought at least since Euclid. It is a human propensity that expressed itself in sixteenth century theology no less than in mathematics. What is sometimes forgotten is that empiricism – fumbling trial and error with a vague goal in mind, observation sharpened by keen perception of needs, or simply random mutation selected for survival by a cruel physical or social environment – these activities of the mind and senses have been around even longer. No defined theory of mechanics guided the shaping of the first stone axe. It came, we must conceive, as an intuitive extension of the use of an unshaped or accidentally axe-shaped natural stone. Altogether the neolithic revolution took at least 5000 years to work out the basic techniques in agriculture and the industrial arts accompanying farming – ceramics, weaving, and metallurgy. And another 4000 years were required for these arts and techniques to spread over the globe from their one or several sources of origin. But only the three centuries that include Newton, Lavoisier, Priestley, Faraday, Liebig and Mendel *et hoc genus omne* has been needed to develop techniques that allowed scientists to analyse these processes in the laboratory, and mental constructs that gave predictable control over them. The reasons are clear: (1) experiment done consciously in the presence of statistical controls and interlaced with a continuing effort to frame valid theory is a vastly more powerful tool than random discovery; (2) the application of science not only to basic discovery but to communication of the results, in a world society directed consciously toward similar goals of material progress, produces a vastly enlarged scale on which even random trial and error takes place. The result is a greatly accelerated rate of useful, or dangerous, discoveries about nature.

Why the rationalistic and the experimental impulses of human thought and behaviour began to join in the seventeenth century into a method that, despite vagueness and ridiculous extremes in its early stages, grew into nineteenth and twentieth century scientific and engineering research is a subject, I would insist, in intellectual history, not to be reduced to a socio-economic explanation except by a really crude and insensitive mind. Both the scientific impulse and the impulse to modern capitalism derive from, or were immensely strengthened by, the materialism and the individualistic humanism that we see displayed in Renaissance literature and art – the element that distinguishes fifteenth-century culture so start-lingly from the twelfth and thirteenth. But since early history is full of examples of capitalism without science and of science without capitalism, it is impossible to call one the cause of the other. Instead one must translate both back to some higher or deeper human source from which they appeared jointly in the Renaissance – and partially Protestant – culture of northern Europe. And apart from the coincidence of timing (which in the loftier heaven of the history of the intellect and the spirit may be no coincidence), there is the matter of the scale and variety in which scientific thought flourished across Europe, from Warsaw to Amsterdam, Paris and London. For in science as in nature, hybridisation within the range of acceptable cross-fertilisation can produce a range of breeds adaptable to a variety of environments. Here the growth of trade and commercial communication as well as war and the interrelations among royal courts no doubt can claim credit. This scale phenomenon is even more important, however, at just a little later point in this story.[12]

We come then to the argument often made, particularly by those economic historians who like Gradgrind pride themselves in dealing in 'facts', that the inventors of the Industrial Revolution were not scientists but humble men – 'tinkerers' is the usual denomination given them. The hard facts are hard enough in the cases of Darby, Highs, Kay, Arkwright, Hargreaves. The scientific training, even perhaps the mathematical aptitude, of the American inventors – Whitney, Fitch, Fulton, McCormick, Goodyear – was low, even zero. The facts are a little squishier in the case of Watt, as the research by Musson and Robinson (1969) has shown. And French inventors even this early had perhaps a better connection with the speculations of natural philosophers.[13] But does the fact that Shakespeare knew 'little Latin and less Greek,' according to Ben Jonson who knew an abundance of both, make him less of a Renaissance man? He was a working inventor saturated with what a sociologist would limply call the 'value system' of his times. Could the eighteenth century inventors have been equally well sixteenth century men? And if a few of them could have been so, (and indeed were – hence the stocking frame and the ribbon loom that stand out like sore thumbs in the early history of textile technology) could so large a body of 'simple tinkerers' have been at work simply tinkering, along so many different and interconnected lines and in such close touch with the economy 300 years earlier?

We come here to the second feature of the eighteenth century invention – again to the phenomenon of scale – not the scale of science indeed, but of the economy. The articulation of a single price system across Europe – detailed by Braudel and Spooner (1967) – the accession of England, with its better world trading location, resource base and more complex society, to world leadership in trade and commerce – the whole involvement of a major nation state in all its branches in commercial economy – this in the presence (unlike the case of ancient Rome) of a body of already developing technology, built for the first time into the economy itself and into its production structure an invention industry – or to put it more grandly, an eco-technic process.

I like to put the matter to economics students in this way. Mantoux in his great book (Mantoux, 1961) explains the sequence of the textile inventions in terms of successive bottlenecks – the flying shuttle created a demand for yarn which induced the development of – or focused inventors' effort on – spinning inventions, and these in turn overshooting the mark, gave rise to bottlenecks in weaving that induced the power loom. It is all very simple and neat. It seems to be built on some impressionistic evidence of yarn shortages in the 1770s but we have no measure of the actual diffusion of the flying shuttle among weavers, and moreover, as Usher insisted (1954, p. 287–8), the development of a power loom continued to be held up by purely technical difficulties. Evidently the supply side of an invention industry also must be taken into account. But there is a more fundamental problem – how does this square with the purely competitive model which, one might suppose ought to have worked, if it is to work anywhere, in the England of the Industrial Revolution? If yarn was short and weavers in surplus supply, why did not some weavers become spinners, and later on, vice versa? The answer, of course, is 'labor immobility', 'non-competing groups'. The answer then is that some immobility is good for invention. But for the society to profit from it rather than to stagnate, it must have available the supply of eager, ingenious inventive tinkerers with a good eye to what is practical and economic.

Here then, I think, we come to the essential element in the transition from the purely Smithian to the Schumpeterian dynamic of the world economy. That element is simply that capitalistic economic organisation had come to exist on a large enough scale, with penetration of its price system deeply enough into the production structure in agriculture as well as in the market for family labour, that the opportunities for immediate profit became evident in invention as well as in trade, exploration, resource discovery and altered industrial organisation so that invention moved in to resolve bottlenecks even faster than capitalists and labourers could do so themselves. Moreover, this was occurring on a large enough scale, and over a wide enough industrial terrain, with sufficient communication among inventors and with sufficient knowledge of investment opportunities that a self-reinforcing process of technical change was set in motion. One small gap was closed and that in turn made other gaps smaller. Improved iron was used in improved steam engines, which powered the improved and more finely accurate machinery.

CONTROLS ON SCHUMPETERIAN GROWTH

'It is no accident,' as Marxists like to say, that these inventions appeared first most strongly as substitutions of natural resources – fuels, waterpower, and iron – for human or animal labour. One observes the delicate balance of factor proportions and types of market demand required for the Industrial Revolution to get under way. Some population growth appears to have been desirable to increase the absolute size of the potential agricultural surplus and to bring scale economies in trade and industry into play. This the population growth of the sixteenth century appears to have been able to do, especially in conjunction with the centralisation of the state administrative systems and the mini-industrial revolution and technical changes of the Renaissance. The suspension of population growth still left an appreciable amount of underemployed agricultural labour in the eighteenth and even nineteenth centuries available to be drawn into factories and mines, and the resumption of population growth in the centres of rural industry in the eighteenth and early nineteenth centuries added to the pool. But labour did not become as abundant as in some Asian or some Latin American countries today, and in any case it remained sufficiently immobilised to give the incentive to labour saving inventions in regions where water power and coal were cheap. But the more important determinant of the path of technical change came from the supply side of inventions: the relatively easy access to a knowledge of mechanics, that is of that part of engineering involved in economising on power. I have argued elsewhere (Parker, 1972) though not with much elaboration, that the order of progression of scientific and engineering discovery must be traced back to fundamental structural conditions of the human mind in approaching nature through the medium of scientific method. That method – with its theories, laboratory techniques, mathematics and instrumentation – was not much more than 100 years old by the start of the major technical changes in England, and it was obviously most directly applicable – and was so applied by scientists and inventors from Galileo through Newton and by tinkerers and inventors from Newcomen through Stephenson – to problems of mechanics, most of which had been defined by Archimedes. The electro-chemical revolution came later because its secrets lay more deeply hidden, were less apparent to the naked eye, and the real agricultural revolution waited till recent decades because of the enormous complexity of life processes and perhaps because of some human fears about direct experimentation with the sources of life.

A track of invention then can be traced in the nineteenth and twentieth centuries out of the difficulties from the supply side which progressively yielded to increasingly more powerful applications of scientific method. As a branch of knowledge grew to the point of direct applicability to useful invention, the choice among lines to pursue was no doubt strongly affected by markets, bottlenecks and factor costs, as well as by many random accidents that dot the biographies of the inventors.

Now there are, it seems to me, two sorts of error that are injurious to the health of a reasonable study of nineteenth century technical history. One – deriving from the side of the history of science since Thomas Kuhn (1962) – emphasises that science is a series of 'paradigms', separate and discrete, like pearls in a strand, each with a delicate and internally supportive structure, spun, like a pearl, around a single irritant, a single grain of sand, a single problem which has crept into the shell of a single social oyster. Kuhn's theory is not a Marxian theory, since it interprets scientific change almost wholly in terms internal to scientific thought itself. A new paradigm is created by an act of insight, as a growing body of observation has become increasingly hard to accommodate within the categories and logic of its predecessor.[14] Nevertheless, this way of looking at the history of science has an intellectual affinity to the Marxian theory of history, with its stages and its revolutions from stage to stage. It contains a truth, and a truth which may be well fitted to an age that seems, like the sixteenth century, to be in some sort of revolutionary psychological and spiritual upheaval. Any notion of history as a string of stages or paradigms, the logic of whose shifts and revolutionary displacements is derived either from internal 'slippage' or from outside the activity, that is, from society, technology, the logic of the superstructure, techniques of warfare, or whatnot – any such notion is itself a paradigm, emphasising one truth whose relevance (to use that demonic word of ten years ago) – may already have seen its best days. Scientific revolutions, like political or industrial revolutions, furnish a problem for historical explanation. The mind is driven back to Tennyson's verses learned in high school:

> Our little systems have their day:
> They have their day and cease to be.
> They are but broken lights of Thee:
> And Thou, O Lord art more than they!

Such lines, supportive of the paradigm-mongers can yet be turned against them. Scientific revolutions are themselves incidents in scientific evolution; just as political and industrial revolutions are parts of total history. We know (or fondly believe) there is a great historical totality in which all is compounded, even Marx, or Braudel – even what I am saying here. The growth of modern science – many of us still believe – is a cumulative process whose correct model is not the pearl in the oyster but the successively more stately mansions of the chambered nautilus. But if this is so, and if this succession of what I would persist in calling 'advances' has been in a major way guided by some internal intellectual and structural logic of its own, then one has here a potent exogenous variable in the structure of explanation of the modern economic world.

   In the understanding of so profound and majestic an historical movement, a further obstacle is presented by modern economists' delicate theorisings over the trivia on the demand side of applied science. They have an unquestionable value in contemporary studies of problems of allocation of research resources. And the observations of the value of 'focusing', and the subtle effects of factor scarcities in shaping technological change in the small are original and essential insights in understanding the biographies of specific inventions or lines of invention. But taken as a vessel to hold the history of technology, these have about as much use as a little boy's effort to scoop out the ocean with a teacup. To understand the history of technology in the large, one must unfortunately know something about technology in all its branches, and that is a dark and thorny terrain into which none of us with training in the humanities or social sciences has been brave enough to enter.[15]

THE NEXT TRANSITION?

With the Industrial Revolution, an interactive process between technology and the economy was built into the structure of modern capitalist development. In marrying technological change, the economy and the entrepreneurs who were its guiding force, delivered society into the hands of science, which has moved where it listeth. There is, it seems to me, no controlling its internal development. The efforts of socialist or fascist societies to place science directly, obviously and totally in the service of the state have been catastrophic for the development of knowledge and for the innocence of the state. No large political and bureaucratic power structure – whether of public officials or of private capitalist lackeys – can be trusted not to blow itself up in the pursuit of more power. This is its internal logic, the dynamic of capitalist or socialist imperialism. Under the capitalism of large scale organisations, power goes disguised under the name of profit, because these organisations still live in a world of accounting, of money and markets. Under socialism, these organisations move under the name of social welfare. But the naked thrust for political dominance and the paranoic drive to destroy everything in the name of security for a system, are the same.

The fourteenth century and to a degree the seventeenth and early eighteenth in Europe are understandable by Malthus; the sixteenth and much of the eighteenth and early nineteenth by Smith. The nineteenth and early twentieth require that a Schumpeterian insight be added to the Malthusian and the Smithian to account for the complexity of the growth, and for its variety as it extended beyond the Atlantic, the Mediterranean and the Urals. But where is to be found the figure for the age that is now perhaps already 30 years into its development?

Clearly, it seems to me the uncontrolled and evidently un-controllable development of natural science, pure and applied, is the deepest problem of the modern world. This is hardly a novel observation. First atomic physics and now modern biochemistry are causing us all to shudder. Yet our fears get buried constantly, first under the glamour and science fiction of space exploration, and

then under the much more immediate power struggles of international politics. It is ironic that at the same time as our fears of
science are growing, we find ourselves pressed by the obsolescence of
the nineteenth century power-using technologies to turn toward
science in a kind of desperate hope. The problem is epitomised in
the dilemma of nuclear power. But – and here is the grain of truth in
the paradigm about paradigms – society appears in history to have
an ability to breed around its intellectual and social problems,
though often only after catastrophe and at a frightful human cost.
Somewhere in that ability, the ability simply to grow in a different
direction, intellectually, spiritually, and materially, may lie
salvation.

   I am reminded of the experience I had once on a jury, after we
had retired to the jury room to deliberate on our verdict. It was not
too serious a case, except to the defendant, but the jurors took it
seriously, conscientiously to the point of self-importance, and came
at it with very different perspectives, perceptions, value systems and
bodies of experience and prejudice. They also were acting under
different degrees of stress with respect to how long they were willing
to remain locked in the jury room with one another. For some the
discussion was a positive good, and they behaved like academics.
One or two others wanted quick dominance and instant discovery of
the truth so apparent to themselves. Most wanted simply to fight
their way through to agreement to give themselves the feeling they
had done a decent job that the judge would respect so he would
release them back to their families. As we discussed the case, going
back over the testimony, expressing assessments of the credibility of
the policemen, the witnesses, and the defendant, we would come to
points of absolute disagreement around which no accommodation
seemed possible. I noted that at such times the discussion drifted.
People began to talk about other things than the case, to make
personal inquiries, to voice complaints, to discuss the hat and make-
up of the woman in the front row of the courtroom. After perhaps
five or ten minutes of such talk someone would begin to steer the
discussions back toward the case, the various small group discussions would consolidate and it would seem that the evidence had
taken on a different cast. Sometimes it seemed that the previous
opinion leaders had suffered, as a result of the inconsequential
discussions, a certain loss of respect, found themselves less listened
to, felt their replacement by others whom the group appeared to
deem more reliable. In this way, not by direct argument over the

points, though that occurred too, but partly by the development of a
reliable leadership, a leadership which seemed in human terms to be
worthy of trust, or to express best the consensus of value, a group
opinion emerged powerful enough to face down and embarrass
hold-outs into acquiescence.

Do societies – which are but broken parts of the whole society of
mankind – do the same thing as history is lived out? Is there any
possibility of a global consensus on what is worthwhile in life, a
consensus in which comfort, knowledge, art, individual achieve-
ment and the thrill of group endeavour, personal 'fulfillment' – that
last refuge of the Renaissance value system – and a joyous social
intercourse do not at last contradict one another? In such a Utopia,
what is the model for economic behaviour and economic change?
The Malthusian model was based on the joy of unlimited
procreation, and as the population experience of the tropical world
shows, it is a hard model to put down. The Smithian model was
based on the excitement of spectacular wealth from trade and the
comforts derived from a rational, natural and orderly organisation
of the work process through trade. The Schumpeterian model took
its dynamic from the thirsty incorporation of the results of scientific
and engineering discovery into an expanding array of synthetic
materials and machinery for both production and destruction. The
corporate and state power derivable from the domination of this
process has become the dominant motivation of twentieth century
economic activity. Uncertainty remains, as strong as in the
nineteenth century, though afflicting larger scale units than the
small farms and manufacturing enterprises of that period. And
the temptation is present to try to dominate the uncertainty by
extending economic power not only over individual actors, but over
the development of scientific activity itself. Before that happens – if
it has not happened already, is it possible that societies will simply
grow away from the whole rationalistic and scientific way of looking
at the world, that science and the exploration of the material
universe will simply wither away out of disinterest? That seems
hardly possible, and if it were to happen as the passions and
excitements of a new generation develop – for one must remember
that extinction or savagery are always for society only one
generation ahead – is it possible that present levels of 'good'
technology, in agriculture, medicine, communications – can be
sustained? Will a race of men develop which, like some primitive
tribe, knows how to do traditional things, but has no interest in the

bases of their power or in extending it? The arts came to civilization before science, presumably out of the perpetuation of random useful accidents. Perhaps they will remain, even revive, when the Faustian pact that western man sealed with the devil of total knowledge has been paid in suffering and fear. Still when one considers that science and the use of the mind is in fact also a kind of art, perhaps that is not what can or should happen. Perhaps the prophet, or the theorist, of the twenty-first century will be not an Anglican parson, or a dour Scottish bachelor, or a Viennese intellectual, but a figure who better expresses the inherent sense of balance which, along with passions and excesses, also characterises the movements of human society as a whole over its history. Marx, Weber, Parsons, Toynbee, Mao – have all been candidates for the job – yet history seems to have outrun them all. And perhaps it is too much to ask that a new phase of socio-economic organisation should furnish its analyst before it is fully born. The owl of Minerva, Hegelians love to remind us, flies abroad not at dawn, but at dusk. Still, after the owl has flown about all night, the rooster (or the Rostow) may wake to crow again, causing the sun to rise.

NOTES

1. Knowles (1926) does not deal with the agricultural revolution, but Mantoux (1961) devotes an important chapter to it.
2. An interesting starting point for the study of modern population growth is the brief and bold sketch in Slicher van Bath (1963), 77–98, which collates M. K. Bennett's (1954) estimates with those of Russell (1948) and Abel (1955). Bennett is based, it appears, on Beloch (1900) while Russell and Abel cover less than all of Europe. The movement of the series is very roughly the same, but obscurity surrounding the movement of the French population, which exceeds Germany and England combined, gives rise to doubts. The most recent survey appears to be the third (1968) edition of Reinhard, Armengand and Dupaquier. The same trends are observable in the regional and provincial data. See also the rather brief sampling in C. Wilson and G. Parker (eds), (1977).
3. The work of the Cambridge group in England has done somewhat more than this, thanks to a sampling of 404 parish records from 1540 to 1840. The gap between baptisms and burials indicates population growth from 1560 to 1660, then stability to 1740 (with some moderate rise after 1700), then a noticeable rise in baptisms with relatively stable numbers of deaths on to 1840. See the summary in C. Wilson and G. Parker (eds), (1977) pp. 115–19.
4. This flippant literary dismissal of the problem will do perhaps for the moment. But the problem is somewhat different from Keats's in trying to distinguish

between truth and beauty. Obviously if nature, or political events rather than 'internal dynamic' produce population 'cycles', then history requires a much broader model, as wide as the whole creation, for its explanatory structure.

5. Henry Palairet and Rosalind Mitchison (Edinburgh) in discussion of this paper reminded me of the limitations on the concept of a 'surplus above subsistence'. They pointed out: (1) that food intake varies with activity and vice versa, and (2) that over time a population adjusts physiologically to a surprising degree to the size and nutritional content of its standard diet. 'Subsistence' then consists not of a single physical daily intake of each nutrient, but a zone within which more or less activity can be carried on with limits which can change over time as the size and build of individuals in a population responds to conditions of food supply. These functional relationships between 'subsistence', physical activity and body size must be taken into account if the size of the potential agricultural 'surplus' over and above such limits is to be measured. But they do not, it seems to me, invalidate the concept of such a surplus.

6. Two interesting recent pieces of research suggest how the market had developed by the late seventeenth century. See Lindert (1980) where a sizable sample of burial records and scattered early urban occupational censuses is examined, and R. M. Berger's (1980) study of retail trade in three towns and scattered places in central and southern England.

7. See the balanced and suggestive concluding chapter (7) in de Vries (1974).

8. J. R. Hicks's (1969) essays on the subjects of this paragraph provide many valuable and plausible insights.

9. C. Wilson and G. Parker (eds), pp. 103–5, 139, 181, 216–18 give an all too brief, up-to-date review of the price history.

10. D. C. Coleman's (1956) incisive critique of the various 'industrial revolutions' of modern history, and especially of Nef, is an essential reference here.

11. As the reader will observe, the comments in the preceding and following section are a kind of home brew, made up of bits of a Dobb, a Sweezy, a Hobsbawm, a Trevor-Roper (Aston, 1967, Hilton, 1976) and their associated controversialists, as well as information and impressions gleaned from 'bourgeois' historians (Trevor-Roper rates as an aristocratic, rather than a bourgeois, writer in this context), insofar as these writers seem to me to provide evidence of the *economic* processes at work in the period. That the controversies over the interpretation of this period remain unsettled, and capable even of being reviewed, as in the recent work of J. Wallerstein (1974) and Gunder Frank (1978) is partly due to ideological differences, but also to lack of a thoroughly quantitative attack on the data, though much has been done by individual scholars. P. K. O'Brien, St. Antony's College, Oxford, for example, has made an effort to quantify the extent of the overseas trade in British trade, and to relate the volume of profits to British net investment. An outside estimate of volume would place it at not more than ten to fifteen per cent of British foreign trade in the mid-eighteenth century. Figures on profits are too uncertain as yet to give a good indication of their size relative to net investment. However, the profit and savings rates both would have had to be fantastically high to have permitted a body of mercantile capital accounting for so small a fraction of national product to have generated any large proportion of net savings. See also the comments in note 13, below.

12. The relations among humanism, capitalism, science, and the Reformation form still a lively and fundamental issue in the historical understanding of all these linked phenomena. In recent literature, I have found the controversy in *Past and Present*, originating out of Christopher Hill's 1964 article (Hill, 1964) and contained in nos. 27 to 31 most helpful in getting my bearings. See also Mandrou (1978) and the earlier articles by Trevor-Roper, 1963, and Lüthy, 1964. With respect to both science and capitalism, it seems now possible to argue that it was not Protestant doctrine as such that offered a more receptive atmosphere to modern thought or business practice, but rather that its individualism, its lack of social content, and in the end its weakness as an instrument of social and political control allowed 'modern culture', or 'bourgeois society' to grow strong in Northern Europe and the USA.

13. The work of Musson and Robinson has greatly clarified the relationship of science and technology in the Industrial Revolution. See Musson and Robinson (1969), A. E. Musson (ed.), (1972), esp. Chapter 1 (by P. Mathias), and 2 (by A. E. Musson). An interesting statement of the relationship in France is offered by C. G. Gillespie in Ch. 4 of the same collection, reprinted from *Isis*, 48 (1957), 398–407. Gillespie's views, based on research into the origins of industrial chemistry, give support, I feel, to the impressions voiced here and in my earlier article (Parker, 1972).

   See also Rostow's able survey of this aspect of the early modern history (Rostow, 1975, Ch. 1, 4). While allowing 'science' an independent causative role in the formation of modern industrial society, Rostow also emphasises mercantilist politics and trade. Like Usher and most of us in the Anglo-American tradition in economic history, he has little to say about social structure, social and group psychology, intellectual and religious doctrines and values that created the 'Renaissance' man, in the arts, religion, government, science and commerce. I wonder if he is as uneasy as I am about this neglect. The treatments by Hicks (1969) and North and Thomas (1973), powerful and searching as they are in some of their insights, leave one with a similar sense that we have not yet got to the bottom of all these matters.

14. Brown (1980) gives a good survey of the state of the discussion of Kuhn's much-discussed 'paradigm model' and makes many telling points of his own, by reference to Kuhn's earlier writings in the history of science. I do not quite feel that he fully states the point which bothers me, that is, the question of a standard against which the succession of paradigms is measured. No doubt I am being naive.

15. I refrain from footnoting these rather bad-tempered comments. References will be furnished by correspondence to scholars presenting proper credentials.

REFERENCES

Abel, W., *Die Wüstungen des ausgehenden Mittelalters*, 2nd ed., (Stuttgart, 1955).

Aston, T., (ed.), *Crisis in Europe, 1560–1660* (New York, 1967).

Beloch, J., 'Die bevolkerung Europas', *Zeitschrift für Sozialwissenschaft*, 1900, *3*, 405–23 (in Mittelalter); 765–86 (zur Zeit der Renaissance).

Bennett, M. K., *The World's Food*, (New York, 1954).

Berger, R. M., 'The Development of Retail Trade in Provincial England, ca. 1550–1700', *Journal of Economic History*, (1980) *40*, 123–8.

Boserup, E., *The Conditions of Agricultural Progress*, (London, 1965).

Braudel, F. and Spooner, F., 'Prices in Europe from 1450 to 1750', in E. E. Rich and C. H. Wilson (eds), *Cambridge Economic History of Europe*, IV, (Cambridge, 1967) Ch. 7.

Brown, F. M., 'Putting Paradigms Into History', *Marxist Perspectives*, 3:1 (Spring, 1980), 34–63.

The Cambridge Economic History of Europe, IV, *The Economy of Expanding Europe in the Sixteenth and Seventeenth Centuries*, edited by E. E. Rich and C. H. Wilson (Cambridge, 1967).

Coleman, D. C., 'Industrial Growth and Industrial Revolutions', *Economica*, 523, (1956) 1–22.

Davis, R., *The Rise of the English Shipping Industry in the Seventeenth and Eighteenth Centuries* (London, 1962).

de Vries, J., *The Dutch Rural Economy in the Golden Age, 1500–1700* (New Haven, 1974).

de Vries, J., *The Economy of Europe in an Age of Crisis, 1600–1750* (Cambridge, 1976).

Dobb, M., *Studies in the Development of Capitalism*, revised edition 1963, (London, 1946).

Gunder Frank, A., *World Accumulation, 1492–1789*, (New York, 1978).

Hill, C., 'William Harvey and the Idea of Monarchy', *Past and Present*, 27, (April 1964).

Hicks, J. R., *A Theory of Economic History*, (Oxford, 1969).

Hilton, R., (ed.), *The Transition from Feudalism to Capitalism*, (New York, 1976).

Jones, E. L., *Agriculture and the Industrial Revolution*, (Oxford, 1974).

John, A. H., 'Agricultural Productivity and Economic Growth in England, 1200–1760', *Journal of Economic History*, (1965), 25; 19–34.

Knowles, L. C. A., *The Industrial and Commercial Revolutions in Great Britain During the Nineteenth Century*, (London, 1926).

Kuhn, T., *The Structure of Scientific Revolutions*, (Chicago, 1962).

Levasseur, E., *La population française*, (Paris, 1889–1892), 3 vols. Vol. 1, Book I, Ch. 7–12 (14–18C.), esp. p. 288, summary table.

Lindert, P. H., *English Occupations, 1670–1811*, Working Paper 14, (University of California, Davis, 1980).

Lopez, R. S., 'The Trade of Southern Europe', in M. M. Postan and E. E. Rich, (eds), *Cambridge Economic History of Europe*, II, Ch. 5, (Cambridge, 1952).

Lüthy, H., 'Once Again: Calvinism and Capitalism', *Encounter* 22 (1964) 26–38.

Mandrou, R., *From Humanism to Science, 1480–1700*, The Pelican History of European Thought, III, (Harmondsworth, 1978).

Mantoux, P., *The Industrial Revolution of the Eighteenth Century*, 2nd edn, (London, 1961.).

Musson, A. E., and Robinson, E., *Science and Technology in the Industrial Revolution* (Manchester, 1969).

Musson, A. E., (ed.), *Science, Technology and Economic Growth in the Eighteenth Century*, (London, 1972).

Nef, J. U., 'The Progress of Technology and the Growth of Large-Scale Industry in Great Britain, 1540–1640', *Economic History Review*, 4 (1934), reprinted in E.

Carns-Wilson (ed.), *Essays in Economic History* (London).

Nef, J. U., *The Rise of the British Coal Industry*, 2 vols. (London, 1932).

North D. C., and Thomas, R. P., *The Rise of the Western World*, (Cambridge, 1973).

North, D. C., 'Ocean Freight Rates and Economic Development', *Journal of Economic History*, *17*, 1958, 537–547.

Parker, W. N., 'Technology, Resources and Economic Change in the West', in A. J. Youngson, *Economic Development in the Long Run*, (London, 1972), 62–78.

Postan, M. M., 'The Trade of Northern Europe', in M. M. Postan and E. E. Rich (eds), *Cambridge Economic History of Europe*, II (Cambridge, 1952), Ch. 4.

Reinhard, M., Armengand, A., Dupaquier, J., *Histoire générale de la population mondiale*, 3rd ed., (Paris, 1968).

Robinson, E., and Musson, A. E., *James Watt and the Steam Revolution: A Documentary History* (London, 1969).

Rostow, W. W., *How It All Began* (New York, 1975).

Russell, J. C., *British Medieval Population* (Albuquerque, 1948).

Trevor-Roper, H. R., 'The General Crisis of the Seventeenth Century', in T. Aston (ed.), *Crisis in Europe, 1560–1660* (New York, 1967), reprinted from *Past and Present*, 11 (1959).

Trevor-Roper, H. R., 'Religion, Reformation and Social Change', *Historical Studies*, 4, (1963).

Usher, A. P., *A History of Mechanical Invention*, 2nd ed. (Cambridge, Mass., 1954).

van Bath, B. H. S., *The Agrarian History of Western Europe, 500–1850*, (London and New York, 1963.).

Wallerstein, I. *The Modern World-System* (New York, 1974).

Wilson, C., and Parker, G., (eds), *An Introduction to the Sources of European Economic History*, I, Western Europe, (London, 1977).

2 *Obrajes* and the Industrialisation of Colonial Latin America

W. P. GLADE

Popular understanding of Latin America's economic past holds that local industry was systematically discouraged by 'mercantilist' policies throughout the colonial era. This reading of the colonial experience, which finds echoes in a sizable body of writing with scholarly pretensions, has been sometimes construed as part of the reason for the region's inability to industrialise successfully during the nineteenth century. As an economic counterpart of the political proposition that the roots of republican-era instability lay in the crown's proscription of local participation in governmental processes, the view has the appeal of explanatory symmetry. And for those, in Latin America and elsewhere, enthralled by the *leyenda negra*, it has the additional advantage of placing the onus for national economic and political inexperience on the misguided policies of Iberian rulers. Yet, the falsity of this version of economic history has long been recognised in serious scholarship, notwithstanding the fact that proscriptive decrees can indeed be found among the voluminous economic legislation of Spain and Portugal and that it is certainly the case that Spanish America and Brazil seem to have been ill prepared to cope with the problems of the industrial age.

THE SPREAD OF COLONIAL INDUSTRIAL DEVELOPMENT

From a variety of sources a clear picture emerges that, although agriculture and mining were the mainstays of the colonial economy, a considerable amount of resources went also into construction (to implant the physical infrastructure for Iberian civilisation in the New World) and, to a lesser degree, into a bureaucratic service (with both civil and ecclesiastical arms) designed to establish and administer the elaborate social order that composed the Iberian way of life. Cross and crown were, in effect, joined in an intimate union for monitoring and guiding social organisation in the Americas. Contrary to what one might expect from the abundant but misleading references to colonial 'feudalism', the system rested on a Roman-style salaried, professional government in the cities, which asserted its jurisdiction, not always effectively, over surrounding rural precincts. Besides these uses of resources, however, and the resources that were tied up in both intercontinental and intracontinental merchanting and transport, no little effort was devoted to the fabrication of goods and construction materials.

Indeed, there can be little doubt that the great bulk of the goods consumed throughout the American kingdoms of the Spanish monarchy were fabricated on the western side of the Atlantic, in spite of the prominence historians have appropriately accorded the trading fleets which brought European and, in the case of the Manila galleon, Asiatic specialties to the markets of the New World. For the category of non-traded goods, the need for local production capabilities is obvious. Musicians and criers, barbers, physicians, barber-surgeons, horseshoers and veterinarians (*herradores*), mining technicians, muleteers and carters, bakers, millers, confectioners, lawyers, notaries, carpenters, masons, painters, merchants, tailors, cobblers, and so on plied their trades throughout Spain's overseas kingdoms, especially in and around the viceregal centres and provincial urban centres. From almost the very beginning of the colonial age, a mixture of immigrants from Europe, Negro slaves, and the indigenous population – in some instances schooled in mechanical arts under ecclesiastical or governmental auspices – provided the skills needed to cater to the prevailing consumption preferences of that day.[1] In time, the range of such skills became ever more diversified, stimulated in no small part by the vast construction programme needed to build the new towns and cities and to equip these with the ornate ecclesiastical and generally simpler civil structures that served as a *mise-en-scène* for the colonial enterprise. The elaborately designed churches of Cholula, Quito, and Cuzco, for example, were hardly the products of a society devoid of skills, while on the frontiers – in California and

Paraguay – missionaries instructed their charges in medieval Spanish arts and crafts even as they inducted them into a new belief system.

Since transfer costs were high on account of the expense of maritime and overland shipping and because of the heavy reliance of the fiscal system on trade taxes, the range of goods fabricated locally was fairly ample. Besides the trades just noted, the American urban centres were, in due course, supplied with a considerable variety of other artisan crafts.[2] Among the smiths, for example, were silversmiths, tinsmiths, goldsmiths, blacksmiths, locksmiths, gunsmiths, and swordsmiths, drawing in some instances on materials provided by local founders. In the softgoods lines, the ranks of the New World artisans included hatters, hosiers, tanners, saddlers and other leatherworkers, silkworkers, and the range of skills – fullers, weavers, dyers, and so on – associated with woollen and cotton textiles, to which must be added such related trades as the provision of cochineal and indigo. Printers and bookbinders, chandlers, makers of musical instruments, cabinetmakers, potters and glassblowers together with other artisans in ceramics, tobacco workers, sculptors and woodcarvers, ropemakers, shipbuilders, and cartwrights, helped fill out the array of skilled craftsmen on which firms and households could draw for local sourcing. In the countryside, winemakers, sugar mill mechanics, and distillers of spirits added to the complement of colonial trades. The central Mexican highlands, the Peruvian coast, and the Andean highlands from Colombia through Bolivia encompassed by far the largest share of the artisan population, which, by the end of the colonial age, was probably mostly *mestizo* in ethnic composition, with some Indians, Negroes, and *criollos* making up the rest. Guatemala, the Chilean central valley, and northwestern Argentina were artisan regions of lesser importance.

ORGANISATION IN COLONIAL INDUSTRY

While the diversity of artisan skills available to the colonial economy is reasonably well established, the exact pattern of the relations of production is rather less clear, owing to the variety of organisational forms within which artisans accomplished their work. In the viceregal capitals and larger provincial centres, many of the trades were organised into guilds, which, fashioned after those of western Europe, had been set up soon after the conquest.[3] Regulated by municipal ordinances which were subject to ratification by royal authority, guilds sometimes reflected the surrounding class and ethnic structure by barriers which blocked certain groups from attaining the status of master craftsman even when progress from apprentice to journeyman was allowed.

As in Europe, the strength of the guilds varied from city to city as well as among crafts, and rural artisans were less likely than their urban counterparts to be included in guild organisations. Public authority, however, probably held the upper hand in regulation more than it did in Europe. A certain petrifaction seems to have characterised the regulatory structure of at least some of the guilds, so that by the close of the colonial period even high officials had come to perceive the antiquated elements of the system.[4] In the case of the mining guilds, the crown eventually took action, not altogether successful in the end, to try to up-date the state of the industrial arts applied in that field, but in other areas of production remedial action seems to have been more discussed than implemented. After 1789, for example, royal functionaries revised various guild regulations so as to make them more conducive to innovation and some guilds were even abolished, but by and large the private sector failed to respond to this encouragement.

Not all artisans were in guilds, however, even outside the rural areas. In at least some of the more outlying districts of the empire, such as the River Plate region, there appear to have been urban craftsmen who, for one reason or another, failed to secure authorisation to organise guilds and who, insofar as they were regulated, worked directly subject to municipal ordinances. Among Indian communities and the missions, skilled artisans were also less formally organised, except where confraternities were established for religious and philanthropic purposes. Accounts indicate that slaves, another segment of the labour force, were employed for skilled work even outside of agriculture, sometimes with an opportunity to use their earnings to purchase freedom, but they could not be members with full standing in the guilds.

As might be expected, much, even most of this artisan production took place in small shops or as domestic industry. There were, however, some larger-scale economic organisations of an industrial character, alongside the rural *haciendas* and the deeper mining enterprises. Sugar milling, for instance, was sometimes carried out on a relatively substantial scale, while tobacco factories,[5] a royal monopoly, were also of considerable size. Shipbuilding, too, was among the larger undertakings, especially in Guayaquil, Nicaragua, and Panama.[6] Of special interest for the student of industrial development, though, is the *obraje*, the workshop of varying size which concentrated workers in one location to surpass the production limits of the individual artisan shops that composed the guild sector proper.[7] A type of proto-factory, the *obrajes* made their initial appearance in the first quarter century of the Conquest and endured, albeit amidst vicissitudes of labour-market fluctuations and regulatory changes, to the end of the colonial era. In them, the ownership of capital was dissociated from the supply of labour, and production was almost invariably disposed of at least partly outside the confines of the communities in which the *obrajes* were located. Although *obrajes* were established in other industrial pursuits such as indigo production and ceramics, the major sector in which they operated was the textile industry, wherein they turned out the coarse fabrics (of wool and cotton, chiefly) and such related products as rope, bed-ticking, ship riggings, hats, fibre sandals, and so forth, bought for everyday use. Finer materials came to the New World markets through the import trade. This product differentiation between local and foreign supply sources needs to be kept in mind, for, as we shall see, it makes it difficult to argue that the nature of the market constituted the crucial impediment to progress of the factory system. Popular demand for *obraje* output must have been far greater than the restricted demand for various luxury imports in the textile line.

The origins of the *obrajes* appear to be triple. In the first place, a good many of the earliest such ventures may well have been organised as community ventures by the indigenous population, at the instigation of either Indian *caciques* or royal officials, to supply tribute in kind to the crown. In this they simply built upon the traditional textile arts of the pre-Columbian peoples, who had long been accustomed to supplying such in-kind tax payments to their native overlords. In at least some of the community *obrajes*, the managers or administrators were, for a long time, Spaniards appointed by the viceroy or another royal office, but later a number of community *obrajes* were leased out. It is also clear that other *obrajes* were, in a related development, established by *encomenderos* as a means of generating the wherewithal to finance their sinecures.[8] Still other *obrajes*, such as those in sixteenth-century Puebla, were founded by Spanish settlers as outright business ventures. Over the years some *obrajes* initiated under Indian auspices may have passed into private Spanish ownership as a means of settling debt transactions. The majority of *obrajes* were operated under private ownership, even, in instances, ownership by royal officials. But all along there were some operated directly on crown account, while others were owned and operated by religious institutions, or leased by the clergy to private operators. There is evidence that a fair number of *obrajes*, including some belonging to church bodies, were illegal.

By no means should it be supposed that those *obrajes* that were privately held were purely market-based operations. By the 1570s, viceregal ordinances began to be issued in some quantity to regulate wages and working conditions in the *obrajes*, although as early as 1549 the crown had attempted to prohibit the *encomenderos'* practice of locking up Indian women in a central workshop in order to oblige them to produce fabric for tribute. In both New Spain and Peru, other ordinances were promulgated with a view to mitigating the abuses of *encomienda* grants, abuses which began to develop from almost the very beginning of the colonial system, and by 1621 *encomienda obrajes* were outlawed altogether. Humanitarian considerations seem to have inspired much of this legislation, giving it the flavour of protective regulation. Because of growing labour shortages, however, it also became the practice to assign conscript labour to the *obrajes* in an officially installed forced-labour system that was called the *repartimiento* in New Spain but in Peru was more often referred to as the *mita*. Both versions of the corvée, used also to raise labour supplies for public works and, on occasion, agriculture and mining, were open to many abuses, to judge from contemporary accounts. In time this particular regime of forced labour in the *obrajes* was ended. This occurred by perhaps 1621 in New Spain, but not until 1704 was the practice officially suppressed in the Quito *audiencia*. The *mita* continued to be employed, for some uses, later still in what are today Peru and Bolivia, and it appears that the 1704 proscription of the *mita* was even ignored for some considerable time thereafter. (One need not suppose that the formal extinction of the system was scrupulously observed.) In any case, by the eighteenth century the recruitment system tended to rely more on free labour, but indenture and other forms of debt peonage as well as convict labour and, on occasion, slave labour continued as 'imperfections' in the labour market.

For that matter, the establishment and sale of *obrajes*, the range of products that could be produced, and even product specifications were subject to official regulation, though this is not to suggest that these controls were always effectively imposed, any more than the protective and welfare legislation was. *Entre dicho y hecho, había mucho trecho.* Nevertheless, cumulatively a rather elaborate corpus of interventionary measures came into being to define the institutional corridor through which the *obraje* enterprises were authorised to move.[9] No doubt this awesome body of regulation did constrain some of the firms' behaviour, but one result, perhaps predictably, was that a great deal of the time *obraje* operations seemed to hover on the margin or, more often, beyond the pale of legality. In this transactional penumbra, purely economic relations were not necessarily those which determined the success of an undertaking.

In some parts of the Americas, yet another element of coercion came to be associated with the *obraje* sector: the *repartimiento de efectos.*[10] This was a system of compulsory marketing under which indigenous communities were, in effect, allocated purchasing quotas for *obraje* output. Provincial magistrates known as *corregidores* and *alcaldes mayores* administered the system, which, in the Peruvian viceroyalty, operated on a large scale and which had the effect of bringing the indigenous sector into closer interaction with the Spanish-organised sector,[11] although some of the supplier *obrajes* were, it seems, also located within the indigenous sector. The *repartimiento de efectos* figured somewhat less prominently in the viceroyalty of New Spain, where it was evidently less needed to ensure the prosperity of the manufactories, although it was a consideration of some importance for the officialdom of the Oaxaca region. In Peru, the *repartimiento* apparently gained in importance during the eighteenth century. Indeed, the record suggests that the last century of colonial rule found the manufacturing sector of the southern region rather on the wane, whereas the fortunes of the *obrajes* were generally rising in the northern portion of the empire. The reasons for this difference are not altogether clear, an ambiguity which also surrounds the additional difference that the southern manufactories tended mainly to be located in the rural setting of the sierra, whereas those of New Spain were mostly located in urban centres.

At the northern end of the empire, the early centres of *obraje* production included Puebla, Mexico City, Coyoacán, Xochimilco, Texcoco, Tacubaya, Cuernavaca, Tlaxcala, Toluca, and, more distant from the economic and political centre of gravity, Oaxaca.

In time, however, the institution spread so that during the eighteenth century, other centres included Querétaro, San Luis Potosí, San Miguel, and Valladolid (the Morelia of today). The Guatemalan highlands contained a few *obrajes* as well. In South America, the most important *obraje* regions were: the highlands of present-day Ecuador, the Peruvian highlands from Cajamarca south through Jauja and from Abancay to the shores of Titicaca, and Sicasica province in Bolivia. Peripheral zones of *obraje* development were located in areas that today compose parts of Colombia, Chile, and Argentina.

In spite of the increasing scholarly attention accorded this economic unit, the evidentiary base for analysing the *obraje* is still quite fragmentary,[12] in part because so many were illegal (that is, unlicensed), in part because many licensed *obrajeros* were thought to keep multiple sets of books, and in part because contradictory numbers have filtered down through the various reports, official documents, and secondary accounts. Moreover, just as new firms were initiated from time to time, others went out of business, so that even for the licensed operations no clear and consistent picture yet emerges for the whole area and era. These scattered figures, then, must be taken in a very impressionistic sense. In the 1578–95 period, for example, the number of manufactories operating in Puebla, Mexico, stood at about forty, with a labour force of some 1200 workers. A few decades later, Puebla is reported as having thirty-two *obrajes*, employing 1400 workers, while the valley of Mexico contained forty-nine *obrajes* employing 2205 Indians. By the close of the colonial period, Mexico City and Querétaro had become the chief manufacturing centres with some twenty-one to twenty-eight *obrajes*, involving approximately 1600 workers, operating at the latter place in the 1780s.[13] By the late seventeenth century, the number of licensed manufactories operating in the kingdom of Quito stood at about fifty, some three-fifths of which were privately owned, but the total work force employed was reported to be over seven thousand. In Peru, however, the three hundred *obrajes* reported to be operating around 1700 had dropped to about half that number a century later. In size, *obrajes* seem to have ranged from small workshops employing no more than a dozen workers to establishments employing as many as two hundred or more. Often a putting-out system was employed to organise the spinning phase of the production process.

Finally, there is the question of the relation of the *obrajes* to the ownership structure of the economy, apart from those manufactories belonging to the native communities, the crown, and the church. Mention is made of some, perhaps only a few, that seem to have been established by master craftsmen. Others, in the early years of the empire, were set up by *encomenderos* as was previously noted. Others were set up by royal officials, in contravention of the law, while some *obrajeros*, in the field of woollen textiles, were sheepranchers, particularly in the Andes. A few owners were of the titled aristocracy. Merchanting, however, seems to have constituted the business background of the largest single group of *obraje* entrepreneurs, at least by the early seventeenth century, although this category of *obraje*·owner included local shopkeepers as well as merchants engaged in longer distance trade. In time, the composition of the *obrajero* group underwent some change, so that by the early eighteenth century in Querétaro, the largest group, 47 per cent of the *obrajeros*, also owned farms and ranches, while merchant-*obrajeros* accounted for 38 per cent of the total.[14] Government officials, it should be remarked, were nearly a fifth, 19 per cent, of the group. From the data available on this sample, almost all *obrajeros* had other business interests.[15] Often, these other business interests supplied the venture capital needed for establishing or purchasing an *obraje*, or the collateral for a loan with which to set up such operations. But once in operation, reinvested earnings were commonly relied on to maintain the *obraje* as a going concern and *obraje* profits could be used to acquire other assets, including, on occasion, titles and public office. The evidence is unclear on the point, but unless the *obrajes* of Querétaro were an exceptional case, there was, by the latter half of the eighteenth century at least, a perhaps surprising degree of turnover of manufactory owners. Here and there, guilds of *obrajeros* were established, but little is known at this time of just how they functioned.

THE *OBRAJE* AS A SPRINGBOARD FOR INDUSTRIALISATION

A question almost unavoidably arises: why was not the *obraje*, together with the wide array of artisan skills practiced in the overseas kingdoms of Spain, a springboard for nineteenth-century industrialisation in Latin America? The answer is that, to a very small degree, it was. Although part of the early nineteenth-century textile industry in Mexico was founded in Orizaba, which had hitherto had no substantial *obraje*-artisan experience, most of the industrial development of the 1830s and 1840s took place in Puebla, the valley of Mexico, and Querétaro. For example, what is said to be the first modern factory in Mexico, the *La Constancia* textile operation established by Estevàn de Antuñano, was opened in Puebla in 1835. Yet, if colonial manufacturing provided a base for subsequent development, it was a very weak base indeed. The industrial firms that sprang up in Mexico in the early years of the republican period were few in number and not long-lived. In the Andean region, there was even less to show. Moreover, substantial organisational discontinuities are involved. At least at this time, we do not have a single documented case in which an *obraje* firm evolved into a factory in the nineteenth-century sense of that term.

What, then, were the factors which inhibited the ability of the *obraje* to function as the midwife of the factory? A comparison with contemporary European experience might be useful in generating some hypothetical insights, even though our thinking about the phenomenon must remain at the level of hypothesis pending a much more comprehensive and systematic mining of the archival sources.

One possibility suggested by European experience is that manufacturing progress was suffocated by the conservative effects of the guild tradition and/or the regulatory structure imposed by the state. Another possibility is that it was limited by the luxury character of the products turned out. Factors such as these seem, for example, to have operated adversely in the case of northern Italy, where Sella has noted that

> The manufacturers of the Lombard cities were certainly closer to their medieval predecessors than to their counterparts of the factory age . . . not only was it [their production] carried out, for the most part, in diminutive shops rather than in large industrial plants, but, by and large, the goods produced (whether silks, suits of armor, or high-grade cloth), intended as they were for a select clientele rather than for a mass market, owed their success more to superior workmanship, exquisite design, and even individual styling than to low prices and an ability to satisfy the ordinary needs of large numbers of consumers. In other words, urban manufacturers, despite the fact that they came to employ thousands of workers, retained all the features of medieval crafts. Not surprisingly, the labor force, although paid wages by the

merchant-manufacturer under the putting-out system, continued to be organized in such typically medieval institutions as the craft guilds and to find in them the best safeguard of those attitudes that for centuries had been the hallmark of the urban artisan class – namely, adherence to traditional standards of workmanship, a determination to monitor closely and, if necessary, to restrict new admissions to one's trade, and punctilious defense of a guild's privileges and exclusiveness.[16]

Some scholars, of course, have seen somewhat similar factors – burdensome interventionism, the strength of guilds, and a structure of production skewed toward elaborate specialty goods – holding the onset of modern industrial development in France behind that of the United Kingdom.[17] But there is little evidence that it was these conditions that substantially retarded early manufacturing development in Spanish America. *Obrajes* were regulated in production technique and labour relations by the state, and guilds served as a regulatory mechanism for other artisans. Yet, compared with European experience, the general laxity of law enforcement and weakness of many, if not most, guilds do not build a convincing case for the regulation of production processes as a primary impediment to development. This is not to say that official surveillance and guild conduct were conducive to technical advancement. They were anything but that and certainly, save in rare cases of official promotion at the beginning and close of the colonial period, did not encourage innovation. But while the Spanish American guilds were less adaptable than, say, the Venetian ones had been, there are not a great many concrete cases at hand in which overt guild intransigence defeated or substantially delayed an attempted introduction of a superior manufacturing technology. And state regulation, while extensive and relatively intricate, seems not to have borne the onus it assumed in Venice and some other instances for frustrating the introduction of cost-cutting measures and shifts to more economical and competitive levels of product quality.[18]

As for the composition of demand and the nature of the products produced, *obrajeros* did not lose out because they were producing excessively specialised and high quality wares. As noted above, colonial manufactories catered chiefly to the popular market, even though by the end of the eighteenth century, some of the Mexican manufacturers could, thanks in part to encouragement from such

progressive viceroys as the second Revillagigedo and Azanza, begin
to produce rather more sophisticated fabrics on a small scale. South
American industry appears to have been even more limited in the
grades of products it turned out. By and large, manufactures of
higher quality and refined technique came from Europe throughout
the colonial period, not only in textiles but in other lines of goods as
well. True, Greenleaf's research reveals that around 1800 a variety
of interests, American as well as peninsular, viewed a potential for
upgraded production in the *obraje* sector with some uneasiness. And
Viceroy Marquina was directed by the monarchy to ascertain the
degree of threat posed by *obrajes* to the markets of peninsular
manufacturers and mercantile interests involved in the transoceanic
trade, as well as to mining and agricultural firms with which the
manufactories may have competed for workers in some few labour
markets. But royal officialdom was by no means of one mind on the
matter and, in any case, European international conflicts quickly
diverted governmental attention to other problems. A provisional
conclusion suggested by the admittedly sketchy evidence is not so
much that technical advances were squelched by public or guild
authority as that they were not being sought or promoted with any
notable vigour by the owners of the *obrajes* in the first place.

European experience with early industrialisation does, however,
point in the direction of at least two promising explanatory paths. In
the first place, there is the market factor which led Adam Smith to
assert the famous dictum linking productivity with the extent of the
market. Simplistic though Smith's understanding of the relationship may have been, it was not altogether amiss in several important
respects. Almost every significant instance of industrial progress in
western European historical experience seems to show a close
connection between expanding markets and advances in production technique. Doubtless the relation was interactive: expanding
markets provided the inducements and the ploughed-back earnings
for heightened capital formation while product improvements and
lowered costs of production made it possible to reach wider markets.
The intricate web of international economic relationships was no
less crucial, in many instances, for its role in securing a variety of raw
materials from distant sources. This close connection of growth
industries with the brisk advance of foreign trade has attracted
frequent scholarly attention, as has the stimulating impact of
transport improvements for both domestic and foreign commerce.[19]
In Spanish America, however, colonial markets were, outside the

few sites of mining booms, growing only slowly, and, dispersed as
they were over an exceedingly difficult and sparsely settled terrain,
they were only weakly articulated with one another – a fragmen-
tation accentuated by the formidable regulatory and fiscal apparatus of the empire.

From the beginning of the colonial period until the trade
liberalisation measures of the later eighteenth century, in other
words, the inland *obraje* centres of the Americas were shielded from
much participation in long-distance trade within the hemisphere,
let alone from direct commercial intercourse with trading partners
lying beyond the bounds of the realm, by both heavy overland
transport charges and the complicated institutional structure in
which they were so deeply embedded. While it could be remarked
that in Europe the organisational matrix within which manufacturing enterprises operated was also complex, there the structures
involved multilateral networks of credit systems, marine insurance
arrangements, transport services, and commercial information
flows, all of which converged on a region that had become the centre
of an immense global entrepôt trade. Not so the remote *obrajes* of the
New World. The complex institutional edifice with which they had
to contend, even after the Bourbon reforms, was of a different, more
archaic character, and for most purposes the peninsular centre of
government and economic organisation was still interposed as a
filter between them and the rest of the world. As sheltered
workshops operating in a system which saw them chiefly in their
provisioning function, the *obrajes* were deprived of the support of the
whole capitalist institutional apparatus which, by accretion, had
grown up in north-west Europe during the three centuries after
1492.

For that matter, it is evident from the historical record that even
while participation in world trade may be a necessary condition for
industrial progress, it is far from being a sufficient condition. Both
Lombardy and Venice were heavily engaged in international
commerce, as were the seventeenth-century Dutch,[20] yet all fell by
the way in respect of their international industrial standing as time
went on. The explanation for any case of economic retardation is
clearly multifactorial. In the instance of Spanish America, other
possible explanatory elements also seem to have much to do with the
administratively imposed isolation of the overseas kingdoms. If,
within the Americas, interregional differences in production costs
tended to be less than intermarket transfer costs for a large number

of products of local manufacture, then the former set of costs needs as much as the latter to be factored into an explanation for the very limited market dynamism of colonial industry. Here a picture of relative technological stagnation emerges.

What seems conspicuously lacking in all the available observations on the *obraje* sector is any indication that the production functions were undergoing significant change. When, for example, the *obrajes* of Puebla were displaced by the *obrajes* of Querétaro, the advantage of the latter appears to have been a purely locational one in relation to the expanding market of that day.[21] The contrast with Europe is striking. There, both products and production functions were subject to variation as the continent moved towards the industrial revolution. In Spanish America, however, one must conclude that the policy structure of empire filtered out a great deal more than just the heretical notions with which the Inquisition – an institution so emblematic of the system as a whole – was preoccupied.

In the Middle Ages and early modern period, technical and organisational progress seems closely associated with international commerce. Communication at long distance was relatively easier by water, and there was a considerable international diffusion of capital and enterprise, even at a time when internal mobility was hampered. For example, the putting-out system seems to have developed earliest in the low countries and northern Italy in manufacturing for export, from which region it spread to many other parts of Europe by 1600, and it was the Hanseatic merchants who first fostered Polish agricultural development, an expansion of Swedish iron production, and sheepraising in England. In extreme cases, such as Russia before the eighteenth century, the pioneering role of foreign merchant-entrepreneurs was overwhelmingly important in establishing capitalistic enterprise,[22] but in nearly all cases of sizable industrial expansion in Europe, there is ample evidence of the migration of artisans and technicians, the international movement of ideas concerning product design and specification as well as production technique, and even, on occasion, industrial espionage. Domestic enterprise was, in other words, quite often enriched by the catalyst of foreign specialists and foreign enterprise, and educated by the international contacts in a variety of ways.

By no means all technical advance, in any country, can be credited to cross-national borrowing. Particularly is this the case in respect of the remarkable spate of technological innovations that occurred in eighteenth-century and nineteenth-century Britain. But, surveying the movement of people and ideas from place to place in late medieval and early modern Europe, it is hard to escape the conclusion that the pace of technical change would have been very much slower without this intercourse and that the industrial revolution was truly a product of European conditions, not just conditions in one country, very much as the 'advance of scientific knowlege was a European phenomenon'.[23] As early as the sixteenth and seventeenth centuries, for instance, British cloth manufacture received a distinct boost from the immigration of French Huguenots, Walloons, and Dutch Calvinists, and before that the introduction of continental fulling techniques had marked a significant advance over earlier methods. From time to time, German specialists were brought in to aid the development of British mining and metallurgy in the same general period, and emigrés from elsewhere on the continent contributed to upgrading the quality of British glassmaking. The Saxony wheel which replaced the earlier spinning wheel, the narrow Dutch ribbon-loom, an Italian silk throwing-mill, the pound-lock pioneered in Dutch shipyards, German and French advances in chemistry – all these and more attest to the remarkable circulation of new technical knowledge that went along with an increasingly sophisticated commercial and financial structure and constituted the 'heritage of improvement'.[24] The slowly growing but notable interregional trade in intermediate products was another indicator of the nature of what was going on.[25]

By contrast, the movement of goods, persons, and information, especially the technical/scientific information so much in the forefront of events in Europe, was, in Spanish America, choked to a minimum. Eschewing mono-causal explanations of what was essentially a multivariable interdependent social process, we need not so much essay a full accounting for the phenomenon as simply remark this characteristic. In contrast to northwest Europe, Spanish America presented a rather sclerotic institutional ambience, notwithstanding the control-oriented reforms ushered in at the instigation of the Bourbon monarchs. Successful as these reforms were from the standpoint of certain aspects of governance, they were of only limited efficacy in rejuvenating economic life before the colonial era came to an end.

Spain, the source of almost all European emigration to the

overseas kingdoms, was not, in the seventeenth and eighteenth centuries, an area displaying much technical and scientific prowess. Indeed, it is relevant that Spaniards figured practically not at all in the notable circulation of technical experts and expertise during the early modern period. Moreover, would-be European migrants with technical expertise had better market options than either the peninsula or Spanish America. Consequently, the culture of the Iberian mother country was unable to supply, either through its own generative processes or through the economic attraction of migrants, the skilled persons who, as conveyors of critical knowledge, were to set industrial development on course elsewhere on the European continent. While the crown sought, belatedly, to deal with this instance of market failure by hiring a few European technical advisors and troubleshooters, such intervention corresponded, not surprisingly, to the most immediate priority needs of the imperial government. Under the circumstances then prevailing, this meant devoting chief attention to the mining sector whence public revenues were most directly obtained. Time ran out before state power could be harnessed effectively to a progressive industrial policy for manufacturing.

While conclusions on this point must be as tentative as any others in this subject area, for the time being one is led by the available documentation to an impression that, for nearly three hundred years, the *obraje* sector was effectively insulated from both technicians and technical knowledge of contemporary foreign provenance. Neither the market nor, as a market surrogate, the public policy agenda accorded the advancement of industrial technology (outside the extractive sector) a high priority. The *obrajeros*, many if not most of whom had other business interests to attend to, were thus plainly out of touch with the manufacturing progress that was slowly building momentum in Europe and that would, in time, overwhelm local manufacturers, *obrajes* and artisan shops alike, as the nineteenth century exposed Spanish America to the full force of European competition.

NOTES AND REFERENCES

1. For the early period in a major governmental and economic centre, see James Lockhart, *Spanish Peru, 1532–1560: A Colonial Society* (Madison: The University of Wisconsin Press, 1968). It should be noted that in the heartlands of the

Spanish empire in the Americas, the artisan trades brought in by the Europeans were joined to a flourishing local craft tradition.

2. An especially comprehensive study is Ricardo Cappa, *Estudios críticos acerca de la dominación española en América*, 19 volumes, (Madrid: Librería Católica de Gregorio del Amo, 1889–1897). Vol. VIII is the one most relevant to this discussion.

3. For a classic study of guilds see Manuel Carrera Stampa, *Los gremios mexicanos: la organización gremial en Nueva España, 1521–1861* (Mexico: Edición y Distribución Ibero Americana de Publicaciones, 1954).

4. A recent discussion of some of these efforts is found in Dorothy Tanck de Estrada, 'La abolición de los gremios,' in E. C. Frost, M. C. Meyer, and J. Z. Vásquez (eds), *El trabajo y los trabajadores en la historia de México* (Tucson: University of Arizona Press, 1979). See also Pedro Santos Martínez, *Las industrias durante el Virreinato, 1776–1810* (Buenos Aires: EUDEBA, 1969).

5. The late colonial history of one such enterprise is traced in Marco Antonio Fallas, *La factoría de tabacos de Costa Rica*, (San José: Editorial Costa Rica, 1972).

6. See L. A. Clayton, *The Guayaquil Shipyards in the Seventeenth Century: History of a Colonial Industry*, thesis, (Tulane University, 1972) for a particularly informative account of this industry.

7. There were instances in which *obraje* workers belonged to guilds, but in other instances the *obrajes* either substituted for guild production or competed with it.

8. The *encomenderos* made up a class of worthy individuals who, in effect, were awarded pensions by the crown, to be raised in an ostensibly regulated manner from a given indigenous population. In 1549, personal services were, by decree, commuted into tribute payments in the *encomienda* grants, providing a strong incentive for the *encomenderos* to organise production enterprises amongst their charges.

9. For examples of the regulated industry status of *obraje* operations, see Luis Chávez Orozco, *El obraje, embrión de la fábrica* (Mexico: *El Nacional*, Jan. 1936) and Silvio Zavala, *Ordenanzas del trabajo, siglos XVI y XVII* (Mexico: Editorial Elede, 1947).

10. For a recent interpretation, see Jürgen Golte, 'Redistribución y complementaridad regional en la economía andina del siglo XVIII,' Lateinamerika-Institut der Freien Universität Berlin, Diskussionspapiere, 1976. A good discussion of the system is also found in Brian R. Hammett, *Politics and Trade in Southern Mexico, 1750–1821* (Cambridge University Press, 1971). This institution, in which royal functionaries worked in cahoots with private entrepreneurs (especially the merchants who financed such schemes), was obviously subject to many abuses. These evidently took place frequently and occasioned many an episcopal and royal denunciation. For much of the period the *repartimiento de efectos* was, strictly speaking, illegal, but by the mid-eighteenth century the crown, despairing of ever effectively proscribing the practice, opted to regulate it. It was, in some ways, in the interest of the monarchy to permit the practice in hopes that, having access to *repartimiento* profits, the local officials would be less inclined to embezzle the royal revenues they were entrusted with gathering. Towards the close of the colonial period, however, the *repartimiento* was abolished.

11. These forced purchases, together with the need to pay a capitation tax, obliged

the Indian population to hire themselves out and to produce commodities for market sale.

12. Besides works already cited, see Richard E. Greenleaf, 'The *Obraje* in the Late Mexican Colony', *The Americas*, vol. XXIII, no. 3 (January 1967), pp. 227–50; William M. Dusenberry, 'Woolen Manufacture in Sixteenth-Century New Spain', *The Americas*, vol. IV, no. 2 (October 1947), pp. 223–34; Richard E. Greenleaf, 'Vice-regal Power and the *Obrajes* of the Cortés Estate, 1595–1708', *Hispanic American Historical Review*, vol. XLVII, no. 3 (August 1968), pp. 365–79; John C. Super, 'Querétaro *Obrajes*: Industry and Society in Provincial Mexico, 1600–1810', *Hispanic American Historical Review*, vol. LVI, no. 2 (May 1976), pp. 197–216; Jan Bazant, 'Evolution of the Textile Industry in Puebla, 1544–1845', *Comparative Studies in Society and History*, vol. VII (October 1964), pp. 56–69; Fernando Silva Santiesteban, *Los obrajes en el virreinato del Perú* (Lima: Museo Nacional de Historia, 1964); Héctor Samayoa Guevara, *Los gremios de artesanos en la ciudad de Guatemala, 1524–1821* (Guatemala: Editorial Universitaria, 1962); Samuel Kagan, 'The Labor of Prisoners in the *Obrajes* of Coyoacán, 1660–1693', in Frost, Meyer, and Vásquez, op. cit., pp. 201–14; John Phelan, *The Kingdom of Quito in the Seventeenth Century* (Madison: University of Wisconsin Press, 1967).

13. By the eighteenth century, the Puebla *obrajes* had experienced decades of decline. To some extent they had been replaced by clusters of smaller shops called *fábricas* which were not subject to the *obraje* regulatory scheme. Whether these smaller establishments were part of larger organisations articulated by merchant-capitalists in a type of putting-out system is not clear.

14. Super, op. cit., *Obrajes* located on the *haciendas* were included among the assets of some of the most prominent nobility and large landholders as Ladd and Harris have noted. See Doris M. Ladd, *The Mexican Nobility at Independence, 1780–1826* (Austin: University of Texas Press, 1976), and Charles H. Harris III, *A Mexican Family Empire* (Austin: University of Texas Press, 1975).

15. This fact may have facilitated the shutting down of *obrajes* in times of business adversity, for the year-to-year variation in number of workshops seems more than might be expected.

16. Domenico Sella, *Crisis and Continuity: The Economy of Spanish Lombardy in the Seventeenth Century* (Cambridge, Mass.: Harvard University Press, 1979) p. 25.

17. See, for example, John U. Nef, *Industry and Government in France and England 1540–1640* (Ithaca: Cornell University Press, 1957); Shepard B. Clough, 'Retardative Factors in French Economic Development', *Journal of Economic History*, vol. VI, supplement (1946), pp. 91–102.

18. Richard T. Rapp, *Industry and Economic Decline in Seventeenth-Century Venice* (Cambridge, Mass.: Harvard University Press, 1976).

19. The examples are many, but among recent works see Phyllis Deane, *The First Industrial Revolution* (Cambridge University Press, 1979); J. A. Van Houtte, *An Economic History of the Low Countries 800–1800* (London: Weidenfeld and Nicolson, 1977); and A. J. Youngson, *Possibilities of Economic Progress* (Cambridge University Press, 1959). R. M. Hartwell, *The Industrial Revolution and Economic Growth* (London: Methuen, 1971) p. 152, cautions, however, against placing too much explanatory weight on foreign demand and holds that 'The largest growth market must have been the home

market . . . demand which was local and obvious and which had an
immediate response from industrial producers'.

20. Joel Mokyr, *Industrialization in the Low Countries, 1795–1850* (New Haven: Yale
    University Press, 1976), indicates how the Netherlands lost their early
    industrial superiority to others, including Belgium, in the eighteenth and
    nineteenth centuries.
21. The aforementioned regression in Puebla to smaller-scale production units is
    interesting in this regard.
22. Joseph T. Fuhrmann, *The Origins of Capitalism in Russia: Industry and Progress in
    the Sixteenth and Seventeenth Centuries* (Chicago: Quadrangle Books, 1972).
23. Peter Mathias, 'Who Unbound Prometheus? Science and Technical Change,
    1600–1800', in A. E. Musson (ed.), *Science, Technology, and Economic Growth in the
    Eighteenth Century* (London: Methuen, 1972), p. 80.
24. A useful account of the pre-industrial ferment in one country is found in B. A.
    Holderness, *Pre-industrial England, Economy and Society 1500–1750* (London:
    J. M. Dent, 1976).
25. See M. M. Postan, *The Medieval Economy and Society* (London: Weidenfeld and
    Nicholson, 1972), p. 196, for an early example of this aspect of interregional
    trade.

3 Variations on the North American Triangle from Yorktown to Waterloo: Substitution, Complementarity, Parallelism

F. CROUZET

I

The role played by the United States in the economic history of the 'Napoleonic wars' period is easily underestimated. Of course, they stood apart from the two main contenders, Britain and France, and not only in the geographical sense. They were a 'small country', with under four million people in 1790, over seven in 1810, as against twenty seven and thirty respectively at the same dates for France,[1] and over fifteen for the United Kingdom in 1801. They were also a 'new country', of recent settlement, with economic structures less complex and sophisticated than in Western Europe. Thirdly, they kept out of the European wars up to June 1812, and Mr Madison's war lasted just thirty months; though they had been previously involved in the (not too serious) quasi-war with France of 1798–1800, and though their diplomatic relations with France and still more with Britain were under severe strain from 1807 onwards (with serious consequences for American trade), their experience was entirely different from that of France and Britain, which were in a state of war for twenty years, with only the fourteen month long break of the Peace of Amiens (not to mention the civil strife in

44

France during the 1790s and the Waterloo campaign). However, this very neutrality, which was something new for Americans who, either as 'colonials' or as 'rebels', had been belligerents in previous Anglo-French wars, and which was preserved longer than for any European neutral (such as Denmark), gave to the United States a unique position; combined with their resources endowment, their geographical position, the enterprise of their merchants and shipowners, it made them play a crucial part in international trading between 1793 and 1812.

This paper will try to explore some aspects of the triangular relationship between the United States, Britain and France[2] – a connection which might have turned into a three-cornered fight, if some American politicians, who wanted to declare war against *both* Britain and France, for having violated American rights, had had their way.

The first point is a substitution phenomenon. As a consequence of the European war, the United States found themselves suddenly having to substitute for France (and other countries) as a sea-trading power; they also infiltrated some trades which had been hitherto British preserves.

On the eve of the French Revolution, France had a large and prosperous (with, however, some concealed weaknesses) foreign trade, the value of which equalled that of Britain. She had also a large merchant navy: over 5000 ocean-going ships of 729 000 tons burden (1785), second only to the British merchant fleet, with its 12 000 ships of 1 200 000 tons.

However, the grand design, which had existed, of taking advantage of American independence for snatching from the British the valuable United States market, had failed utterly.[3] French exporters were unable to compete with the British in supplying textiles and iron goods for current consumption, while American importers and consumers reverted quickly to British manufactures to which they had been accustomed before the Revolution. French merchants were also unable to grant long-term credit on the same scale as the British. Moreover, many French firms which had been involved in trade with America during the war, had badly burnt their fingers, and first class houses kept to their traditional West Indian or East Indian connections. Anyway new trading and credit networks take some time to be woven, while it proved easy for British merchants to resume contacts with their former correspondents in the 'colonies'. The depression and instability which were rampant in the Confederation must also be taken into account.

In any event, once war with England had started in 1793, French shipping and trade were left completely unprotected. During the eighteenth century, the French Navy had been inferior to the Royal Navy, both in numbers (of ships and – this was probably more serious – of able seamen) and in fighting capacity: crews, officers and admirals, training, tactics and strategy, were not up to English standards. Even under the favourable circumstances of the American War of Independence, the much-vaunted navy of Louis XVI just managed to hold its own. During the French Revolution, the navy was soon completely disorganised, owing to a breakdown in discipline and the emigration or dismissal of many officers. While the revolutionary governments built up a new army which became a formidable force, they never managed to restore the navy to a satisfactory condition. A number of encounters with the British ended up in serious losses which further weakened the French and it was a much depleted fleet which Napoleon inherited – to send it to be uselessly butchered at Trafalgar. Later on, however, he made a serious effort to restore his navy and had a large number of new ships built, but he kept them safely in the ports, waiting for the moment when superiority in numbers over the British would have been achieved; this moment never came before his fall . . .

The French Navy was not able thus to organise and escort, as in earlier eighteenth century wars, convoys of merchant ships, in order to maintain long-distance trade relations, especially with the French colonies. Such convoys were used only once, in 1794, in special circumstances, to save France from famine, by importing large quantities of grain from the United States.[4] The risks of capture for merchant ships flying the French flag were therefore very high, insurance premiums prohibitive. The French flag was wiped out from the high seas and the French merchant navy almost destroyed: around 1800, it had only 1500 ocean-going ships left and in 1814 a few hundred – while the United Kingdom had over 21 000 ships of 2 400 000 tons burden.

What happened to the rest of French shipping is not quite clear. A good number were, of course, captured by the British, but they were mostly ships which were at sea at the beginning of the hostilities. For instance, in 1803, the shipowners of Bordeaux lost 63 of the 155 ships which they had at sea when war was resumed. But once it was known that war was on, few shipowners were foolish enough to send out ships under the French flag: indeed, the British did not have much to capture and this was one reason why they eventually turned against the neutrals. On the other hand, some French ships were sold to neutral owners, including American merchants; such sales could be either genuine or fictitious, in the latter case the ship remaining French property under ostensibly neutral papers.[5] This system of 'neutralisation' was widely used by the Dutch, once they were at war with England, and they transferred many of their ships under 'convenience flags' of tiny North German states, such as Kniphausen and Papenburg. Some fast ships were converted into privateers – privateering being a normal substitute for regular trade (Americans also resorted to it during the War of 1812);[6] and it is likely that many others just rotted away in port.

The picture is not as black for French foreign trade: its history, during the Napoleonic wars, appears as complex, with a number of sharp fluctuations, rather than some sudden collapse or continuous decline; there were depressions and revivals, attempts also at finding new orientations. Nonetheless, even in its best years, the sea-borne trade of France was markedly smaller than before the war, and after 1807 – when Britain brutally tightened her sea blockade – it fell to a very low level, though it was not completely destroyed. However, it is now generally accepted that the 'maritime' or 'Atlantic' sector of the French economy, including industries which had backward or forward linkages with sea-borne trade, suffered during the Napoleonic wars serious and, in some respects, irretrievable losses.[7]

In sharp contrast with this decline stands the meteoric rise of American foreign trade and shipping, from 1793 onwards and up to 1807, when they were faced with serious problems. There is no need to quote more than a few figures: the value of total American exports had been $21 million in 1792; its record level of the period, in 1807, was $108 million, a five-fold increase within fifteen years, that is an average exponential rate of growth of 9.4 per cent per year (but, at constant prices, the advance would be less dramatic, roughly by a factor of three).[8] As for American shipping, the tonnage of vessels engaged in foreign trade, which had already risen markedly from 1789 onwards, increased from 411 000 tons in 1792 to nearly one million (981 000) in 1809.[9] Within a few years, it had replaced the French as the second largest merchant fleet in the world. And the approximate share of the United States in world trade reached six per cent in 1800, while it had been two per cent twenty years earlier.[10]

A very large part of this spectacular progress was a direct consequence of the war between Britain and France, and of the destruction or inactivity of the ocean-going shipping of France and her allies. However, some of this advance had nothing or very little to do with the war: especially the enormous increase in raw cotton exports. Its causes were Whitney's gin, the spread of cotton cultivation in the southern states, the fantastic growth of the cotton industry in Britain (plus a slower growth on the Continent).[11] The value of cotton exports was next to nothing before 1793; it reached $14 million in 1807,[12] so that those exports were responsible for nearly one half the increase in *domestic* exports by the United States, which rose by $30 million between 1793 and 1807.

However, most of the expansion in other fields of American trade resulted from the wars and the new opportunities which they opened and which American merchants and shipowners were quick to grasp.[13]

In some years of the war period, European countries which had suffered bad harvests resorted on a large scale to the United States to obtain the grain and flour they needed; normally, they would have bought from the Baltic countries, the traditional granary of Europe; but during the wars trade relations with Baltic ports were at times entirely cut off, at some others, freight and insurance on trade with them were so high that it made American grain competitive, despite the longer haul over the Atlantic. This happened, for instance, to France in·1794, to Britain in 1801, to Spain and Portugal in 1811 and 1812.

Less spasmodic was the export from the United States to the Caribbean islands of foodstuffs and lumber. This trade was, of course, far from new, but it increased a good deal after 1793. The French colonies had been officially opened to American ships since 1784, but once the war had started, what remained of them became completely dependent on imports from the United States for their food supplies (in 1805, these imports exceeded $7 million). As for the British, after 1783 they had tried hard to restrict trade between ex-continental colonies and their West Indian islands (and to reserve it to British ships), and to have the latter supplied as much as possible from British North America. This system had not been too successful and it became unworkable in war time. To prevent food shortages – which were thought especially dangerous in an era of slave revolts – the British Government had, though reluctantly, to authorise the islands' governors to suspend the Navigation Acts and to open their ports to American foodstuffs and lumber imported in

American ships. The latter had the advantage of lower freights and insurance premiums than British ships,[14] which were driven out from the trade in the 1790s; while, of course, imports from British North America had the additional and decisive disadvantage of distance. It was estimated that in 1803–5 the British West Indies received from the United States two thirds of their food imports and almost all their lumber, with 85 per cent of these imports on board American ships.

However, the most spectacular and important development in American foreign trade, owing to the war, was the capture of a large slice of the 'carrying trade' between European countries and their colonies. As mentioned earlier, owing to British ascendancy at sea, it was impossible for French ships to trade with the French colonies. The same fate overtook the two other colonial powers which willy-nilly joined France in the struggle against England: Holland in 1794, Spain in 1796, and both again after 1803. The French, Dutch and Spanish colonies would have choked if they had not been able to use neutral ships to keep up relations with Europe. At first, a British Order-in-Council of 6 November 1793 had prohibited neutral ships trading with the French colonies, but London retreated soon before American anger; a fresh Order of 8 January 1794 (which was extended in 1798, confirmed by the King's Advocate in 1801, and renewed on 24 June 1803, when hostilities were resumed) only forbade neutral ships to trade directly between an enemy country and its colonies, implying that trade between enemy colonies and neutral ports would not be disturbed.

This allowed the development, from 1794 to 1807, of a peculiar commerce which grew fast and became very large. Neutral ships, mostly American (but including some European neutrals, such as Danes and Hamburgers), carried on trade actually between France, Holland and Spain, on the one hand, and their colonies (in the Caribbean, but also in the Indian Ocean and in South America),[15] on the other. They supplied the latter with foodstuffs, manufactured goods, wines and spirits, even slaves, and they brought back sugar, coffee, indigo, cotton, etc. But, on their way, they called at a neutral – generally American – port, in order to 'break' or 'interrupt' the voyage and to make it lawful in the eyes of the British. In many cases, this was just a 'formal' or even fictitious call: taking advantage of convenient American customs regulations, the cargo was landed and a bond given to pay import duties if the goods were not reexported within a given period; actually the cargo was soon reexported, the bond cancelled and a certificate of drawback granted, which could be used in case of British capture as evidence that this was not a 'continuous voyage' between two enemy ports, though, quite often, the same ship was used on both legs of the journey. Thanks to this system of fictitious 'bonded warehousing' and to the trade routes which were generally followed across the Atlantic, the detour to call at an American port on the way from the Carribbean to the Continent was not a cause of serious additional expense or delay. It was estimated in 1807 that the trade in Caribbean colonial produce was shared between Britain and the United States in the proportion 60 per cent–40 per cent.[16]

The growth of this carrying trade brought about a large increase in imports into the United States (though most of them did not stay long on American soil) and a still larger one of reexports of foreign goods. American reexports had been quite small before the war: $1.8 million in 1792; as soon as 1796, they had jumped to $26 million; in 1801, they reached $47 million; they fell back during the peace of Amiens, when direct relations between European countries and their colonies were resumed, but they flourishd again when the war broke out anew, to reach their peak in 1806 and 1807, at $60 million, thirty-three times more than in 1792, having risen much faster than American *domestic* exports. Ideed, in every year but two between 1797 and 1808, the value of reexports exceeded that of domestic exports; they were the most powerful factor in the rise of total American exports, being responsible for 68 per cent of their increase between 1792 and 1807.

American ships were also employed in other new trades and in tramping activities with intricate patterns; like the seventeenth-century Dutch in Colbert's words, they had become the *rouliers des mers*. They entered the coasting trade in Europe, between ports of countries which were at war with Britain: for instance, they carried wine fom Bordeaux to northern Europe. As for the trade with India (the Jay treaty had opened British ports there to American ships) and China, it was also helped by the war, as Americans reexported or even carried directly to Europe and to non-British colonies in America, large quantities of Indian printed cottons, tea and spices. Exports from British India in American vessels increased from 23 to 31 lacs of rupees (yearly average) between 1796–1800 and 1801–5.

All this growing and eventually enormous carrying trade was bringing in a large invisible income: American net freight earnings are estimated to have risen from $7 million in 1792 to $31 million in

1801 and to $42 million in 1807, making good a large part of the United States merchandise-trade deficit. Of course, thousands of American ships were captured or seized by the British and the French (though capture did not mean inevitably condemnation and confiscation), but this was a business risk that could be reduced to a cost by insurance and up to 1807, it was a supportable cost.

This upsurge of American foreign trade and shipping has been the theme of discussions which shall be only briefly mentioned. D. C. North and G. R. Taylor considered that it was a major factor in the fast economic growth which, according to them, took place in the United States during the very prosperous years from 1793 to 1807. The fluctuations in the American economy were directly correlated to those in foreign trade and to the military-political situation in Europe. The carrying trade enriched the main port-cities and stimulated a number of ancillary industries and services; moreover, it had a multiplier effect through the whole economy. This view of an export-led growth has been criticised by P. David: he does not see much evidence of a boom in the economy or of a large increase in per capita income; moreover, the economy was not open enough for a rise in exports to have a serious impact on the whole of it; the increase in foreign trade and shipping can therefore have made a small contribution only to the growth of national product. It can be added that the reexport of unmanufactured produce, however massive, has little stimulative effect upon an economy as a whole, and especially upon technological progress.[17]

According to a recent article by C. D. Goldin and F. D. Lewis, American maritime expansion has been 'romanticised', but loses much of its legendary importance when confronted with statistical analysis, which leads them to conclude that 'had there been no change in the foreign sector from 1793 to 1807, per capita income would have been reduced by approximately three per cent', that is less than two dollars in 1800. On the other hand, they stress that 'though the rate of growth was modest', the buoyant foreign sector 'contributed significantly to the growth that did occur', increasing it 'by about one-quarter of a percentage point or slightly more than 25 per cent' (and 40 per cent if other assumptions are made). However, 'even though the increase in trade . . . did not dramatically increase incomes', it had longer range effects, such as urbanisation and other structural changes, so that the period of neutrality 'may have led to the emergence of a nascent national economy'.[18]

A similar controversy has taken place in France, though at a far less sophisticated level: it has been maintained that the growth and prosperity of French sea-borne trade from the early eighteenth century up to 1789 was something superficial – epidermic, as E. Labrousse was fond of saying – without much impact upon *la France profonde*, so that the decline and collapse of the maritime sector during the Revolutionary and Napoleonic periods did not have far-reaching consequences (except at the local level, in the ports and in coastal districts) and did not prevent France from being rather prosperous during most of Napoleon's rule.

II

The rise of the American carrying trade and of the American merchant navy which transported it, was basically a substitution for the direct relations, in their own ships, among France, Holland, Spain and their colonies, which the war had made impossible. On the other hand, there was no inverse correlation (except as far as shipping was concerned) between American and French (and Dutch and Spanish) maritime prosperity, but rather a good deal of complementarity, a sort of symbiotic relationship across the Atlantic. It was mainly thanks to the mediation of American ships that France and her satellites were able to retain some long-distance, transoceanic trade and especially some relations with their colonies. A counter-proof is the quasi-war of 1798–1800, during which French ports suffered a sharp fall of traffic (eight American ships entered Bordeaux in 1800, as against sixty-four in 1796), many bankruptcies and a serious depression. On the contrary, during the years 1803–7, which saw American trade at its zenith, French ports such as Bordeaux, Nantes and Marseilles, enjoyed a phase of 'semi-prosperity' (P. Butel), which was actually the best (or the least unfavourable) of the whole war-time period. In 1805, 201 American ships entered Bordeaux, which was a large number, and in 1807 Marseilles received 97 of them.[19] Ostensibly, their cargoes were American property, in order to escape British capture, but part of this trade was actually on French account.[20] A network of relationships, which had not existed in the 1780s, had been built up, especially as a number of French merchants had settled in the United States, often as refugees from the French colony of Santo Domingo (Haiti), after the slave revolt.[21] It was during those same years that the irregular and volatile Franco-American trade made up a significant share of each country's total trade,[22] though much of it was not really between France and the United States, but between France and her colonies through American ships and ports (it is typical that sugar was then the largest 'American' export to France). Still, American shipping helped France to preserve some remains of her former trading position, and the Continent to be supplied with non-British colonial produce and without Britain's mediation.

However, in November 1807, the British cabinet issued its famous Orders-in-Council, which prevented *de facto* neutral countries to trade with enemy ports; in conjunction with Napoleon's Berlin and Milan decrees, as well as with Jefferson's embargo, this was a deadly blow to the American carrying trade. It revived somewhat (but not with France) after the raising of the embargo and the British Order-in-Council of 26 April 1809, which put France, Holland and northern Italy – and them only – under strict and rigorous blockade and therefore allowed neutrals to trade with the outer fringes of Napoleonic Europe, in northern Europe and the Mediterranean. But the highest figure for American reexports from 1808 onwards, $24 million in 1810, was a far cry from their 1807 peak.[23] Anyway, if the Order-in-Council had struck this trade suddenly, it was doomed in the longer run, owing to the conquest by British forces of the last colonies which remained under French rule (in 1809 and 1810, and the Dutch East Indies in 1811), while the Spanish colonies had sided in 1808 with the Spanish patriots and therefore with Britain against Napoleon.[24] Eventually, Britain monopolised the carrying trade in the produce of both East and West Indies and 'became the grocer of Europe'.[25]

Nonetheless, though the sea-borne trade of France fell to a very low level after 1807, it somewhat revived at times, for instance when both the British Government and Napoleon found that their interest was to relax the rigour of their respective blockades and to grant licences for a direct trade – in grain, wines or sugar – between the two countries. And there were the blockade-runners, ships which tried to break through the British sea-blockade. From July 1810 onwards, Napoleon granted special permits to American ships to trade directly between the United States and France. This was a highly risky venture, but it was attempted by a number of fast American ships, sailing mostly from Baltimore and during the winter, to take advantage of the long nights. Over thirty of those blockade-runners arrived each year in Bordeaux, which was their main destination, in 1811–13. When leaving France, they were obliged to export French goods for a value equal to that of the imports they had brought in, with a given proportion of some articles such as silks (eventually 50 per cent of the total cargo), wines and brandies.[26] It is possible that those exports, though actually forced upon the American market, did help to create there a taste for French goods which had not existed before, but which developed after 1815, when the United States became the largest foreign market for the silk industry of Lyons.

There is no need to dwell on the obvious complementarity between the American and British economies (J. Potter has written of a neo-colonial economic relationship),[27] in which the former almost specialised in primary production, the latter having a large manufacturing sector, which was exporting a significant part of its output, while its most dynamic industry was increasingly dependent on the United States for its raw material supplies. Moreover, from 1783 to 1802, exports were for Britain a major engine of growth, and the United States market played a crucial part in the fast growth of British domestic exports; at current prices, it took 21 per cent of them in 1784–6, 27 per cent in 1794–6 and 25 per cent in 1804–6; it was responsible for 26 per cent of the increase in total domestic exports from Britain between 1784–6 and 1804–6 (but 34 per cent for the period 1784–6 to 1794–6).[28] The United States were Britain's first customer and up to 1807, more than made good the losses of markets in continental Europe. As for American domestic exports, Britain bought over a third of them in the early nineteenth century: 1802–7.

However, in the case of Britain – or rather the British Empire as a whole – there was also a good deal of competition with the United States. Shipping was, in this respect, a basic factor. For obvious geographical reasons, shipbuilding costs were much lower in the timber-rich America than in deforested Britain, which had to import from northern Europe much of the materials. American ships were generally better built than the British, and their running costs were not higher. Their owners could offer cheaper freight rates while, as neutrals, they paid lower insurance premiums. Therefore, they drove out British ships from the sea routes which were open to competition and, to begin with, from the direct trade between Britain and the United States. Before 1793 British ships were at least on a par with Americans on this route, but in 1802–4 American ships accounted for 82 per cent of the total tonnage of shipping which entered British ports from the United States and left them for the latter destination; in 1805–7, their share had risen to 92 per cent. They had also practically monopolised the traffic between their country and the British West Indies. As a result, shipbuilding declined in Britain and her colonies after 1803, while it boomed in the United States, which in 1805 built 129 000 tons as against 71 000 in Britain and 90 000 in the whole Empire.

Moreover, the rise of the American carrying trade in colonial produce had eventually baneful consequences for the British colonies. This did not happen in the 1790s, because of the 'destruction' of Santo Domingo, the world's first producer of sugar, which created a shortage of this commodity; but most sugar-growing territories increased their output in answer to higher prices, so that sugar prices peaked in 1798 and declined on trend afterwards, the seller's market having turned into a buyer's market.[29]

In the cut-throat competition that followed, the British were at a disadvantage: most of their Caribbean possessions were high-cost producers and, thanks moreover to lower transportation costs in American ships, foreign – mostly 'enemy' – sugar could undercut British-grown sugar on European markets.[30] From 1802 to 1806, reexports of sugar from Britain fell by half, while imports increased (owing to British conquest of some enemy colonies), and while reexports from the United States advanced sharply. In 1806 and 1807 the British West Indies suffered an acute depression and many planters were ruined or at least threatened with ruin.[31]

British North America was also depressed; owing to the war, it had lost to the United States, as mentioned earlier, the Caribbean market for its grain, lumber and fish.[32] As for the exports of cod from Newfoundland and the present maritime provinces of Canada, they suffered from French control over the Catholic countries of Southern Europe which were their chief market; a growing share of 'British-caught fish' had to be sent to American ports, in order to be reexported on American ships toward Europe. At the same time, American fisheries, which had been the main beneficiaries of the disappearance of French fishing boats from the Newfoundland Banks, were enjoying an insolent prosperity. Lastly, the rise of American trade with India, which has been alluded to earlier, short-circuited British East Indian trade and harmed British imports and reexports of Indian printed cottons.

On the whole, there was a crisis of the imperial economy, which developed after the renewal of the war in 1803 and became serious in 1806–7. Undoubtedly, its direct cause was American competition, including an American infiltration within the imperial economic system (for instance, British North America appeared to be on the way to be economically satellitised).[33]

No wonder, therefore, that the United States, and especially their carrying trade in colonial produce from enemy colonies, came under heavy fire not only from mercantilist die-hards like Lord Sheffield, but also from some powerful pressure groups, first of all the West India interest, but also a 'North American' lobby, the 'shipping interest' and the East India Company, which were all suffering from American competition. It was maintained that the United States were 'objective' (as one would say currently) accomplices of France and her satellites which, through their help, were able to preserve relations with their colonies and to trade almost as freely as in peace time; under such circumstances, the Royal Navy was almost neutralised as an offensive weapon, Britain's vital interests – especially her sea-power – were in jeopardy, her colonies and her reexport trade (which actually stagnated after 1803) were threatened with ruin.[34]

On the other hand, it could be pointed out that this very American carrying trade, which harmed British colonies, was most beneficial to British manufactures. The United States balance of payments had a deficit with the British Empire, but a large surplus with continental Europe, which was remitted to merchant banks in England and used eventually to pay for English manufactures which were exported to America.[35] This triangular system of international settlements had been essential to the progress of British exports to the United States.

III

In any event, the enormous American carrying trade existed only on sufferance from Britain. She tolerated it for years, but it suffered from some harassment in 1805[36] and eventually, in November 1807, the new Tory government prohibited it *de facto* altogether. The motivations for this change were complex, the main one being the necessity of countering and defeating Napoleon's Continental Blockade, but the influence of the anti-American lobbies which have just been mentioned cannot be denied, so that, in some respects, the Orders-in-Council were directed as much against the United States as against France.

From 1805–7, American neutral rights were therefore less and less respected by the belligerents; Napoleon, for his part, was no innocent and, on several occasions, behaved abominably with America;[37] still, occasions for incidents with Britain, as the dominant sea-power, were more frequent than with France, and there was also the burning issue of impressment and the question of the west. Confronted with the same problem as France, Britain's overwhelming sea-power and the way she was wielding it, the United States attempted to retaliate by policies which were not too different from those followed by France. Those policies and the War of 1812 which came on top of them brought about eventually some similarities and parallelisms in the economic development of France and the United States during the later years of the wars.

Jefferson and Madison wanted Britain (and France) to be more respectful of American rights, but also to avoid war with her; it was obviously absurd to make war to protect American trade, which would soon be destroyed if hostilities broke out with England. So Jefferson resorted to 'peaceful coercion', that is economic sanctions. He tried, through the embargo, to deprive Britain and France of American produce, American markets and the use of American ships, which in his view they badly needed, in order to retaliate against their exactions and to force them into concessions; the embargo, therefore, was an American *self-blockade*, a refusal to trade with countries which were trampling on American rights.[38] The same calculations and the same device of self-blockade can be found in the other economic sanctions – or would-be sanctions – which were taken by the United States against the delinquent great powers, from the abortive first Non-Importation Act of 1806 to the Non-Intercourse Act of 1809 (though this was a bad joke, as nothing was easier than to violate it), and to the second – and more effective – Non-Importation Act of 1811.

Now those various measures of self-denial of trade by America were akin – though less drastic and following a native patriotic tradition of 'threats to the British pocket-book'[39] – to Napoleon's Continental Blockade, which was basically a self-blockade, the refusal to admit any ship coming from Britain and any British merchandise into France and the countries she controlled. There was, of course, the difference that Napoleon's blockade was part of a warfare system aimed at defeating England, while American 'sanctions' were diplomatic weapons, intended to bring back to its senses the British cabinet, without resorting to war: they were an 'alternative to war', as B. Perkins has called the embargo. But the two sets of measures had in common the fact that they were rather inefficient substitutes for the sea-power which neither France nor the United States had, but which would have been the only effective weapon against England. They had moreover the common fate of being violated on a grand scale: America had its equivalents of Heligoland (the island off the north German coast which was the base for intensive smuggling of British goods), such as Amelia Island on the border between Georgia and Spanish Florida. And the British Government resorted to the same devices to encourage the citizens of the United States and Napoleon's subjects to break the prohibitions against British trade which their own rulers had issued. Still, when it came to happen in 1811 and early 1812 that the American and the French self-blockades were enforced rather efficiently at the same time, the effects upon British industry were serious; so, under the pressure of manufacturers and the fear of workers' riots, the British cabinet repealed the Orders-in-Council on 23 June 1812; four days earlier, President Madison had proclaimed a state of war with Great Britain.

C. P. Kindleberger has written that 'war is the ultimate protective tariff',[40] but the self-blockade measures which had preceded 1812 had already afforded American industry an intermittent, but not ineffective protection. Jefferson's embargo did not affect directly the importation of British goods, and the Non-Importation Act of 1806, which was enforced during part of the embargo period, did not apply to several important British manufactures. However, many British exporters and American importers were worried by the danger of war between the two countries; they wondered also how exports to America would be paid since the embargo was preventing the United States from exporting. So, at the end of 1807 and for most of 1808, British businessmen restricted their shipments; exports of British goods to the United States fell from £11.9 million in 1807 to £5.2 million (current values) in 1808. The second Non-Importation Act, which was more comprehensive and more seriously enforced, brought about a more drastic fall of British exports to the United States: from £10.9 million in 1810 to £1.8 million in 1811. Officially, the American market was closed to British goods from April 1811 to the Peace of Ghent – though there was a good deal of smuggling.[41] This situation resulted in higher prices for manufactured goods, which made their production in the United States a more economic proposition than formerly, when

British goods were coming in freely and paying low duties under the tariff of 1789. On the other side of the Atlantic, the Continental Blockade was not purely an offensive weapon against England; it had also a defensive aspect, as it acted as a system of extreme protection against British competition, which fostered the growth of industry in France and some other parts of the Continent (though, at least in France, protective measures had been adopted well before the Berlin decree).

'Jefferson's embargo launched a period of Hamiltonian development in the United States', which 'entered (like France and Belgium from, say, 1800) a period of protracted industrial expansion'. One cannot but agree with those remarks by W. W. Rostow:[42] the Napoleonic period in France, the years 1808–14 in America, did see an upsurge in industrial production under the shelter of protection and war. The parallel is made closer by the fact that the most striking developments in both countries took place in the same branch – the cotton industry.

This is a well-known story and one needs only to stress that cotton was, at the time, the industry which was the most liable to grow fast, but also where British competition was the most formidable, so that its progress, on both sides of the Atlantic, was dependent on economic warfare against England. In France, machine-spinning of cotton did not develop really before the late 1790s, when the Directory tried to enforce a prohibition of English goods and when some manufacturers managed to smuggle in from England blueprints and spare parts of 'modern' machinery. Renewed and striking progress of the cotton industry was achieved under Napoleon's rule, especially after a decree of February 1806 which prohibited the importation into France of cotton yarn and cotton grey cloth (for printing). There was a boom in machine-spinning from 1806 to 1810, with a four-fold increase in the output of machine-spun yarn. At the fall of Napoleon, France had built up a respectable cotton-spinning industry of about one million spindles (but Britain had five million of them!) and hand-spinning had disappeared. The industry's total output, as measured by its raw-cotton consumption, might have been, in its peak year, 1810, three times its 1789 figure – a sign that weaving and printing had not grown as fast (nor technically changed as much) as spinning.[43]

In the United States there had been since the 1780s a number of attempts to establish a cotton industry, but most of them had failed. The stimulus given by the embargo was remarkable: the 'cotton craze' increased the number of mills from 15 in 1807 to 87 in 1810 (with 8000 and 80 000 spindles respectively). Non-importation and the War of 1812 gave a further stimulus: in 1815, the United States had 213 mills with 130 000 spindles; the industry had attracted a number of men with large capital, especially the 'Boston Associates', and the factory system had taken definite roots in New England. Moreover, though weaving remained a domestic hand-loom activity, the output of cotton cloth in New England, according to R. Zevin's calculations, jumped from 84 000 yards in 1807 to 181 000 in 1808, 801 000 in 1811 and just under two million in 1814 – a fantastic rate of growth of 55 per cent per year.[44]

In other industries, the impetus from the war and the self-blockades, though widespread, is less striking – and also the similarity between France and the United States. The large French wool industry was not too exposed to British competition; still it achieved some modernisation: by 1815, most of the carding and spinning of wool was done by new machinery imitating English models. On the other hand, the United States had very little in the way of a wool industry strictly speaking, though a good deal of spinning and weaving of wool was done within households. After 1807 there was some progress, especially owing to government orders of cloth for the army during the War of 1812; in 1815, Connecticut, the main centre of the wool industry, had 25 factories employing 1200 workers – figures which illustrate both the rise and the very modest scale of this industry in the United States. As for the iron industry, it is interesting that both in France and in America it underwent very little technical progress during the wars and started its industrial revolution after they were over (actually much later in the United States). But there was more change in the secondary metal trades, and the origins of the 'American system of manufactures' go back to the work of Eli Whitney and Simeon North for supplying firearms to government during the quasi-war with France.

On his way back from Moscow in 1812, Napoleon, who was meditating rather gloomily, suddenly said to one of his companions: 'After all, I have created French industry'. This was, of course, a gross overstatement, but with the grain of truth that his policies had helped the beginnings of the industrial revolution in France; indeed many scholars would maintain that modern industry was born in France during his rule. Likewise, it would be wrong to claim that the embargo, non-importation and the War of 1812 created American industry: before 1808, large quantities of manufactured goods of many varieties were already made in the United States. But those political events 'produced substantial change in the course of economic development', as C. P. Kindleberger has written, and gave to industry a strong stimulus (just what some people in Britain had feared as an indirect effect of the Orders-in-Council). Up to 1807, the large profits to be made in foreign trading ventures and in shipping as well, of course, as in agriculture (owing to high farm prices), had attracted all available capital; later on, a good deal of merchants' and shipowners' capital, which was idle owing to the interruption of sea-borne trade, was shifted towards industry. So the United States had an industrial expansion 'which helped to prepare the way for the later passage of New England into sustained industrial growth',[45] *a* beginning, if not *the* beginning of the industrial revolution.

Both the American and the French industrial developments of the war period (especially in the cotton industry) have been criticised as 'hothouse' expansion, achieved under artificial conditions, and as a wasteful diversion of national resources into import-substitution. This problem will not be discussed here, but a last similarity between the United States and France will be mentioned. In both countries, many industrial firms which had mushroomed during the war but which had much higher costs than their British rivals, could not stand the latter's competition when hostilities ended, inasmuch as the low-duties American tariff of 1789 was no protection against the flood of cheap British goods and the restored Bourbons announced in April 1814 a liberal trade policy. The result was an industrial 'infanticide',[46] which made the tariff question acute. In France there was such an outcry that the government had to retreat quickly; as early as December 1814, a new and strongly protectionist tariff law was passed; additional legislation during the few years that followed gave France an ultra-protectionist system which lasted, without much alleviation, until 1860. In the United States, things did not go as far, but many petitions demanded protection for the nation's infant industries and the tariff of 1816 was decidedly protectionist, especially in respect of cotton goods. A lasting consequence of the Napoleonic wars was thus to create in both France and the United States a strong protectionist tradition.

IV

During the 'Second Hundred Years' War' (1689–1815), the control of North America, of the Caribbean and the glittering prizes of the carrying trade between *les deux Indes* and Europe had been major stakes in the Anglo-French struggle. Despite many set-backs – especially the loss of her North American empire in the Seven Years' War – France had managed to hold out as far as trade was concerned. However, during the final phase (1793–1815) of their long-drawn struggle, France was decisively defeated by Britain and dropped out of the race for naval, colonial and commercial supremacy. Though she started at the same time to modernise her industry and – much more slowly – her agriculture, and though she remained up to 1871 the second commercial power in the world, her role in international trade was minor in comparison with Britain, which during the war period had 'moved from a major to a dominant position in the world trading framework'.[47] Of course, Britain's economic lead had helped her win the wars (as Malthus wrote in 1820, 'in carrying on the late war, we were powerfully assisted by our steam-engines'),[48] but military victory strengthened markedly her economic position. P. O'Brien and C. Keyder have observed that the gap of about fifteen per cent between British and French per capita incomes during the nineteenth century resulted mainly from British superiority in shipping, banking and commercial services supplied to foreigners, and that 'this particular advantage was a pay-off' for earlier British 'investment in naval power and imperial conquest'.[49]

As befits a new and fast-growing country, the United States underwent at a much quicker pace an evolution which has some common features with that of France. A basically agricultural country, they came unexpectedly and without having wanted it, to be in possession of the heritage of France as a great sea-trading power,[50] and therefore, willy-nilly, the rivals of England. There is no 'perfect' neutral and American neutrality was, according to circumstances, 'objectively' profitable at one time to France, at another time to Britain. For instance, the American carrying trade in colonial produce created severe competition for the British West Indies and for British reexports of colonial produce and was helpful to France and her satellites. When Jefferson enacted the embargo, he actually sided with Napoleon in waging economic warfare against England. On the other hand, when the non-intercourse policy and still more the Macon Act of 1 May 1810 were adopted, the United States accepted to trade more or less freely with Britain (and on a massive scale in 1810), but to be deprived of any trade with France; they became indeed Britain's satellite. However, with the Non-Importation Act of 1811, they changed sides and became Napoleon's allies. During the War of 1812, they were in the boat where France had been for many years: their sea-borne trade was strangled by the British blockade, but they enjoyed an outburst of industrialisation. Anyway, because of overwhelming British sea-power, they had not been able to retain their role of *rouliers des mers* for more than a dozen years and the rise of their carrying trade was as short-lived as it had been spectacular. Though the American merchant navy remained up to the Civil War a dangerous competitor for the British, its registered tonnage in foreign trade had fallen in 1820 to 584 000 tons, against 981 000 in 1809, this latter figure not to be exceeded again before the 1840s. Roughly speaking, after 1814 the United States turned away from high-seas ventures and toward 'internal improvements', which is not too different from what took place in European countries like France, Prussia and Belgium. However, they had a continent to improve – in the long view an elementary but basic datum.

NOTES AND REFERENCES

1. The 1810 figure does not include the population of the territories which were then annexed to France.
2. With some stress on the Franco-American side. This writer apologises for taking the short or medium and not the long view. He can, however, plead that he deals with a particularly 'Rostovian' period; indeed part of this paper tries to gloss on some ideas which have been put forward by W. W. Rostow who stressed, for instance, that during the wars the American economy was 'both beneficiary and victim of (the) new trading environment', *The World Economy. History and Prospect* (London, 1978) p. 200. The close intermingling and interaction between economics and politics during a period when battles and diplomacy determined much of economic short-term change have also seemed relevant.
3. Recent contributions to this question include: E. C. Papenfuse, 'An Uncertain Connection: Maryland's Trade with France during the American Revolution, 1778–1783', in *La Révolution américaine et l'Europe* (Paris, 1979) pp. 243–64; J. .Meyer, 'Les difficultés du commerce franco-américain vues de Nantes (1776–1790)', *French Historical Studies*, XI, 2, (Fall 1979) pp. 159–83; also a forthcoming article in the same journal by C. Fohlen.
4. This was the occasion for the battle of 'The Glorious First of June' in British

parlance (*13 prairial an II* to the French). However, convoys of small coasters, creeping along the shore, were regularly organised.

5. Paul Butel has kindly informed this writer that he has evidence of Bordeaux merchants' interests in several American ships in 1805-8.
6. But French privateering was less active under Napoleon than in the 1790s, because of increasing British command of the seas.
7. This aspect is only mentioned since the present author has already written too much about it, for example F. Crouzet, 'Wars, Blockade and Economic Change in Europe, 1792–1815', *The Journal of Economic History*, xxiv, 4 (December 1964) pp. 570–2.
8. Imports rose more slowly, from $32 million to $139 million. All figures for US trade and shipping are from *Historical Statistics of the United States* (Washington, 1960).
9. The percentage of US imports and exports, by value, which was carried on American ships, increased from 24 per cent in 1789 to 89 per cent in 1800; W. Woodruff, *America's Impact on the World. A Study of the United States in the World Economy, 1750–1970* (London, 1975) p. 262, Table XII.
10. W. W. Rostow, *How It All Began, Origins of the Modern Economy* (New York, 1975) p. 117, Table 5.
11. It is likely that the war helped the substitution of British cottons for other textiles, which it prevented from reaching their usual markets, but this was not significant.
12. As cotton prices fell after 1799, the increase in volume is the most striking: 138 000 lbs in 1792, 66 million in 1807, 94 million in 1810.
13. J. F. Shepherd and G. M. Walton, 'Economic Change after the American Revolution: Pre- and Post-War Comparisons of Maritime Shipping and Trade', *Explorations in Economic History*, 13, 4 (October 1976) p. 420, stress the 'drastic change' which took place in 1793, inasmuch as in previous years 'the relative importance of foreign trade was declining' for the American economy, but also that the existing 'commercial base' was crucial for the ability of the US to take advantage of the new opportunities.
14. Which were liable to capture by French privateers.
15. After Spain had entered the war against England in 1796, US trade with Spanish America increased very fast; exports to that area reached $13 million in the year 1806/7; 175 American ships entered the port of Havana within four months of 1805 alone.
16. In 1806, the US re-exported 146 million lb of sugar and 47 million lb of coffee.
17. D. C. North, *The Economic Growth of the United States, 1790–1860* (New York, 1961);
    G. R. Taylor, 'American Economic Growth before 1840: An Explanatory Essay', *The Journal of Economic History*, xxiv, 4 (December 1964) pp. 439–42; P. David, 'The Growth of Real Product in the United States before 1840: New Evidence, Controlled Conjectures', ibid., xxvii, 2 (June 1967) pp. 186 *et seq.*; also W. W. Rostow, *The World Economy*, p. 391.
18. C. D. Goldin and F. D. Lewis, 'The Role of Exports in American Economic Growth during the Napoleonic Wars, 1793 to 1807', *Explorations in Economic History*, 17, 1 (January 1980) pp. 6–25, and especially 15–16, 18–23 (and 24, Table A2, which shows that at constant – 1790 – prices, earnings from domestic exports and the carrying trade roughly doubled from 1793 to 1807).

19. Many American ships laden with colonial produce went also to Antwerp and Amsterdam: the latter received 211 of them in 1806. Actually, in 1805, reexports from the USA to Holland – $15 million – were markedly higher than to France – $9.9 million.

20. Still the French had lost the freight earnings on the colonial produce and other goods which in peace-time had been carried on French ships.

21. Unpublished paper which P. Butel has kindly allowed me to quote.

22. From 1804 to 1807 exports to France averaged 12 per cent of total US exports; higher percentages were reached for the abnormal years – 1795 and 1813.

23. A number of American ships went to Holland during a brief period after the aborted Erskine agreement of April 1809, and others to Tonningen in Denmark. Later on in 1810 and 1811 the US had a relatively large trade with Russia, as one of the few markets left open; cf. A. W. Crosby, *America, Russia, Hemp, and Napoleon: American Trade with Russia and the Baltic, 1783–1812* (Columbus, 1965) e.g. pp. 191, 224.

24. As the Spanish colonies – and Brazil – were opened to the British in 1808, when American trade was interrupted by the embargo, they managed to keep the lion's share in their trade, despite an active traffic by the Americans (but the latter lost the reexport to Spanish America of German linens, which had been important before 1808).

25. R. B. Sheridan, 'The Wealth of Jamaica in the Eighteenth Century: a Rejoinder', *The Economic History Review*, XXI, 1 (April 1968) p. 60.

26. There was thus a peak in American imports from France in 1811–13.

27. J. Potter, 'The Effects of the American Revolution on the Economic Relations between the former Colonies and the Mother Country', in *La Révolution américaine et l'Europe*, pp. 267–74.

28. F. Crouzet, 'Toward an Export Economy: British Exports during the Industrial Revolution', *Explorations in Economic History*, 17, 1 (January 1980) pp. 70–2, 78 *et seq*. The percentages quoted have been computed from R. Davis's current values. The role of the US market was especially important from 1788 to 1798 and from 1803 to 1807.

29. Though prices somewhat recovered from 1802 to 1805; but coffee prices fell also from 1805 onward.

30. J. R. Ward, 'The Profitability of Sugar Planting in the British West Indies, 1650–1834', *The Economic History Review*, XXXI, 2 (May 1978) pp. 199–200, Tables 1 and 2, on the rise in freight rates and insurance premiums on sugar from the British colonies to London.

31. J. R. Ward, ibid., pp. 208–9 and S. Drescher, *Econocide: British Slavery in the Era of Abolition* (Pittsburgh, 1977) pp. 76 *et seq*., 131 *et seq*., are less pessimistic than L. J. Ragatz in his classic book *The Fall of the Planter Class in the British Caribbean, 1763–1833* (New York, 1928), but they stress the growing dependence of British plantations on the international market – where they were confronted with American competition.

32. In 1803–5, it supplied under ten per cent of the food imports of the British West Indies.

33. On the contrary, the North American colonies were to prosper during the American embargo, when they exported on a large scale to the Caribbean and were a base for a smuggling trade with the US. From 1809 onwards, they benefited greatly (as also did the shipping interest) from the rise of their timber

exports to Britain, thanks to the preferential duties on colonial timber which were then established.

34. F. Crouzet, 'Groupes de pression et politique de blocus: Remarques sur les origines des Ordres en Conseil de novembre 1807', *Revue Historique*, 463 (July–September 1962) pp. 45–72, where more complete references to some facts mentioned in the present paper can be found.

35. Many American ships which had imported colonial produce into continental ports left them in ballast for England; it was said that three-fourths of the proceeds of American sales in these ports were remitted to London.

36. As a result of the condemnation of the ship *Essex* (July 1805), which encouraged British naval commanders and privateers to capture American ships, but not on government orders; it proved to be a false alarm and American traders carried on.

37. He suspected American ships to be used for smuggling British goods into continental ports; although this happened now and then, the US carrying trade was on the whole beneficial to France.

38. Of course the embargo had also initially a defensive purpose: to save American shipping from the massive depredations that were expected from Britain and France but, as time went on, the coercive side became dominant.

39. B. Perkins, *Prologue to War, England and the United States, 1805–1812* (Berkeley and Los Angeles, 1961) p. 150. And the emphasis in the embargo was on preventing exports from and not imports into, the US.

40. C. P. Kindleberger, 'U.S. Economic Foreign Policy, 1776–1976', *Foreign Affairs*, vol. 55, no. 2 (January 1977) p. 396.

41. And the hasty but massive shipments which had been made from Britain between the repeal of the Orders-in-Council and the news that the US had declared war, were eventually admitted in America.

42. W. W. Rostow, *How It All Began*, p. 202; and *The World Economy*, p. 122.

43. F. Crouzet, 'Wars, Blockade, . . . ', pp. 576–80.

44. R. B. Zevin, 'The Growth of Cotton Textile Production after 1815', in R. W. Fogel and S. L. Engerman (eds), *The Reinterpretation of American Economic History* (New York, 1971) p. 123, Table 1.

45. Rostow, *The World Economy*, p. 122, also p. 119 and *How It All Began*, p. 203.

46. C. P. Kindleberger, 'U.S. Economic Foreign Policy, 1776–1976', p. 396.

47. Rostow, *The World Economy*, p. 122.
    C. Carrière, *Négociants marseillais au XVIIIe siècle*, 2 vols (Marseilles, 1973), has rightly stressed that there was definitely a rupture for French trade when war started in 1793, and that when it ended over twenty years later, the international trading system had completely changed.

48. P. Sraffa (ed.), *The Works and Correspondence of David Ricardo*, vol. II (Cambridge, 1951) p. 361.

49. P. O'Brien and C. Keyder, *Economic Growth in Britain and France, 1780–1914* (London, 1978) p. 197.

50. And also later of Holland and Spain.

4 The Spoilers Foiled: The Exclusion of Prussian Finance from the French Liberation Loan of 1871*

D. S. LANDES

I

If we are to believe Bismarck, it was the representatives of defeated France who first offered the Germans a money indemnity in the hope of saving territory. To this, his first reaction was one of scorn. 'We don't need money', he proclaimed to one unofficial peacemaker. 'I pray of you to say, when you go back, that we are neither children nor fools'.[1] That was in mid-September 1870, two weeks after the Battle of Sedan. Shortly thereafter the bankers of Prussia were negotiating with one another the modalities of what

---

* The essay that follows is based on the Nachlass of Gerson Bleichröder, which was made available to me by the late Friedrich Brunner, partner in the firm of Arnhold & S. Bleichröder of New York. Mr Brunner, who was a devoted student of banking history, was most eager for me to complete a history of the Bleichröder Bank in the nineteenth century on the basis of these materials. I have yet to do so. The essay that follows was intended to be a part of that story and is small part payment for Mr Brunner's encouragement, assistance and hospitality. I only regret that I have worked so slowly that he is not here to see this.

Readers of the essay who want to follow up the end-note references to the archives may do so in the Baker Library of the Harvard School of Business Administration, to which Mr Brunner donated these papers during his lifetime. The box numbers I have used in my citations are those assigned before the donation; these have subsequently been changed, but since the materials are still classified by subject, person, and date, the researcher should have no trouble locating the letters in question.

67

had come to be known as the Kriegs-Kontribution, and Prussian claims on French territory had grown with the contemplation. In the end, the French paid lots of money, more than they thought anyone could ask; and they gave up considerable territory, again more than they ever thought their enemies could ask them.

To be sure, one must never take Bismarck's curt rebuffs at face value. This was his style; to make his interlocutor so unhappy that the slightest concession was seen as a hard-won triumph. It is possible, even probable, that the moment the French hinted at an indemnity, Bismarck began to calculate the prospects – without in any way abandoning those territorial ambitions that had been nourished for some time by German chauvinist intellectuals and were now the primary concern of the Army high command. He almost surely consulted Bleichröder, Camphausen, and other financial experts in this regard, for by mid-October a number of German bankers were already girding themselves for the business battles that would obviously follow the military conflict.[2]

There was good historical precedent for a war indemnity. The obvious model was the compensation extracted from France in 1815: 700 million francs, to cover the damages and costs imposed on the Allies by twenty-three years of revolutionary and Napoleonic aggression. On the same principle, the indemnity for the few months of combat in 1870 should have been substantially smaller. But as in 1815, the purpose of the imposition was to punish as well as to compensate; and a much richer France could obviously support a much larger burden than it could a half-century earlier. Bismarck's calculations, therefore, in spite of *pro-forma* references to widows' and orphans' pensions, the cost of feeding prisoners, and compensation to the South German states, were governed solely by what he felt could be extracted from France without driving his defeated enemy to desperation.

The historical record of the negotiations leading to the fixing of the final sum of 5 billion (thousand million) francs is confusing and contradictory. Obviously, different feelers were put forward at different times by both sides; and in their subsequent recollections, the actors concerned did their best to show themselves in the best possible light. It is difficult, moreover, to verify some of their later affirmations by the contemporary record, for none of them at the time could afford to be entirely candid about what he was doing. Bismarck, who was long afraid that intervention by other nations might rob Germany of her spoils, did not want to appear insatiable. In his talks with French representatives, therefore, he was reluctant to commit himself too early to a definite figure. The French, in turn, were only too happy to interpret Bismarck's ambiguities in the most favourable sense, the more so as they had a difficult task persuading their countrymen to accept the Prussian conditions. The principal French negotiators were Jules Favre, Adolphe Thiers, and later on, Pouyer-Quertier. The most important of these was Thiers, the grand old man of French politics – journalist and vocal opponent of the Restoration regime in the 1820s, a ministerial prodigy in the 1830s, the incarnation of bourgeois virtues under the July Monarchy, historian and opposition leader under the Second Empire. Talented enough to make several careers, he had begun as a dissenter, worked his way into the Establishment, and was now concerned to save his country from revolution. In the face of these unconscionable demands for territory and money, he was above all anxious to settle as quickly as possible, thereby restoring peace, affirming the authority of the temporary government, and aborting the alliance of popular unrest and anti-German anger. He was also more concerned to save francs than Frenchmen: land and people could be reconquered, but money spent was money gone. Once, when he was reproached by the members of a parliamentary committee for having yielded up Alsace-Lorraine to the enemy, he tried to deprecate the loss: it was, after all, only a small part of France. To which came the reply: 'There are times when cutting away a small part of a man leaves him no longer a man'.[3]

According to Thiers, his first conversation with Bismarck on this subject, in early November 1870, saw the Chancellor ask for the equivalent of two French budgets, that is, two years' government expenditures. For Bismarck, that meant about four billion francs – an unprecedented sum that far exceeded the total of German war outlays and losses. Thiers protested that the swollen budgets of the late Empire were an unnatural standard; that a normal budget ran to about one and a half billions; and that even was far too much to ask. 'He [Bismarck] seemed to weaken,' Thiers writes, 'and I supposed [*je crus deviner*] that two billions plus Alsace and a part of Lorraine, but not Metz, might be the terms of peace if we signed at once'.[4]

Thiers misjudged his man. Bismarck had already heard Favre mention five billions; at least he thought he had; and once he sniffed that kind of money, he was not going to settle for two. Besides, the war dragged on, and the combination of unreasonable French resistance (didn't they know when they were beaten?) and mounting losses increased German appetites. Once the armistice was

declared and both sides prepared for peace negotiations, the
German press in chorus issued a spate of articles (an inspired spate?)
to justify the forthcoming demands. The wrongs and sufferings of
the French occupation of 1803–13 were revived; readers were
cautioned that they could not compare the quick, cheap campaign
of 1866 (eight weeks) and the hard, costly one of 1870–71 (34
weeks); journalist-accountants vied with one another to provide the
most all-inclusive list of justifiable claims, and then concluded by an
open-ended reference to things not yet measured or measurable;
and a number of thoughtful editorialists made a point of France's
ability to pay what would be no more than a fraction of the national
wealth.[5] Enormous sums were bandied about, to the consternation
of sober men. On 14 February 1871, Abraham Oppenheim, writing
his good friend Gerson Bleichröder at German headquarters in
Versailles, offered some thoughts on the subject that, seen from the
vantage point of a century's painful experience with war and
reparations, constitute a paradigm of sensible statesmanship.

> If the public prints have been driveling up to now about seven to
> eight billion francs, that is to be excused on the ground that these
> are people who have no accurate notion of what that is, a billion
> francs. We financial types, however, will be guilty of a serious
> crime if we sing the same song and do not take into account what
> so rich a country as France is in a position to do, after so bloody a
> war, in which her financial resources have been used in an utterly
> irresponsible way, without succumbing to total ruin. My personal
> view is that we, if we be moderate and want to have the gratitude
> of the neutral powers, must be content with three billion francs
> plus compensation for the cost of maintaining war prisoners. Four
> billion francs, however, should be the outside limit of our
> demands and would probably be accepted by the French without
> grumbling. These four billions could be raised by the French only
> on very onerous conditions and would add a charge of at least 250
> million francs to their annual budget. When one adds to that how
> much of France has been laid waste by the war, how many
> families have lost the greater part of their fortunes, and what
> further expenditures are required to recover bit by bit from the
> calamities of the war, one is surely not out of line in predicting
> that it will take them at least ten years to get back on their feet.
> The task of raising so large an indemnity without plunging the
> country into a financial crisis that would ruin it completely is
> really no small matter. To facilitate it, reasonable due dates must

be accorded, and, in addition to specie, other forms of payment that serve the purposes of our government must be permitted.

Another call for moderation came from Friedrich Lehmann, *prokurist* in S. Bleichröder and Gerson's *Vertrauensmann*. Replying on February 20th to a letter from Gerson (unfortunately not preserved) that had apparently spoken of two billion Thaler (7.5 billion francs), he pointed out that France could probably pay this amount, especially if she reconciled herself to peace and disarmament. 'One can therefore see the French, as you do, actually deriving advantages from the indemnity' – Bleichröder always tried to see the pros and cons of every deal, especially the pros for the other side.

In all honesty, however, I do not think it *fair* [in English and in italics in the original] that young Germany should set the sum of the contribution higher than absolutely necessary to cover the real costs of war – compensation for the refugees, pensions for the wounded soldiers and for the dependents of warriors fallen on the field of honor, confiscations, etc. I consider 800–1,000 million Thaler (3 to 3.75 billion francs) for this purpose a very high estimate.

Lehmann then went on to point out that what Germany needed was land for the security of her territory; and that excessive monetary demands would embitter the defeated neighbour and put Germany 'on the precipitous path of either a permanently defensive posture or of a conqueror-state; – the blessings of peace then would not be ours, and the burdens of Germany will not be lightened'. Elsewhere in the letter he remarked that France would be ruined either by a sharp drain of specie or a sharp increase in the circulation of paper money. The world would not excuse young Germany for either of these.

Bleichröder went along with this reasoning. Henckel von Donnersmarck, Bismarck's other financial expert at Versailles, did not.[6] In any event, the times were not made for wisdom. There was no holding the chauvinists in Berlin who wanted to cripple France so that never again could she play the bully and push Germany around. It never occurred to them that roles in international politics change with power, and that Europe's bully for generations to come would be Germany. When Thiers next saw Bismarck on this subject, in late February 1871, the price was up to six billions, plus Alsace, plus part of Lorraine, this time including Metz. That's impossible!

protested Thiers. And he went on to prove with figures that France's heavy war losses left her far too poor to repair her wounds and raise such a sum. Besides, he is said to have expostulated, this number is so large that if someone had started counting out six billion francs one by one in the time of Jesus, he still wouldn't be finished. To which Bismarck replied: 'I have an adviser who started counting at the Creation'. The reference was to Bleichröder. The story is apocryphal, but it is almost too good not to be true.

Bismarck took the position that the sum had been decided on in Berlin; that he was only a mouthpiece; that he would have to wire back for instructions; and that once he had received these, he would send his two specialists, that is, Bleichröder and Henckel, to Paris to pursue the negotiations. They came the next day with the same number of six billions. Thiers, always impressed by his own powers of persuasion, recalled the interview as follows: 'We proved to them that a financial operation like this was impossible; that one could never pry so large a sum out of the capitalists of Europe. M. Bleichsröder [*sic*], more honest [*de meilleure foi*] than M. Henckel, understood this and more or less agreed'. The next day (Friday 24 February), Thiers and Favre called on Bismarck at Versailles. The Chancellor informed them that Berlin had consented to one billion less. That was the end of the matter: five billions. As Thiers puts it, he could see that Bismarck was ready to break off on this point.[7] Thiers consoled himself with the thought that he would include in this sum the amounts the Prussians had already exacted from the French in the course of their occupation. It was only a thought, and the Germans never conceded the point.

For the indemnity was only the largest part of the monies extracted from France. The Prussians levied in addition a 'war contribution' of 200 million francs on the city of Paris. This, like the war indemnity, was essentially a ransom. (It was nominally intended to cover the damages of those German residents of Paris who had been expelled by the authorities after the outbreak of war.)[8] Further exactions included the value of property requisitioned by the Germans, the taxes they collected in the areas under occupation before the conclusion of the armistice, and the costs of the occupation itself. Not all of these gave rise to transfer payments, that is, entailed a movement of funds from France to Germany. The occupation costs, for example, were largely paid in kind or spent in France; though as we shall see, a certain portion of these found its way to Germany. Even so, it is not unreasonable to estimate the overall transfer burden at about six billion francs, which in turn was something less than half of what the war and its aftermath cost the French people.[9]

An indemnity of five billion francs! Outside observers were appalled. An editorialist for the London *Economist* argued that such monumental greed was a bad precedent: 'For a State to go to war to get money would be considered infamous, and to exact huge sums of money as a consequence of victory suggests the belief that money may be next time the object as well as the accidental reward of battle'. He felt, moreover, that Germany would 'suffer for years from the suspicion of all nations irritated by the idea that she is not only the strongest Power in the world, but is willing to use that power to fill her exchequer'. He was both right and wrong on both counts.[10] The indemnity was a disastrous precedent, less as an incentive to war, however, than as a compensation for it – witness the reparations of the First World War; and Germany did suffer the jealousy and resentment of other nations, to say nothing of the hatred of France, not so much for the money she took as for the power she showed in winning and taking.

At the time, however, the sympathy of outsiders was small consolation. France was confronted with an extremely difficult task – not impossible, but extremely difficult. Never had the capital markets of Europe raised or transferred so large a sum. French credit, moreover, was at a low ebb. In addition to the capital losses mentioned by Abraham Oppenheim, there was the amputation of Alsace-Lorraine, which deprived the country of the greater part of its most active iron manufacture and of its most enterprising cotton centres; and these material injuries were compounded by the uncertainty of the domestic political situation. The population was restive, especially in the capital. The legitimacy of the Government of National Defence was widely challenged, and there was no consensus on the form the new government should take. Radicals and socialists, after two decades of more or less authoritarian rule, were everywhere coming out of hiding, and gaining confidence with every demonstration and riot. All of this came to a boil in Paris during the month that followed the signing of the preliminary treaty of peace, and on 18 March the city was abandoned to the insurrectionary National Guard and the radical populace. Ten days later the Commune was proclaimed.

In these circumstances, the stock market, that barometer of the fears and hopes of the investing public, showed clearly how great was the loss of confidence: the 3 per cent *rente* was down at end December and again at end March to almost 50, a loss of nearly one third from the pre-war level; one had to go back to the revolutionary period 1848–9 to find a lower price. The shares of the Bank of France, the most highly prized of blue chips, plunged from 2940 frs. to 2260 in 1870 and remained depressed until the fall of the Commune. In the meantime, the presence of the invader was a heavy burden and was linked to the payment of the war indemnity: the sooner France paid, the sooner the Germans would go.

How to pay? This was really two questions: how to raise the money; and how to deliver it to Germany without upsetting the international balance of payments to the point where the exchanges would be significantly altered and the franc would lose value relative to other currencies.[11] The problem was rendered in some ways more difficult by the German refusal to accept either French paper money or French promises to pay (bonds or *rentes*.) No French paper money, because then it would be too easy for France to pay her debt with the printing press; and no bonds or *rentes* that might be repudiated at some later date or paid in depreciated money. On the other hand, Germany *was* ready to take the paper of the great private banking houses; and this was a remarkable testimony to their solidity and trustworthiness. Since then, creditors have tended to put their faith in governments and done much less well.

These questions in turn comprised, and to some extent concealed, others. On the surface, for example, the task of raising the money quickly resolved itself into a choice between taxes and loans; and since taxes at the moment could not even cover the ordinary budget and the costs of restoration at home, France had to borrow. Yet a loan has to be repaid, and the underlying question was, how would France raise the money required to pay the carrying charges on this new debt. Any doubt of her ability to do this would affect her ability to borrow and increase the charges incurred. In the same way, the mere transfer of the indemnity to Germany, however complicated, was only the beginning of the story. Some of the money could be raised by borrowing in Germany itself, which reduced by that much the amount to be transferred; and some could be borrowed in third countries, which changed a bilateral imbalance into a multilateral one. Yet much, if not most, of the money had to be raised in France, for as *The Economist* (London) pointed out, the French could hardly expect support for their loans abroad unless they themselves were prepared to subscribe at home.[12] These remittances from France in turn had to be either made in bullion or specie or covered by French claims on Germany, or by the purchase of other countries' claims on Germany. In other words, payment now by means of commercial paper or bankers' acceptances was not enough; sooner or later, these had to be compensated (paid for) by a real flow of funds in the opposite direction. One way to accomplish this was to sell off foreign securities and liquidate holdings abroad; another, much longer and more difficult, was to build up a favourable balance of trade on commercial account, that is, sell more to other countries than one bought from them. For the moment, however, recourse to bankers' drafts gave the whole arrangement far more flexibility than it would otherwise have had. In the hands of skillful men, it made possible the completion of the transfer with only the slightest and briefest weakening of the franc – so slight as not even to pass the gold point, that is, the point where it actually paid to ship bullion or specie rather than remit paper. It was like crossing Niagara on a tightrope with a full glass of water and not spilling a drop.

The raising and transfer of a sum of this size was a feat that called for the collaboration of the greatest banking houses, strong with accumulated wealth and unquestioned credit. Very few firms met this standard; but many more thought they did, and others felt they could grow big in the doing. The prize, after all, was enormous. First, there would be the indemnity loans themselves, bringing with them a commission for the issuing houses, plus fees for expenses, plus a further commission on such part of the loan or loans as the issuing houses underwrote or purchased firm. There was also the prospect of a speculative gain on the securities issued, if, as seemed probable, the fortunes of France and the stability of her government improved over time. Then there would be further fees for the collection of the loan proceeds and the payment of interest to the bondholders or *rentiers* in the months and years to come. It seemed reasonable, moreover, to assume that the houses entrusted with the loan would also be favoured in the award of contracts for the transfer of funds from France to Germany; and for German banks especially, there was the additional task of remitting the monies allocated to the lesser German states from Berlin to their recipients. Finally, there was this large mass of liquid capital that would be flowing into various German treasuries and sitting there for longer or shorter periods awaiting disbursement. Again, it did not seem unreasonable to assume that those bankers who handled the German end of the transaction might have the use of these monies pending their ultimate disposition. This prospect had its counterpart on the French side: the French government would be collecting foreign currencies and commercial paper in anticipation of maturity dates and would no doubt be ready to deposit these funds with bankers rather than let them lie idle.

When the first hints of an indemnity transpired in the fall of 1870 – probably as a result of Bismarck's consultation with Bleich-röders and other German houses – the initial reaction was to equate the opportunity of performance with the privilege of conquest; that is, the German banks thought that just as France would have to pay for her sins, so she should be made to pay through German intermediaries. This was an arrangement that Bleichröder is likely to have commended to Bismarck, with a view to taking the matter in hand himself. It was all perfectly logical. Reliance on German bankers offered the victors the greatest possible security for France's performance of her obligations; and no German house enjoyed connections like those of Bleichröder – with the Rothschilds on the one hand and Bismarck on the other. In an affair where confidentiality and expeditiousness would be of the utmost importance, the Bleichröder–Rothschild alliance provided the perfect financial bridge between the Prussian and French governments.

Not everyone saw the matter in the same light. Gerson's old friend, Abraham Oppenheim, delighted to be asked in, thought that precisely because of the close link between Gerson and Bismarck, the latter might prefer to keep Gerson in the background and push Abraham to the fore; the reverse arrangement, he felt, might be misinterpreted. Besides, if Bleichröder had Rothschilds, he had Foulds – not so big, no doubt, but a solid house nevertheless. It was important, he wrote Gerson on 20 October 1870, for the two of them to work together and to join in advising Bismarck on these matters. 'At his first sign, you should therefore be ready to proceed along with me to Headquarters to develop our plans to him orally'. Bismarck, he was sure, would be favourably disposed. In this way Otto von Camphausen's efforts (he was Minister of Finance) to shift the business away from Bleichröder and Oppenheim to another person (unnamed, but very probably Adolph Hansemann, director of the Discontogesellschaft, whom Camphausen had worked with before) would be thwarted.[13] Clearly a serious financial competition was already under way. If Gerson had any doubts about this method of proceeding, Abraham thought he might write directly to the king, with whom he was on friendly terms – unless of course Gerson thought Bismarck might take offence.

We do not have Gerson's reply, but he was certainly not happy at the thought of Abraham Oppenheim sharing the ear of Bismarck and taking Gerson's place at the head of a German bank syndicate; or of Abraham's turning this kind of plum over to Foulds and thereby depriving Gerson of the chance to play the benefactor to Rothschilds. No, thank you. When it came time to visit Bismarck at Versailles in February 1871, Gerson went alone.[14]

Abraham took the disappointment well. On learning of Gerson's invitation to Versailles, he wired him congratulations (31 January): 'Please have no further hesitations on my account. Wish you a happy and pleasant trip. Keep me informed. Letter follows.' Even so, he did not give up hope. In the letter that followed he reiterated, for the fifth or sixth time, that he was at the Chancellor's disposal and would await his call at any time; and he asked Gerson to tell in that event what would be 'the *very smartest* way' to get to Versailles. This offer was further renewed in later letters, along with the assurance to Gerson that he really hoped that his trip would not be necessary. It was not.

Meanwhile Bismarck did his best to persuade the French that it would be to their advantage to handle the indemnity through German intermediaries. Six billions were too much? He had with him two of the most important German financiers, who had worked out an arrangement whereby the French would be able to pay the levy, heavy as it appeared, almost without being aware of it. If you accept their collaboration, he cajoled, we will have settled one of the major questions, and the others will take care of themselves.

The next day saw the visit of Bleichröder and Henckel to the temporary quarters of the Ministry of Foreign Affairs. This is the way Favre tells the story:

Anyone who is engaged in business in Europe knows, at least by name, M. Black Schröder [sic] and the Count de Heukel [sic]. Their immense fortune, their vast notoriety, their undisputed shrewdness place them in the first rank, and this particular circumstance, that they happened to be, at just the right time, at headquarters, ready to coin money at a signal from our pitiless conqueror, gave to their personal merits a singular character of opportunism [*un singulier caractère d'àpropos*]. . . I don't think there is any point in reproducing, even by analysis, the ingenious systems they proposed to us. They all worked out to an increase of our crushing ransom by half again. To be sure, these gentlemen were ready to take full responsibility for advancing the sums required and for settling with the German government. We couldn't accept such services. It was already cruel enough to have to submit to the tribute levied on us by the victor. It would have been too much to have to confide its collection to his bankers. I cannot convey how deep was the painful impression left by this interview, in which these two princes of Prussian finance, always smiling, voices of honey, embroidering their speech with a persuasive, almost affectionate politeness, did their best to prove to us how much they wanted to carry out a colossal operation with our billions.

They kept at it a long time, with an answer to every objection, except those that politeness prevented us from uttering. It was time to call a halt. We made them understand that France, in spite of her misfortunes, would take care of herself.[15]

We can only regret that Favre chose not to preserve for posterity the details of the bankers' proposals. There is no record of them in the Bleichröder archive. It is possible, even probable, however, that Gerson's scheme was not much different from the one eventually adopted by the French. There are certain intrinsic constraints in an operation of this kind, and any proposal, from whatever source, would have had to adapt to them. One of them, as we have seen, was the need for international collaboration on the largest scale; any banking consortium, therefore, that Gerson might have organised would not have looked very different from the one that eventually floated the loan. The major difference is that it would have been headed by Gerson and included a large German component; and for him, of course, that would have made all the difference in the world. In addition, if one can reconstruct some of Gerson's thoughts on the subject from the letters he was getting from Abraham Oppenheim in Cologne and his home office in Berlin, it would seem that he envisaged an operation that combined borrowing and payment; that is, the banking syndicate would on the one hand take French *rentes* or other security, probably at a fixed price, with the right to sell as and when it could, and on the other, remit the indemnity to the German government in the form of bullion, specie, or commercial paper.[16] Since the participating bankers would not be able to cover such an enormous amount of paper within the customary short maturities (up to 90 days), the German government would presumably have to be persuaded to renew diminishing amounts of these notes over a longer period; their security could be the solidary liability of all members of the consortium, or at least of the French members.

This last proviso was suggested by Oppenheim, who was far more cautious in these matters than Gerson. On 23 February 1871, the very day when Bleichröder and Henckel were giving their sales talk in Versailles, Abraham wrote to say that he was looking forward to joining with Bleichröders in any riskless operation [*welche mit einem Risico nicht verknüpft sind*], but that he wanted to be consulted by telegram on anything that entailed a serious risk. He explicitly included in this category the purchase of *rentes* from the French government. On the other hand, to accept, that is, endorse, the paper of a consortium of the leading French banks, such as Rothschild, Fould, Marcuard, André and Cie, Hottinguer, the Banque de Paris, Seillière, Mallet, and Pillet-Will, signing solidarily – that, he felt, was no risk, and he was ready to go up to 10 million Thaler (37.5 million francs) or more. Abraham Oppenheim, obviously, was not thinking big, and Gerson Bleichröder was.

One thing is clear: an operation of this kind, as Jules Favre remarks, would have cost the French government far more than the loan-payment combination that was finally arrived at. The Prussian bankers were thinking in terms of 5 per cent *rentes* at a fixed price somewhere in the mid-70s; the French wanted, and eventually got, a price between 80 and 85. The Prussians, by handling everything as part of the same package could reasonably expect a commission on the full amount of the payment; the French hoped to raise a good part of the transfer monies required, in a form acceptable to the German government, as part of the eventual loan operation; and they could acquire the rest on a competitive basis. Even if considerations of national pride had not been overriding, it would not have paid the French to accept the propositions of the two smiling bankers.

Yet the Prussians did not discourage easily. During the conversations of the next two days with Thiers, Bismarck broached the matter again, more than once, but Thiers would not hear of it. Bismarck was vexed; still, there were more important things to fight about, and he abandoned the issue.

From this point on, it was clear that the French would take the matter in hand and find their own way to pay. In the meantime the representatives of the two powers met in Frankfurt to convert the preliminary treaty of peace, signed at Versailles on 26 February, into a definitive treaty. This was concluded on 10 May and stipulated that payment of the indemnity would begin thirty days after the re-establishment of the authority of the French government in Paris. The Commune fell on 28 May, and Bismarck notified the French government that he considered that order had been restored on 1 June and that the first instalment of the indemnity would thus be due on 1 July. France had roughly four months then in which to put her financial house in order, to say nothing of her political house, and raise an initial payment of 500 million francs.

II

From the hindsight of history, it would seem that the French had no choice but to borrow the money; yet it was not so obvious to contemporaries. The first suggestion was to ask for voluntary contributions. Critics of this proposal were quick to point out that it penalised the generous and rewarded the selfish, but it did not take a moralistic debate to convince the authorities that such a solution was impracticable: a campaign to solicit gifts from the public, which admittedly received little encouragement from the government, raised the sum of 6 850 000 frs. – about one thousandth of what was needed.

More feasible was a tax on capital: estimates of the French national fortune ran from 100 to 150 billion francs, so that a levy of $3\frac{1}{2}$ to 5 per cent would raise the money required. Once again, however, moralistic objections were heard. For one thing, not everyone has his capital in the same form, so that those material assets that constitute taxable capital are not the true measure of a person's means. A professional man – doctor, lawyer – might well have most of his wealth invested in his training (what economists today call human capital) and can draw on this to earn a substantial income; whereas a retired shopkeeper or employee would probably have capitalised his modest savings in the form of a house and *rentes*. The one would largely escape a capital levy, while the other would bear a disproportionately heavy burden. Furthermore, even admitting the principle of such a tax, how was one to assess it equitably on capital assets as conventionally defined? The way would be open to all kinds of evasion, and once again, the honest man would be punished for his virtue. (The difficulty seemed especially serious in France, where defrauding the fisc was a habit born of inequities of the Old Regime and cherished ever after; and where most of the securities issued by private corporations were made out to bearer. Under the circumstances, the coupon clippers would escape lightly and the heaviest burden would fall on the landowners, who could hardly hide their acres.) Finally, it was pointed out that a levy on capital would exceed in many cases the liquid resources of the taxpayer, so that he would have to realise assets in order to pay. The result would be an abrupt, massive dumping of all forms of wealth, with disastrous consequences for the sellers, and a serious diversion of money into unproductive and socially subversive speculation.

This left the solution of a loan or loans, which offered the advantage of tapping the wealth where it was available; whereas taxes take it whether available or not. The form of the loan gave rise to some debate: should it be amortisable (bonds) or perpetual (*rentes*)? And if amortisable, should the French government sweeten the issue(s) by making it a lottery loan and drawing for premiums as well as amortisation? Such a prospect would certainly make the issue more attractive to many investors, and they would be prepared to pay more for the bonds or (the same thing) accept a lower rate of interest. The French Government, in other words, would pay less for its money. On the other hand, lottery loans were forbidden in a number of European countries, particularly in Britain, for reasons of morality. An issue of this kind could therefore not be quoted on the London Exchange and the French would lose in advance an important segment of their prospective clientele – all the more important because the French needed to raise some of the indemnity in foreign currencies.[17] A lottery loan, then, was excluded; and so, on contemplation, was an amortisable loan, partly because it was not susceptible of conversion if and when French credit should improve and the state should be able to borrow more cheaply, partly because the French Government traditionally borrowed by means of perpetual *rentes* and any departure from this practice could only disconcert and perhaps deter investors.[18] At least this was what was argued at the time.

On 6 June 1871, therefore, after long consultation with the budget committee of the Chamber and private banking opinion, Pouyer-Quertier, Minister of Finance, deposited a bill with the Chamber simply authorising the government to issue *rentes* in the amount required to raise 2½ billion francs.

The proposal was too simple. The legislature felt that the law should specify the modalities of the loan; in particular the deputies wanted the government to offer the loan at public subscription rather than contract it out, as had been the practice under the Restoration and July Monarchy.[19] They also felt that $2\frac{1}{2}$ billions was too much. As a result, the law as finally passed on 20 June provided for the creation and sale at public subscription of enough perpetual *rentes* at 5 per cent to produce a capital of two billion francs. The price and terms of sale were left to the discretion of the Executive, although Thiers gave the Chamber to understand that the loan would come out at 81, 82, or 83 francs. This was followed by two decrees on 23 June. The first, by Thiers, set the price at 82 frs 50. The second, by Pouyer-Quertier, announced that the subscription would be opened on 27 June and continued until complete; that payment by subscribers would consist in an initial outlay of 12 francs for each 5 francs of *rente* (equivalent to about 15 per cent), followed by sixteen monthly instalments running from 21 August 1871 to 21 November 1872; and that payments in advance would be credited with 6 per cent interest. The main point to be noted here is that the French Government would have to wait almost a year and a half to get all its money; whereas the timetable of indemnity payments established by the Germans set earlier deadlines. The law of 20 June, therefore, granted the government the right to borrow from the Bank of France in anticipation of the payments by subscribers to the loan. Behind this, however, lay the necessity for the government and the Bank of France to work with private banking enterprises, first, to collect and borrow the use of paper instruments eligible as payment to the Germans *in advance of* receipts from subscribers; and secondly, to convert these receipts themselves, as required, into similar means of payment.[20]

III

It took the French, therefore, about seventeen of the eighteen weeks available to them from the preliminary treaty to the due date of the first installment of the indemnity to make up their minds how they wanted to raise the money. Much of this delay was unavoidable: France could hardly go out and borrow money at a time when the capital city was in the hands of revolutionists and the legitimacy of the regime was still in doubt.

In the meantime, the French representatives in Brussels, who were negotiating the revision of the preliminary peace treaty, did their best to reopen the question of the indemnity and persuade the Germans that they should take less than the five billions agreed upon. France, they argued, could not possibly pay so large a sum in precious metals and specie (the question of acceptable means of payment was still open); would the Germans not be willing to take some of the indemnity in bills of exchange or even *rentes*?[21] The answer to such an inquiry depended of course on the German appreciation of the value of such securities, and for reasons that are not clear, Bismarck saw this as an attempt to persuade him to take less than the sum originally agreed upon. In letters to Brussels of 29 and 30 April, he spoke first of a French offer of 'at most 4 billions, not counting the risk' and then of 'about 3 billions'.[22] In typical Bismarckian fashion, the Chancellor responded to what he felt was a breach of word with threats of war: tell the French, he ordered, that we will not give them the help they asked for in the overthrow of Paris and that we will arrive more easily by this path at a resumption of hostilities than at a definitive peace.[23] At the same time he consulted Bleichröder, who made haste to check with Alphonse de Rothschild in Paris. Alphonse, presumably on behalf of or at the behest of the French government, quickly repudiated the actions of the French delegates. 'All these propositions come, I can assure you, not from the ministers, but from the desire of certain people to put themselves forward and play the big shot.' As for the financial differences between the two countries, Rothschild was convinced that they would be amicably settled and that, specifically, the French Government would do nothing in contradiction with the preliminary peace agreement.[24]

Bleichröder had a few thoughts of his own to add to these reassurances. The absurdity of the French complaints at Brussels, he said, was shown by their willingness to pay three billions in cash in three years (presumably as payment in full), since if they could do that, they could easily raise the same sum at once by means of a loan. Indeed, Bleichröder thought that a loan of five billions would be easy once order was restored: Britain would take one billion; Germany, Belgium, and Switzerland, one and a half; France, two; and the rest could be covered by credits for contributions in kind. Finally, Bleichröder remarked that he would infer from the tone of Alphonse's letter that it was the Rothschilds who would probably head up the loan syndicate. That Bleichröder should have to infer such a thing about the house that had always been his sure and closest connection is evidence of the degree to which relations had cooled as a result of the war and Bleichröder's new prominence. Alphonse was apparently telling Gerson as little as possible for the moment.

This lack of communication was not for want of initiative on Bleichröder's side. The moment Gerson had digested Jules Favre's rebuff and accepted the fact that the French were not going to put themselves into the hands of German bankers, he had taken steps to work out a partnership with Rothschilds. Again, we do not have the project itself and must infer its character from comments about it. It apparently envisaged the formation of an international banking syndicate to float the loan, with Rothschilds at its head and Bleichröders standing in for a consortium of German participants; and then special arrangements for Bleichröder's group to handle the remittances from Rothschilds and associates in France. Gerson first broached the matter to Alphonse in a letter of 26 or 27 February, that is, only two or three days after Bismarck had yielded on the question of German intermediaries; and then again, in a more detailed letter of 10 March. Neither of these has survived. We do, however, have replies from Alphonse himself and from Emil Brandeis, Rothschilds' specialist in German matters, which convey a certain hesitation and reserve: the Minister of Finance was at the temporary seat of government in Bordeaux, and no real business could be done until his return.

In the meantime Rothschild was interested in having Gerson speak to the Minister in Berlin [Camphausen? Bismarck?] and convey to him the importance of accepting payment of the indemnity in other places than Berlin, above all, in London. To compel France to remit the entire sum to one point, Alphonse felt, would create 'a crisis for all Europe'. His main concern, obviously, was the balance of the exchanges, which was already exerting a decisive influence on some of the operations that Rothschilds were then engaged in.[25]

One was the reimbursement of divers German banks for the funds they had furnished on behalf of the city of Paris. The reader will recall that payment of the 200-million-franc indemnity had been made on 12 February. Historians have tended to view this as the end of the matter and have not asked the question, where the money came from. Yet, that, for us, is the important point, because this transaction was a practice run for the transfer of the war indemnity. The city borrowed the money from the Bank of France and paid with the following instruments: 100 million francs in banknotes, of

which 50 to be replaced by specie by 19 February at the latest; 37.5
millions in bankers' drafts on Berlin, issued by a syndicate of Paris
houses grouped around Rothschilds, endorsed by the city of Paris,
guaranteed by Bleichröder, and payable to the Seehandlung; and
63 millions in short paper on London issued by the same syndicate.[26]
These drafts in turn had to be covered and the Berlin drawees
reimbursed. To this end, Rothschilds opened with Bleichröders in
early February a special 'V de P' [Ville de Paris] account, which it
proceeded to build up in subsequent weeks by the sale of foreign
securities in the bullish Berlin market – mostly Russian bonds and
Italian *rentes* and railway debentures – and by the remittance of bills
of exchange on London and Berlin.[27]

At the same time, Rothschilds were busy buying all the gold they
could with London paper, with a view to furnishing the city of Paris
with the specie required by the agreement of 11 February. Among
the suppliers of this metal, ironically enough, was the Bavarian
Kriegskasse[War Chest], which was prepared to sell to the French
16 million francs of gold and silver, so that they in turn could send
the money back to Germany. Rothschilds was paying 3/4 per mill
for gold in Berlin, 2 and even 3 per mill in Paris,[28] and the rising
demand for specie made the exchange rate on London crucial to the
success of the operation, which by mid-March was beginning to
turn sour.[29] Hence Alphonse's concern to increase or at least sustain
the price of bills on London by getting Germany to permit France to
make payment there. How hard Bleichröder tried to persuade the
Minister of the need for such a concession, is impossible to say. Since
it went against his own interest, which was to have as much of the
amount as possible pass through his hands in Berlin, he may have
been wanting in his usual zeal on the Rothschilds' behalf. In any
event, the Germans never conceded the point.

In the meantime, the first serious conversations concerning the
modalities of the forthcoming loan got under way between Pouyer-
Quertier and the Rothschild group; and there is no question that,
had it not been for the intervention of political events, the great loan
would have taken place in April. The proclamation of the
Commune, however, by placing the solidity of the regime in
question, made an international loan impossible. In the meantime,
the Rothschilds began to assemble *Zahlmittel* – instruments of
payment that would be suitable for the Germans in settlement of the
indemnity; in particular, they began large-scale purchases of
Prussian treasury notes (*Schatzanweisungen*) that had been issued

with the proviso that they would be acceptable for this purpose. As usual, Bleichröder had his troubles filling the order: the Rothschilds had set an outside price and stipulated notes at 3–3/4 per cent discount, but demand was so strong that Bleichröder had to settle in part for 3–1/2. 'I'll take them over myself if you don't want them', he wrote Paris on 8 May. Paris went along.

These purchases by Rothschilds reflected their foresight and their intimate conviction that they had the inside track on any loan contracts. They were, to begin with, the only banking house big enough to handle the operation; as Mazerat of the Crédit Lyonnais put it, 'the wide European connections of Rothschilds and their capital resources confer on them an absolutely exceptional role'.[30] At the same time, their contacts with the French Government officials, both directly and through the intermediary of an 'in-and-outer' like Léon Say, were unequalled. Say, the grandson of Jean-Baptiste Say of Say's law, was a high school classmate of Alphonse de Rothschild, an editor of the influential *Journal des Débats*, a member of the Northern Railway (the Rothschild fief) from 1857, and a serious student of the finances of the city of Paris. He cut his teeth on the '*comptes fantastiques d'Haussmann*' and followed his campaign against the famous Prefect of the Seine with public lectures on the finances of Paris under the Allied occupation in 1814–15; all of which made him a logical nominee for the committee that represented Paris in the negotiations of February 1871. The same month saw his election as deputy to the new National Assembly and his appointment as reporter of the all-important Budget Committee of the Chamber. In this capacity he prepared two reports on the financial state of the nation that were never read because Thiers felt they might do serious harm to France's credit. What was not good for the public, however, was nourishment to M. Thiers, who had consulted Say on earlier occasions and was once again impressed by the lucidity of his observations. When, therefore, the time came to appoint a new prefect of the Seine in early June 1871, Thiers's choice was Say. As deputy and prefect, Say technically had nothing to do with the arrangements for payment of the indemnity; yet he was privy to the negotiations, and in May we find Henri Germain, president of the Crédit Lyonnais, battling with him in the Budget Committee to compel him to keep the Chamber informed of the financial conversations. Germain would no doubt have been far less zealous in the cause of open covenants had he been in Say's place.[31]

Not that other firms and groups did not try to elbow their way in. Among those to put themselves forward was J. S. Morgan & Co. of London, the ancestor house of the more famous J. P. Morgan & Co. (Junius S. was J. Pierpont's father). It was this bank that had floated the emergency wartime loan of 250 million francs negotiated by the Délégation de Tours (the French Government in retreat) in the dramatic circumstances of October 1870. The loan later gave rise to nasty recriminations: paying 6 per cent and issued at 85, it had been a blow to the self-esteem of a nation that had long since gone over to 3 per cent *rentes*. (The French negotiators had gone to London with the authorisation to go as high as 9 per cent.) In addition, the Morgan bank was felt to have made too much money on the operation: one quarter of the issue taken firm at 25 francs under the issue price of 425; a commission of 3–1/4 per cent of the nominal value (gross of expenses), reduced to 1–1/4 per cent on the portion taken firm by the bank; and further small commissions on the collection of payments from subscribers and on redemption of coupons – all in all, about 10 million francs, or some 5 per cent of the money realised by the French Government. It could be argued, of course, that given the circumstances, such a profit was only reasonable; the loan might well have been a fiasco. In the meantime, all the French could see was that they had paid more for this loan than for any in living memory; and the Morgan bank became for them a symbol of their national humiliation.

This impression was confirmed by an ill-considered early move of Morgans to put itself forward as the contractor for the forthcoming indemnity loan. In mid-February a representative of the bank submitted a proposal that Dutilleul, director of the Service du Mouvement des Fonds in the Ministry of Finance, described as follows: 'There's a neat and quick job. But what the borrower will find a little less neat is that he would have to pay something like 10.5 per cent interest during twenty years of amortisation. It's a little Morganatic – no pun intended, but only to let you know who would be the lender.'[32] Morgans were lucky that Dutilleul's remarks were confined to a personal letter; adjectives of that kind are just made for eponymous immortality.

This was not the end of the story. In a letter to Bismarck of 5 May 1871 Gerson Bleichröder had occasion to write that he had it on good authority that 'Morgan [*der Morgan*] has not yet concluded a loan'. The tone would seem to imply that Morgans were a serious contender; yet the record of these negotiations conveys more the impression of a useful ogre, utilised by the French treasury to keep the other postulants on their best behaviour and to keep up appearances of competition. Certainly the Ministry gave Morgans' overtures short shrift. When, on 12 June, the bank informed the French chargé d'affaires in London that it was ready to underwrite the whole of the loan at 80, the telegram notifying the Minister of Finance of this offer took ten days to reach his secrétariat-général, where it was apparently left to gather dust. This wiped out the critical week before the passage of the law authorising the loan. On 21 June, the day after passage (the first wire had still not been delivered) Morgans sent both a wire and letter to the Minister stating that they had been informed that the French Government was negotiating with certain bankers to take a portion of the loan firm and would accord them 2 per cent commission on that amount. On those terms Morgans were prepared to take £4 million (100 million francs) – just like Rothschilds – and pointed to their role as friends-in-need as justifying their request for equal treatment: 'We base this application on the fact that at a time of its greatest need, we raised for France the sum of £10 million, when no one else would lend her a helping hand'. Nothing was better calculated to wake the dogs of French resentment. There is no record of an answer in the French files, but three days later a subdued letter from London dropped the request for a share in the underwriting and asked merely that Morgans be permitted to seek subscriptions for the loan on the same basis as Rothschilds and Barings: 'Our honor requires us not to disinvolve ourselves from the affairs of France when we have given her our assistance in the most difficult circumstances'.[33] Again, the wrong approach, and once again, there was apparently no answer.

There were other contenders in the lists. One was a German-Belgian group headed by Gebrüder Sulzbach of Frankfurt (once very active in Egyptian finances) and Errera-Oppenheim of Brussels.[34] Another was a syndicate of Paris banking houses and bankers of German origin – A. J. Stern & Co., Samuel de Haber, Antoine-Maurice Schnapper – in combination with the Banque de Paris, a young joint-stock investment bank with close ties to Sterns and Haber.[35] Still another was an amorphous coalition of French joint-stock commercial and deposit banks (inaccurately described as *sociétés de crédit*), working their way singly and collectively into an area that was the traditional preserve of the Haute Banque (the community of great private houses). Among these were the Crédit

Lyonnais, a young, ambitious, pushy firm that had been casting about in every direction, making and unmaking alliances, in an effort to find a niche in international finance; the Crédit Foncier de France, founded in principle to promote land and real-estate development, but more interested in the larger, quicker profits of stock-market promotions; the Comptoir d'Escompte, created in 1848 to sustain French trade in its hour of crisis by furnishing commercial credit against good paper, but also diverted long since into the more hazardous but more profitable paths of loan underwriting.

None of these postulants ever had much of a chance, though the joint-stock banks tried hard enough, urging their resources and good will on treasury officials and crying against the monopoly of the inner circle of high finance. This kind of favouritism may have been compatible, they contended, with the corruption and privilege of the monarchy; but it had no place in a republic. At the same time, the Crédit Lyonnais at least, and perhaps some of the others, did their best to ingratiate themselves with the Rothschilds, who were hostile by temperament and experience to these impersonal, 'irresponsible' (in the sense of limited liability) banking factories. They made rough going. On 27 February, Mazerat, the head of the Paris office of the Crédit Lyonnais, wrote the home office at Lyons: 'It's Rothschild who is the pivot of the financial combinations that are coming up. It is impossible to know what he's up to.' Then further: 'Alphonse de Rothschild told us nothing. He claims to know nothing. We don't know whether he will deviate on our behalf from his antipathy toward credit banks.' Two days later, after telling Dutilleul that the great private banking houses were not the only ones with money, Mazerat could only comment wryly: 'Dutilleul knows less about what's going on than Rothschild'. So back to Rothschilds; on 7 March: 'We're trying to see to it that the Crédit Lyonnais is not excluded from the consortium, in spite of the fact that the corporate banks enjoy little favor'. And so on through the spring: Rothschilds, the Ministry of Finance (the Minister 'hardly knew our name'), the other joint-stock banks, Léon Say, the Budget Committee of the Chamber, and back again.[36]

In the end, the persistent efforts of the Crédit Lyonnais and the other corporate banks did compel the Haute Banque to disgorge a little. Very little: on 26 June the syndicate of private banks headed by Rothschilds contracted with the Minister of Finance to underwrite the second billion of the two billion to be issued, plus 60 millions more for a commission of 2 per cent, that is, 21 000 000 francs; of this plum, Rothschilds and company conceded 65 millions – a little more than 5 per cent – to a syndicate of *sociétés de crédit*: the Crédit Foncier, the Crédit Industriel et Commercial, the Crédit Lyonnais, the Société de Dépots et de Comptes-Courants, the Comptoir d'Escompte, and the Banque de Paris – each for 10 millions; and the Société de Crédit Agricole, for 5 million. Pouyer-Quertier was rather pleased: 'I made a place for the French credit banks,' he wrote Thiers on 27 June. Initially, some at least of the joint-stock bankers were also pleased: 'Considerable!' wrote Letourneur, director of the home office of the Crédit Lyonnais. On second thought, however, they were less happy. They had been left the crumbs, and determined that it should not happen again.

That now we are getting ahead of our story. What about the Rothschild syndicate itself? In particular, what about its foreign members and the place of Bleichröder? This place, the reader will recall, was by no means assured. Alphonse de Rothschild's initial response to Gerson's overtures was non-committal, and as late as May, Gerson clearly was not privy to the negotiations in Paris. In this sense, he was hardly better off than Henri Germain of the Crédit Lyonnais. His uncertainty and anxiety were surely aggravated by – or perhaps they gave rise to – a new flare-up of his chronic eye trouble, which had grown worse with the years and eventually left him almost blind. In early June, however, Alphonse invited Gerson to submit proposals for German participation in the prospective flotation: how much were they prepared to take firm? We do not have this crucial letter of 7 June, but we do have Gerson's replies of the 11th. First a wire: 'Am ready to send you my confidential associate to work things out, but in order to offer definite proposals, need your authority to confer with friends. How big a sum can we have if you handle operation?' Then a letter, promising to build a strong consortium that would include the state banks (meaning primarily the Seehandlung) and the joint-stock investment banks and would raise more money than Rothschild could afford to allocate to Germany.[37]

That was Sunday, and Gerson was obviously buoyant with anticipation. The next day, however, Adolph Hansemann, head of the Discontogesellschaft, began his business week by calling on Gerson in the Behrensstrasse to tell him the results of a trip he had just made to London and Paris. He had been talking with Rothschilds about the indemnity loan. They had charged him, he said, with the formation of a German syndicate to take a portion of the loan, and he wanted to invite Gerson to join. The roof had fallen in. All Gerson could do was mumble generalities and good intentions and somehow get through what must have been one of the most painful conversations of his career. And when, finally, Adolph left, Gerson sat down and wrote to Alphonse de Rothschild a letter in which hurt and indignation struggled with bitterness:

> I have worked on this affair enough after all to know that Hansemann and his friends are thinking of participating in the operation with hardly more than 50 million francs, and any other promises are based solely on conjectures that a breath of air could blow away.
>
> For that reason, it seems to me that either he read far more into what you said than you intended, as a way of getting you to put the matter in his hands, or else, that you in fact told him nothing more than to get in touch with me in this connection.
>
> You, *Hochverehrter Herr Baron*, whose tact and tender feelings [*gefühlvolles Herz*] I have come to know in innumerable instances, cannot possibly have sent H. here with such a mission at the very time when you were summoning me to see you at Ferrières to consider the negotiation of the French loan.

You couldn't do this, he went on, 'if only because it does not seem opportune to yield the field to a man who goes with anyone and is prepared to accord to anyone the most favourable treatment . . .' This last was an appeal to Alphonse's exclusiveness (the last thing a Rothschild would do would be to do business with just anyone) and to his determination to exclude from this operation a number of disagreeable competitors. And Gerson, who had just fired off a wire asking if all this were true, concluded that only after receiving the answer from Paris would he know what kind of response to give Hansemann that would be compatible with his honour and Rothschilds' interests.

Gerson had good cause to be worried. Adolph Hansemann was the Henri Germain of German banking: ambitious, aggressive, always pushing himself into new spheres, including those that had long been the undisputed province of the great private banks. He had inherited control of the Discontogesellschaft from his father, David Hansemann, himself a man of uncommon energy and the most varied commercial experience; and first father, and then father and son together, had turned their small joint-stock partnership [*Kommanditgesellschaft auf Aktien*] into a financial force of the first order. Within a few years of its formation, the Disconto was trying to elbow its way into Rothschild syndicates and, failing that, to mount competitive ventures, even in Vienna, where Rothschilds' financial primacy seemed unchallengeable. Moreover the Hansemanns compounded this original sin by joining forces with Erlangers, a firm and family detested by Rothschilds wherever found. (The founder of the house, Raphael Erlanger, had been a trusted officer of Rothschilds in Frankfurt and had left to set up on his own – under what circumstances, we do not know. But the Rothschilds were always sensitive to the departure of employees who were privy to their affairs and had enjoyed their favour, especially when these same men then competed with the mother firm. Witness their feuds with the Pereires in the 1850s and 60s and Bontoux in the 1870s.)

The Hansemanns' efforts either to force their way into the Rothschild circle or fight them were not always crowned with success. David and Adolph were too proud to accept the state of subordination that Rothschilds were accustomed to impose on their collaborators; and they were as yet too weak, even in alliance with enemies of the great house, to shunt it aside. Still, the Disconto made enough trouble and Adolph Hansemann was persistent and sharp enough to persuade the Rothschilds that it were better to have him as an associate than a rival. Beginning in the mid-1860s, therefore, we find the Disconto joining Rothschilds repeatedly in promotional syndicates in both Prussia and Austria; increasingly, moreover, it was Adolph Hansemann who took the initiative in these affairs and managed the operations. He had just turned forty in 1866 and was at the height of his vigour; by comparison, Meyer Carl von Rothschild, head of the Frankfurt house, though only a few years older, was the tired custodian of an inherited fortune. All of this brought Hansemann into close relations with Bleichröder; the two men became a kind of doubles team at the head of Prussian banking. This did not prevent each from going his own way, as circumstances or judgment indicated. But the presumption in any given transaction was that they would work together.

They were going to work together on the indemnity loan, for the Disconto was certainly one of the firms Gerson was thinking of when he wrote on 11 June that he wanted to bring the German joint-stock banks into his syndicate. But now Adolph wanted to reverse their roles and in effect displace him as Rothschilds' man in Berlin.

Alphonse de Rothschild was not a man known for his 'tender heart', whatever Bleichröder might write, but he did not have to be very sensitive to imagine the impact of Hansemann's visit on his old collaborator. Even before Gerson's wire arrived that Monday, Emil Brandeis, who held down the German desk in the rue Laffitte, wrote him a letter to reassure him and ward off trouble: 'Baron Alphonse said to me he would have preferred that you come rather than Hansemann, but that he could not refuse to hear Hansemann's propositions (this just between us). I'm telling you this so that you'll know that the barons here are still most friendly disposed toward you and want to do the right thing [*alle Rücksichten beobachten wollen*]'. And then, to emphasise the nature of the confidence: '*Don't write anything about this*'. The letter went on to mention, in a way designed to allay Gerson's doubts, the names of firms that Rothschilds wanted to be included in the loan syndicate. Two Berlin bankers, Teplitz and Betzold, had actually come to Paris in an effort to secure a share directly from Rothschilds. Alphonse had simply referred them back to Gerson: 'You want to act entirely *at your own discretion* and Baron Alphonse wanted to be rid of the gentlemen'.

Some of the names mentioned in the letter, unfortunately, are given in code, and this recourse to code complicates considerably at this point the analysis of the correspondence. The problem was that normal telegraphic connections with Berlin had not yet been restored. Only special people, the Paris Rothschilds among them, could use the line, and cipher messages were not allowed. As a result, Rothschilds and Bleichröders adopted a partial code, which substituted names for names, places for places, and things for things – all in apparently clear language. Thus Bismarck became Reiche; Alphonse de Rothschild became Gerbert; and Paris Rothschilds became Merk. French *rentes* were *vis de fer* (or *Schrauben* in German correspondence); and London, or paper on London, was Cöthen. A billion was a *titre*; a thousand was a *pièce*. The trouble is that the correspondents at both ends chose to use the code not only in wires but in letters, where presumably it served no purpose. Had they written the letters in clear, we could have quickly decoded the wires. As it is, however, we have to translate from context, which is sometimes opaque or ambiguous. Moreover, the decoding process is complicated by the carelessness of some of the writers, who lapsed occasionally and gave a man's name now in code, now in clear. In a way, this is worse than having all code, because there is nothing better calculated to put the cryptanalyst off the scent. Even so, one can be sure of the meaning of the most important code words, and one can make informed guesses about some of the others. A few, which appear infrequently, may well remain secret forever, unless a copy of the code itself turns up somewhere in the Rothschild archive . . . The Bleichröder copy, which is mentioned as an inclosure in one of the letters from Paris, has disappeared.

Hansemann's move threw S. Bleichröder into a fit of action. In twenty-four hours the bank gathered all the relevant information and packed Friedrich Lehmann off to Paris. It was a long trip. The train left Berlin the night of the 13th and was due in to Lagny, on the eastern outskirts of Paris (direct service into the city had not yet been restored) on the afternoon of the 15th. It came in late, so that by the time news of Lehmann's arrival reached Alphonse in the rue Laffitte, the office was closed. This was Thursday evening. Friday was then lost getting installed in Paris; Saturday was the sabbath; and it was not until Sunday morning that Lehmann was able to sit down and bring Bleichröders abreast of events.

It was not an easy task. Paris was still recovering from the trauma of the Commune and its gory suppression, and communications with the outside world were exasperatingly slow and irregular. Yet already Cooks and other travel agencies were bringing curious tourists to visit the scenes of street fighting and massacres, to touch the walls that would one day become sites of pilgrimage, to take away pieces of broken statues as souvenirs, to gawk at the Parisians and imagine in every labourer a *Fédéré* and in every washerwoman a *pétroleuse*. There was even a *Guide de l'étranger à travers les ruines*. The French Government was at least as much concerned at the moment with liquidating the insurrection, through courts martial, executions, deportations, and imprisonment, as it was with putting its financial house in order; and the newspapers reflected this order of priorities, being filled with reports of testimony, tales of Communard outrages, stories of innocents caught up with the guilty and subjected to humiliating and abusive treatment, and indignant outcries against the foreign press, especially some elements of the British press, for presenting the restoration of order as a cruel and vengeful act of rage.

In the meantime, the financial and banking world was in a turmoil. Two weeks to go before the first payment of the indemnity, and the details of the loan operation had still not been worked out. The Ministry of Finance had returned to Paris to find its offices in the rue de Rivoli burned out and all its records destroyed. Business on the major European stock exchanges was at a half stop, as banking houses and investors mobilised resources for the coming flotation, which was expected to provide a boost for the entire market. A report on the state of the Frankfurt exchange for the week ending 17 June began: 'I give you three potent words: "*Medio* [the mid-month liquidation day], *Geldknappheit* [tight money], *Milliar-dengeschäft* [the affair of the billions]." This was the triple star that governed the past week.' The report went on to speak of bankers and bank directors running about and passing one another on all the railways of the world. Paris had become a financial Mecca. The reporter thought that the Sulzbach-Errera-Oppenheim group had the inside track for the loan contract. He was, of course, away off the mark; but given the secrecy and confusion, he could hardly be blamed. Even the insiders were not sure what was going to happen.[38]

A good part of the difficulty lay in the slowness and uncertainty of communications. Some letters took two days to get from Berlin to Paris or the reverse; others took five. By the time an offer arrived, it was obsolete and new conditions had already gone forth. Telegrams to private parties in Paris were being stopped at Lille and sent on the rest of the way by post. In order to make sure that they got through to the rue Laffitte, Bleichröders took to sending many of their wires via Lambert, the Rothschild correspondent in Brussels, and Lambert in turn found it necessary on occasion to route his telegrams via James de Rothschild [this was James Edouard, son of Nathaniel of London], staying for the moment at the Hotel des Bains, Boulogne-sur-Mer. Some Bleichröder wires were sent via N. M. Rothschild & Sons in London. In Paris, de Rothschild Frères found it desirable to duplicate many of its wires, sending one copy direct and the other through Brussels – just in case; while for communications with their London cousins, they supplemented the telegraph with the traditional Rothschild system of couriers. Even those telegrams that got through were often hopelessly garbled, and the recourse to code names did not make things easier. The historian has dozens of these texts to puzzle over, sometimes with in-decipherable dates and cryptically elliptical language, and his confidence might well be shaken if he did not have the testimony of the recipients that they too were at a loss to understand the messages.

When Lehmann sat down Monday morning, 18 June, to write his first letter to Gerson, he began by offering assurances about

Hansemann. 'I won't go into details', he said, 'because you must have already received information on this since my departure' (the reference was presumably to Brandeis' letter, since Alphonse does not seem to have taken the trouble to write). Hansemann's position, whatever it may have been to start with, had in fact weakened rapidly since his visit, partly perhaps because of his quickness to humiliate Bleichröder, partly because he was too conservative in his estimate of the possibilities of the loan. After conversations with Oppenheim, Bleichröder, and William Bastow von Günther, president of the Seehandlung, Hansemann wired Paris via London that the success of the loan in Germany would require a price of at most 77 net, less at least 2 per cent commission on the under-writing – assuming that England went along.[39] This was a mistake. The competition for the loan was heating up by the hour, and it was already clear to Paris that one would have to bid higher than that to get the contract. Bleichröder, by comparison, was more sanguine. In a letter of 15 June, he spoke of 79–80 net, with the syndicate contracting at a fixed price of 76–77. Even this was to prove a little low, but it looked a lot better to Alphonse, who felt that a large German participation was indispensable to the success of the operation, primarily to prevent a sharp deterioration in the value of French banknotes.[40] Lehmann made the most of the opportunity, and what he called his 'chess move' in regard to Gerson's higher offer seemed to pay off. Alphonse, he reported happily, was in high dudgeon. 'I don't give a damn [*je m'en fous*],' he said; 'if Hansemann doesn't go along, let Bleichröder wire us his offer *with* or *without* Hansemann and Oppenheim'.[41]

Unfortunately, that kind of instruction was easier given than carried out. Lehmann was desperate at the confusion of com-munications. Alphonse was expecting a firm offer from Gerson momentarily, and Gerson seemed to be under the impression that he had to wait for some kind of signal from Paris. On Monday, 19 June, Lehmann sat in the rue Laffitte writing words that would be obsolete by the time they reached Berlin: 'answer Alphonse's telegram of today by tomorrow morning early; otherwise you may well find yourself excluded from the operation. The Rothschild syndicate must put in its bid tomorrow, and Alphonse cannot give you an order; he can only take your offers and put them in for you.' And again later on: 'I pray to heaven that your precisely framed offers come in by tomorrow morning'.

Each letter from Lehmann brought Bleichröder news of backbiting and machination. Our friend Betzold was back, complaining that Bleichröder was trying to take a commission for admitting people to the German syndicate. (Bleichröder was apparently taking 1/4 per cent commission on the shares of all but a few insiders to cover promotional costs.) Lehmann was indignant: 'The louts deserve to be excluded, along with their clients'. Alphonse, he said, had made no reply to the complaint; just told Betzold to go back to Bleichröder. Lehmann suspected that Betzold might be working in Paris on behalf of Hansemann; in any case he [Lehmann] would find out and wire Berlin at once, so that Bleichröder could air the whole business with Betzold's associate Teplitz before he left town.

All of this makes it clear that even at this late date (19 June), Bleichröders were still not sure where Hansemann stood. Would he join the Bleichröder consortium? Was he covering for people whom Bleichröder and Rothschild did not want to do business with? Troubled by this last possibility, Lehmann wired Berlin that same day, that if and when Hansemann and Oppenheim chose to join, they would have to accept the same moral obligation as the others not to give some of their share to Errera-Oppenheim, Sulzbach, Haber and the rest of 'that crowd'. The Rothschilds did not forgive easily. In fact, they wanted Bleichröder to submit at once a list of all the members of the group. Lehmann thought the whole idea absurd: 'there is more than enough room in the wings for certain actors to conceal themselves'. Later that afternoon, however, in a second letter, Lehmann told Bleichröder to take his time; the whole idea, he said, was a whim of Gustave de Rothschild, Alphonse's younger brother and junior partner. Gerson must have been relieved, if only because he may well have included in his group, for half a million francs, an employee of de Rothschild Frères. The fact is not certain, because Lehmann uses the cover name of Matthias for the person in question. Yet contextual analysis indicates that 'Matthias' was someone in Paris, and Lehmann's remarks on the subject run as follows: 'Emil [Brandeis] wants half a million for Matthias at the base price . . . In view of the manoeuvres of Hansemann and the very solid position that Emil has made for himself, it would seem opportune to make the concession.'[42] Alphonse would not have been pleased to learn that Bleichröders was trying in one way or other to buy the loyalty of one of his important officers.

As this little incident shows, Hansemann was always a source of concern. He turns up again, in these same letters, in connection with a small arbitrage operation. Bleichröder had written Lehmann that French banknotes were selling at a discount in Berlin, and Lehmann had seized the opportunity to make a little money on the side by buying Lombard railway bonds in Paris against payment in paper money. The pause that replenishes: 'Hopefully,' he wrote Berlin, 'these will cover the costs of the trip'. Bleichröder liked the idea and instructed him to buy more. In reply, Lehmann reported that Brandeis had told him that the Lombard railway, which was essentially a Rothschild property, would declare a dividend the following month; so that Lehmann felt they couldn't lose: if they sold, they gained on the exchange, and if they held, they stood to realise a substantial capital gain. And then he suggested that Bleichröders make these purchases henceforth directly through Rothschilds, the better to ingratiate themselves; 'otherwise, Hansemann and his people might gain ground'.

Another potential competitor was the Rothschild house in Frankfurt. It was not a particularly active bank. Frankfurt was a rich but sleepy market compared to Berlin, and Rothschilds was the very paradigm of cautious coupon-clipping finance. Still, it was the dominant force in any operation touching south Germany, and its connections with the other Rothschild houses gave it a kind of veto power over large international flotations in central Europe. It might not want to participate, in any given operation, but the promoters would do well to invite it to do so and to offer it a share and position commensurate with its dignity. There was here, clearly, matter for discontent: Gerson could not be happy sharing his moment of glory even with Meyer Carl von Rothschild; and Meyer Carl could not be happy about taking second place in a German consortium formed to participate in what was in effect a Rothschild loan. The solution was found by setting up two syndicates – one for south Germany and one for the north; and Lehmann warned Bleichröder (letter No. 1 of 19 June) to make sure that no south German firms appeared in his subscription list. As for those houses located in areas that might easily be defined as belonging to the one or the other, Bleichröders should cover these by its own subscription. 'I've already told Rothschilds,' he wrote, 'that you will be taking under your wing a great many of the smaller subscriptions; so that even a very large sum in your name would no longer attract attention'. The letter concluded with the hope that it would not be necessary to return home to Berlin via Bad Kissingen, where Meyer Carl was taking a cure – right in the middle of the negotiations for the biggest loan operation in history. 'There is no time,' Lehmann said, 'for an understanding with him; and now, if only Hansemann and Oppenheim will refuse the higher issue price, we'll have a free hands.'

That was issue day minus seven; and Lehmann could dream his dreams because, in the euphoric excitement of the rue Laffitte, everything seemed possible. From the Berlin side, however, everything looked hopelessly confused and disorganised, and the news from Paris brought a succession of disappointments that overtook every effort at an understanding. The last letters from Gerson to Alphonse, written on 14 and 15 June, just before his ophthalmia rendered him *hors de combat*, expressed serious misgivings about the shape the loan was beginning to assume. The market, he wrote, was depressed; but he felt that the Germans would be ready to take a third of the issue if the French did also. He even spoke of a billion francs for the German syndicate, with 250–300 million available almost at once and the rest in six to eight months. He was not happy, however, with the idea of an underwriting as opposed to a fixed purchase and sale. The difference was that a firm purchase – as in the old style – would have permitted the consortium to profit by whatever increase in price the *rentes* enjoyed; the results, in other words, were open-ended; whereas an underwriting consisted simply in guaranteeing the sale of some or all of the *rentes* at the issue price, and the 2 per cent commission represented the maximum that the promoters could expect. Gerson did not think that really enough to compensate for the risks incurred and even went so far as to say that he thought a successful flotation in Germany depended on a firm purchase.

With Gerson ill, Leopold Schwabach took over the negotiations for Bleichröders. He was younger than his cousin, uncommonly gifted in business matters, especially in market operations, impatient of deferential relationships, and intolerant of inefficiency. He had a sharp pen, and because, unlike Gerson, he had not been nourished from early childhood on the greatness and benevolence of the Rothschilds, he was able to approach a negotiation with them with considerable independence of mind and candor. His first letter to Lehmann (21 June 1871) began with some sharp comments on the state and quality of communications: 'It is no small matter to handle an affair of this scope and work with one another in the face of irregular telegraph service'; and matters were not being made any easier by the ambiguity of Alphonse's language. And it concluded with some advice to Alphonse, couched in the form of a request. 'Ask him', he wrote Lehmann, 'whether he can't do something for the Paris Bourse and push the prices up a little. When the Paris exchange is so soft as it has been today and yesterday, our Exchange in Berlin loses all courage. Things are bad enough already owing to the uncertainty about the modalities of payment. No one is willing to lend on *reports* (that is, lend speculators in futures the money needed to carry them from one month to the next), and if we don't help the market pass the end-of-month liquidation and hold out until July coupons are paid, a successful indemnity loan is out of the question.'

This was Schwabach the market manager talking. The next day, however, a much bigger stumbling block made its appearance, one that was linked to Gerson's earlier doubts about the underwriting arrangements. The reader will recall that the Treaty of Frankfurt (Article VII) required the French to pay a first instalment on the indemnity of 500 million francs within thirty days of the restoration of government authority in Paris. In negotiating with the various bidders for the loan, therefore, the French treasury was concerned above all to assure the availability of this sum and thought initially to limit the underwriting to that amount. Indeed, there were some who thought that, given the political uncertainty and the depressed market, it might be preferable to forego a big loan altogether and confine the operation to a direct borrowing of these first 500 millions. (This was, remember, the proposition of the 'Sulzbach-Haber clique', as the Rothschilds liked to call them.)

From the point of view of the French treasury, the major advantage of a small underwriting was that it saved money on commission. For this reason, the bankers involved cannot have been very pleased with the idea, even though a small underwriting implied a correspondingly small risk. They were, after all, prepared to handle a much larger sum, especially if they could have enough time; as Bleichröder had written on 15 June, Germany alone could raise 250–300 millions immediately and the rest of a billion in six to eight months. Still, if that was what the French treasury wanted, one couldn't very well tell the borrower what to borrow. On 21 June, therefore, Rothschilds (Paris) sent the following telegram to S. Lambert in Brussels:

Wire Bleichröder Berlin that time is passing fast and competition serious. French group set up on following basis: effective guarantee to sum of 500 million to cover eventual share which may not have been subscribed. Net price of iron screws (that is, *rentes*) 7915 (that is, 79 frs. 15) less 2 (per cent) for draft (*tirages*, that is, commission). German group would be on exactly same basis as French group. Ask you to answer yes or no. Until tomorrow. Rothschild.

This wire created enormous confusion; it gave rise to a whole array of interpretations, and as Schwabach put it in his letter of 21 June to Lehmann, 'our best heads have racked their brains in vain over this dispatch'. The crucial question was what was meant by the statement that the French syndicate would guarantee up to 500 millions. Did that mean that the bankers would underwrite only that amount in the total loan? In that case, the Germans would be happy to take whatever part of the guarantee they could get, up to the full amount. Or did it mean that the French would take that amount, the English perhaps the same, leaving the Germans with little or nothing? (The general assumption was that the guarantee would cover perhaps half the amount of the loan, which the Germans still thought would amount to 2.5 billions altogether.) The bankers in Berlin decided they would have to wait for further clarification.

One possibility, however, they did not envisage, since it went against all their experience, and that was, that whatever the size of the underwriting, it would cover the tail end, the unsubscribed portion of the loan. The usual practice, far more favourable of course to the underwriters, was to apply a guarantee of this kind to the initial subscriptions, the front end of an issue; the bankers, in other words, would guarantee a minimum sale and stood to be stuck with unsold securities only if subscriptions fell below that minimum. It thus fell to the borrower to determine what was the least he needed; and whatever sum he chose, his lenders stood to earn a safe commission on the greater part of it or maybe all of it, unless the issue proved to be a fiasco. The first sales are always the easiest.

Yet Rothschilds' wire had really been perfectly explicit in its stipulation: 'to cover eventual share which may not have been subscribed'. It was right there in front of Schwabach's 'best heads'. Their sense of prevailing usage, however, was so strong that they could not read the message.

They got the message the next day, 22 June, when a letter arrived from Lehmann (dated 20 June) describing the direction that the negotiations were beginning to take; and although Lehmann's views were still unofficial, the matter was confirmed by a wire from Rothschilds, dispatched Thursday evening, 22 June, at six and delivered the following morning in Berlin:

> Your wire incomprehensible (that is, Bleichröders' reply to the earlier wire of June 21st). Have proposal of the Minister (*sic*) and are waiting for his answer this evening. Ask you to answer yes or no, without supplementary clause, if you want to join us on same conditions and for what amount. Will see if we can still include it in our proposition, understanding the guarantee as follows. All the groups in the syndicate as one body undertake to take over the sums not subscribed up to the amount of their engagement. Thus if the syndicate guarantees 1,250 millions of nominal capital and only, 1,250 million (*sic*: clearly 250 millions is meant) subscribed, syndicate will take 1,000 million, and so on. Hope you understand.[43]

The picture was now clear, to the intense indignation and disappointment of the German syndicate. On the one hand, they had to reconcile themselves to a fixed commission, which they had never liked; on the other, they had to earn this commission by guaranteeing the last and most problematical subscriptions. Schwabach blew his top:[44]

> Completely new and really astonishing to me was the news that Thiers (code name 'Weber'; possibly Pouyer-Quertier) is to come first with one billion francs. Those are conditions that are flatly unacceptable. You can well imagine that I like to do business, like to make money, and above all would also like to make things easy for Alphonse. If it were only a question then, of five or six bankers who had made this kind of offer with me, I might perhaps have gone along with those . . . (one word illegible; presumably something like 'risks') that I have to run in such an operation. When, however, in order to put together so large a sum as 300 million francs, I have to scrape together the whole Exchange and our entire clientele, when further I get the other people to leave everything to us, get, so to speak, a vote of confidence from our associates, then you can well imagine that I cannot go along with conditions that in all the history of German loan operations have never yet been applied. Rather than accept such terms, I tell you frankly, I'd be ready to lose the market for all time . . .

What is clear from these and other remarks of both the bankers involved and contemporary observers is that the prospects of a successful flotation seemed far less bright in Germany than in France. For many, caution and even pessimism were an expression of wishful thinking; as good Germans they wanted the indemnity to hurt France and did not want to see the French pay easily. The Paris correspondent of the leading German financial weekly, *Der Aktionär* of Frankfurt, is a good spokesman for this kind of chauvinistic forecasting. And although the bankers were presumably more objective in these matters, they were insulated by distance from the competition and excitement of Paris and were almost bound to see those difficulties that the French were inclined to deprecate or overlook. Thus Schwabach was concerned, as we have seen, about the momentary softness of the market and the tightness of money. He was also troubled by the fact that the French *rente* was, for the Germans, a new and unfamiliar type of security; 'we cannot, therefore, undertake to provide the same guarantees that experience tells us we can, for example, with Russian and even Austrian securities'. This to Lehmann on 23 June; the French would have cringed at the very thought of their credit's being compared unfavourably with that of Russia or Austria, the two most improvident great powers in Europe.

Whatever reservations Schwabach had, moreover, were more than matched by the misgivings of Hansemann and Oppenheim. (Hansemann was the crucial man here, since Oppenheim had been included in the negotiations more out of courtesy than necessity.) Both had always been more pessimistic in their appreciation of the loan prospects than Bleichröder; and both felt that they would be exceeding their authority to accept the terms proposed. Schwabach felt that he had to go along with his associates, however much this might draw out the negotiations, although, by way of persuading Rothschilds, he assured them that he was convinced that the disagreement could and would be settled and the affair placed on a 'correct and customary basis' (letter of 23 June). That same day, therefore, he sent them the following wire:

Dispatch of 22nd 6 pm received and understood. In view of the altogether new and unprecedented form here, Hansemann, Oppenheim, and I do not feel ourselves authorized to accept on behalf of syndicate your propositions. We maintain ours, which agree with yours save the one point that we cannot grant Thiers the privilege requested of 1,250 millions. Furthermore our syndicate remains in being and we do not consider negotiations broken off.

In a postscript to his letter, however, directed personally to Alphonse, Schwabach gave vent to his sense of helplessness and discouragement:

> I am convinced, *hochverehrter Herr Baron*, that you will fully understand the difficulty of my position. You know my devotion to you, but I cannot dissociate myself from the objections of my colleagues. Whichever way the decision goes, please make use in any case of my services for a subscription here. I will, needless to say, do everything to produce a favourable result.

It was not an easy spot for Schwabach to be in. The situation called for Gerson's authority and tenacity, but unhappily Gerson's condition did not permit him to intervene. The difficult negotiations and particularly the arguments with Hansemann had worn him down, to the point where the doctors had momentarily feared a recurrence of his inflammation. This was Thursday, 22 June. Furtunately the crisis had passed, but Gerson obviously needed all the rest and quiet he could get.[45]

Schwabach's postscript of the 23rd was prescient. However much he wanted to hold his syndicate together and find a basis of agreement, he simply did not have time to heal the breach; and once the underwriting operation was lost, all that was left was to participate in the issue on behalf of Rothschilds. The morning of 24 June brought Berlin news of the new price set by the Ministry of Finance: 82–1/2 gross, which came to about 79.35 net after deduction of commission and allowance of interest for payment in advance; from which the underwriters could deduct another two points on the 1060 million francs they guaranteed (1 fr. 65 for every 5 fr. of *rente* guaranteed). The dispatches concluded with the request for a definitive response by 'tomorrow morning'. But since the wires had been sent the evening of 23 June, 'tomorrow morning' was already here. Schwabach did his best. He held some hasty conversations with his associates in Berlin, and they agreed, with some unhappiness, to accept the latest increase in the issue price; but they wanted the French Government to permit them, by way of compensation, to exclude from the subscription and hold for appreciation such portion of their respective shares of the issue as they desired; and they refused once again to go along with the underwriting arrangements.

That was Saturday, 24 June, issue day minus three. By the time Schwabach's wire reached Paris, the underwriting operation was closed and the Rothschilds submitted a list that omitted the German syndicate. Monday, 26 June, the contracts were signed. As finally constituted, the underwriting group included some of the leading private houses of Paris, in the amount of 670 million francs; a foreign group whose exact composition I have not been able to ascertain but whose principal elements were Rothschilds (London), Barings, and perhaps the other Rothschild houses in Frankfurt and Vienna, 325 million francs; and the syndicate of French joint-stock banks listed above, 65 million – total guarantee of 1060 million francs.[46]

The gloom in Berlin may well be imagined. None of this transpires in Bleichröders' correspondence with Paris. Lehmann packed his bags and returned home. The Rothschilds themselves were far too busy attending to the subscription to send personal letters for the moment. The business correspondence, as always, was matter-of-fact and confined itself to the usual information about drafts, remittances, and market conditions. And Schwabach, who took Sunday, 25 June, off – at least he did not write Paris, for the first time in days – concentrated on promoting the new issue. In his letters of that week, there is not the slightest expression of regret about the deal that missed.[47] We do, however, by chance, have the testimony of one visitor, Edouard Kleinmann, traveling in Berlin on behalf of the Crédit Lyonnais. Among the firms he called on was Bleichröders. He found the bankers of Berlin in 'bad humor' and commented on their 'unhappy mien'.[48]

NOTES AND REFERENCES

1. In an interview with Edward Malet, second secretary of the British Embassy in Paris, sent by Lord Lyons, the British Ambassador, with the encouragement of Jules Favre of the French Government of National Defense, to sound out Bismarck on the possibility of armistice negotiations. Edward Malet, *Shifting Scenes, or Memories of Many Men in Many Lands* (London, 1901) pp. 265–9, cited in Robert I. Giesberg, *The Treaty of Frankfurt: A Study in Diplomatic History, September 1870–September 1873* (Philadelphia, 1966) p. 30. On the other hand, Baron Wimpffen, the Austrian Ambassador to Berlin, wrote Vienna as early as 13 August of Prussia's intention to demand an indemnity of two billion

Thaler – a figure that comes very close to the high figure advocated by some of Bismarck's advisers in early 1871. Where does the truth lie? Or could Jules Favre, the French representative, have unwittingly opened the way for a Prussian claim that would have been made anyway?

2. Bleichröder Archives, Box XXIX, Letter Abraham Oppenheim, Köln, to Gerson Bleichröder, Berlin, 20 October 1870.

3. Cte de Falloux, *Memoires d'un royaliste*, 2 vols. (Paris, 1888) II, 450.

4. M. Thiers, *Notes et souvenirs de M. Thiers, 1870–1873* (Paris, 1903) p. 96.

5. Some of these began to appear from 17 February on in the so-called *Moniteur prussien de Versailles*, the German occupation newspaper that presented itself as the *Moniteur officiel du Gouvernement Général du Nord de la France* – just in time for the indemnity negotiations that were about to take place. The issues of this newspaper were collected and reprinted, advertisements and all, by Georges d'Heylli [E. A. Poinsot], *Le Moniteur prussien de Versailles*, 2 vols. (Paris, 1872).

6. Heinrich O. Meisner (ed.), *Denkwürdigkeiten des General-Feldmarschalls Alfred Grafen von Waldersee*, 3 vols. (reprint of 1922 edition; Osnabrück, 1967), I, 162. Unknowingly, Waldersee makes use of the same language as Abraham Oppenheim but turns it to different ends: ' . . . our financiers, even Bleichröder, did not understand what a billion meant, and what a country like France could do'.

7. M. Thiers, *Notes et souvenirs*, pp. 119–24.

8. This was one instance where Bismarck did yield on his demands. Initially he would have liked to have Paris pay a billion francs; anything smaller, he said, would be insulting to so rich a city. Favre was authorised to go as high as one half billion but apparently bargained well enough to save more than half that amount. Giesberg, *The Treaty of Frankfurt*, p. 91. The ransom was paid two weeks later (12 February 1871), with a final reckoning to be established under terms agreed on by Henckel von Donnersmarck, Bleichröder, and L. Scheidtmann, acting for Germany, and Dutilleul, Léon Say, and Alfred André acting for France. Both sides obviously found it helpful to use professional bankers and private citizens in these negotiations. On Alfred André, see David S. Landes, *Bankers and Pashas: International Finance and Economic Imperialism in Egypt* (London and Cambridge, Mass., 1958).

9. See the table in Jean Seguin, *Les emprunts contractés par la France à l'occasion de la guerre de 1870* (Paris, 1914) p. 71. Three items presumably comprise, among other things, monies exacted by the Germans over and above what was paid in indemnities and occupation costs: payments by the French Treasury to departments, communes, and private citizens by way of indemnification: 605 million francs; deficit of tax collections in 1870–1, 364 million francs; unindemnified damage to communes and private citizens, 535 million francs. How much of this total of 1.5 billion actually took the form of transfer payments, is impossible to say, but something in the neighborhood of 250 million seems a conservative estimate.

10. *The Economist* (London, 4 March 1871) p. 254.

11. The most useful analysis of this problem in furnished by Fritz Machlup, 'The Transfer Problem: Theme and Four Variations', in his *International Payments, Debts, and Gold* (New York, 1964) pp. 374–95. The four cases studied are Britain, 1793–1816; France, 1871–75; Germany, 1924–32; and the United States, 1950–63. See also his 'Foreign Debts, Reparations, and the Transfer Problem', ibid., pp. 396–416.

12. *The Economist,* 4 March 1871, p. 253.
13. In 1866 Camphausen, then President of the Seehandlung, hence representative of the Prussian Government in loan matters, denounced the contract of 1860, which gave Rothschilds (Frankfurt) a monopoly of Prussian issues, and turned the business over to a consortium nominally headed by the Seehandlung but effectively managed by Hansemann and the Disconto. Helmut Böhme, *Deutschlands Weg zur Weltmacht: Studien zum Verhältnis von Wirtschaft und Staat während der Reichsgrundungszeit 1848–1881* (Köln and Berlin, 1966) pp. 215–16. Hansemann was at this time (October 1870) underwriting the largest share of the unsold portion of the Prussian national war loan, which had failed badly the previous August, in public subscription – a sign of popular misgivings about Prussian military prospects. Hermann Münch, *Adolph von Hansemann* (Munich and Berlin, 1932) pp. 90–1.
14. Abraham's letter (see note 2 above) also took the matter of that part of the French Eastern Railway located in the portions to be annexed of Alsace-Lorraine. Abraham had been considering for some time (*längst*) the acquisition of this line by the Rheinische Eisenbahn in return for payment in Rheinische stock, and thought that here too perhaps a letter to the King might help. Oppenheim was prefiguring here what was to become a characteristic pattern of German business, ever quick to seize on the opportunities of conquest. In 1870, however, he was premature: the Prussian state took over the Eastern Railway and ran it directly.
15. Jules Favre, *Gouvernement de la Défense Nationale,* 3 vols. (Paris, 1875), III, pp. 96–7.
16. It is interesting to consider Friedrich Lehmann's views on the subject. On 10 February 1871 he wrote Gerson in Versailles, 'I am really curious to see in what way people propose to bleed France'. To require payment entirely in metal would not be possible, he maintained, as France could not survive on paper money alone. To take *rentes* in payment would be 'dangerous', and to place that large a sum in *rentes* would be 'a pure impossibility'. He favoured taking 'solid securities' in part payment, for example, railway shares and bonds, so long as they yielded six per cent at par; the rest could be paid in metal and in funds raised by issuing a loan on the London market. (Lehmann did not like the idea of the Germans being asked to subscribe to a French indemnity loan.) Note in this regard that most French railway bonds paid three per cent, so that six per cent at par would mean paying for them at half of their nominal value.
17. Lottery loans were actually forbidden in France as well, but the Chamber could obviously legislate an exception if it so desired. (It had done so, for example, in 1868, for the Suez Canal Company.) They were permitted in Prussia until 1871 and had been used on four occasions from 1796 to 1855. In addition, the state had relied heavily in the early part of the century on a number of straightforward lotteries: the firm of Bleichröder had begun among other things as a retail outlet for lottery tickets. Eugen Richter, *Das preussische Staatsschuldenwesen und die preussische Staatspapiere* (Breslau, 1869) pp. 220–2.
18. See the discussion in Seguin, *Les emprunts contractés,* pp. 84–9. In fact, the wartime Morgan loan was to be amortised in 36 years. And as of early May, Bleichröder (and presumably some of his French friends) favoured the issue of a five per cent loan redeemable at 120 per cent of par within 46 years. Letter of 5 May 1871 to Bismarck.

19. The need to contract out loans, that is, sell the issue at a fixed price to bankers, who were then free to resell the issue at whatever price they could realise, was a sign of weakness. Holland and England were the first countries to liberate themselves from this necessity and go over to public subscription. France had followed it in 1870 and failed; even the enthusiasm of wartime had not sufficed.

20. For the law of 20 June 1871 and the decrees of 23 June, see Seguin, *Les emprunts contractés par la France*, pp. 98, 137; Amagat, *Les emprunts et les impôts de la rançon de 1871* (Paris, 1889) pp. 139–40.

21. The content of the proposal is known indirectly from a report by Balan and Arnim, German plenipotentiaries in Brussels, to Bismarck, 25 April 1871, reprinted in Hans Goldschmidt, *Bismarck und die Friedensunterhändler 1871* (Berlin and Leipzig, 1929) pp. 99–100. In regard to payment of bills of exchange, Rudolph von Delbrück, *President of the Reichskanzleramt*, had noted in the margin: 'In my opinion very possible'.

22. Ibid., pp. 110–11. The deficit was presumably accounted for by a low German estimate of the value of the securities proposed.

23. Letter to Balan and Arnim, 30 April 1871, ibid., p. 111. Bismarck was in rare form. In a similar response to efforts by the French representatives to secure what the Chancellor felt was an exorbitant price for the annexed portion of the Eastern Railway, he instructed the German agent to inform his *vis-à-vis* that if they persisted in their 'shameless demands', the German Government would annul the railway's concession and expropriate the line for such value as it might have without permission to operate.

24. Bleichröder to Bismarck, 5 May 1871. This was the first of two letters of that date.

25. Bleichröder Archive, Box XIV, Letter of Alphonse de Rothschild to Gerson Bleichröder, 13 March 1871.

26. The agreement of 11 February 1871 concerning the modalities of payment of the Paris indemnity is reprinted in Jean Figard, *L'oeuvre d'un ministre des finances après la guerre de 1870–71: Léon Say* (Paris, 1915) p. 259 f. These details differ substantially from those furnished by Gabriel Ramon, *Histoire de la Banque de France* (Paris, 1929) pp. 340–1. The Paris syndicate consisted of de Rothschild Frères, Fould & Cie., F. A. Seillière, Hottinguer & Cie., Mallet Frères & Cie., Marcuard, André & Cie., and Pillet-Will & Cie. All were solidarily liable for any paper issued by any of the members.

27. The details are to be found in the business letters from Bleichröders to Rothschilds, Paris, in the Rothschild Archive. See, among other letters, that of 24 March, which transmits the receipt of the *Discontogesellschaft* for three million Thaler, paid by three drafts of one million Thaler each by Hottinguer, Seillière, and Pillet-Will on Bleichröders and covered by Bleichröders by a debit against Rothschilds' V de P account. One of these huge bills of exchange has been preserved in the Bleichröder Archive as a souvenir – this one for one million Thaler by Fould & Cie.

28. Rothschild Archive, Paris, letter Bleichröders to Rothschilds, 7 March 1871.

29. According to the Convention of 11 February, the remittances in specie were due by 19 February. Apparently, however, this deadline was extended, because in a letter to Bleichröder of 16 March, Emil Brandeis writes that the gold and silver purchases from Bavaria were made 'for the account of the City'. See also Brandeis' letters of 28 February, 9 March, and 13 March 1871.

Bleichröder Archive, Box XVII. Another possibility is that the city of Paris borrowed the specie it needed and had to repay in kind.

30. Letter of 4 March 1871, cited by Jean Bouvier, *Le Crédit Lyonnais de 1863 à 1882, les années de formation d'une banque de depôts* (Paris, 1961), I, p. 403.

31. The best source on Say, though far too sweet of tone, is Georges Michel's biography, *Léon Say, sa vie, ses oeuvres* (Paris, 1899). Say was subsequently four times Minister of Finance. As reporter of the Budget Committee of the Chamber, he issued in 1874 a *Rapport . . . sur le paiement de l'indemnité de guerre et sur les opérations de change qui en ont été la conséquence* (Assemblée Nationale, Document No. 2704, Annexe au procès-verbal de la séance du 5 août 1874) [cited below as Say, *Rapport*] that has served as the basis of all subsequent discussions of the subject. The report was reprinted in Say, *Les finances de France sous la Troisième République*, vol. I (Paris, 1898).

32. Dutilleul to E. Picard (Minister of Finance) 18 February 1871, cited by Bouvier, *Le Crédit Lyonnais*, I, 403 n. 4.

33. Archives Nationales [henceforth A. N.] F³⁰ 215.

34. *Der Aktionär*, 11 June 1871, p. 447. On Gebrüder Sulzbach see Landes, *Bankers and Pashas*, p. 64 n. 2.

35. On Sterns and Samuel von Haber, see Paul Emden, *Money Powers of Europe in the Nineteenth and Twentieth Centuries* (London, n. d.) pp. 259 f., p. 88.

36. Rothschild Archives, Paris, A-12-3/4 agreement of 26 June 1871. The story of the manoeuvres of the joint-stock banks in the months preceding the loan is based on Bouvier, *Le Crédit Lyonnais*, pp. 404–7. Bouvier, however, was not able to obtain information on the composition of shares of either of the two banking syndicates.

37. The letter also informed Alphonse that Berlin had learned on good authority that the loan would be for two billions only; and that Bismarck felt, therefore, that further conversations about the possibility of an immediate complete settlement would be superfluous. The political implications of this passing remark are extremely important: there is some reason to believe that Thiers was not interested at this point in the quick withdrawal of the German occupant, because it was precisely the task of liberating the country that gave him his political leverage. Only his role in accomplishing this task gave him the authority he needed *vis-à-vis* royalists and Bonapartists at a time when the republican constituency had been amputated by the Commune. Cf. the Arnim 'Promemoria' of 1 May 1871, in Goldschmidt, *Bismarck und die . . .* , pp. 116–17; also Maxime du Camp, *Souvenirs d'un demi-siècle*, vol. II: *La chute du Second Empire et la IIIᵉ République, 1870–1882* (24th printing; Paris, 1949) pp. 273–6.

38. *Der Aktionär*, 18 June 1871, p. 470.

39. Hansemann to Alphonse de Rothschild, 14 June 1871.

40. Lehmann to Gerson Bleichröder, Paris, 19 June 1871.

41. Lehmann to Gerson Bleichröder, Paris, 19 June 1871. This is the second letter of that date. The underlinings are as in the original.

42. Letter No. 1 from Lehmann to Bleichröders, 19 June 1871.

43. We have in this instance the rough copy on which the telegram is based and can correct the second sentence to read: 'Have made proposal to Minister and are waiting for his answer this evening'. The error in the arithmetic at the end clearly arises from the confused formulation of a guarantee of 1250 millions on a total loan of 2.5 billions, so that, if 1250 millions were to be subscribed, this

would in fact leave 1250 millions to be taken over by the underwriters. And yet it had already been established by law of 20 June, that is, two days earlier, that the loan was going to be for two billions and not for 2.5. The people in Rothschild were obviously a little overworked by this time.

44. Schwabach to Lehmann, Paris, 22 June 1871.
45. On Hansemann's contribution to Gerson's ill health, see Schwabach to Lehmann, Paris, 22 June 1871.
46. Rothschild Archives, Paris, A-12-3/4, contract of 26 June 1871. Since the exact composition and shares of the French group has not been published before, the reader may be curious to know who participated: Rothschilds (Paris), 248 million; Fould, 65 million; Seillière, 40 million; Mallet, 54 million; Hottinguer, 30 million; Marcuard, André & Cie., 48 million; Vernes, 20 million; Hentsch, Lutscher & Cie., 16 million; Abaroa, Uribarran & Goguel, 16 million; Mirabaud, Paccard & Cie., 8 million; Pillet-Will, 30 million; the syndicate of Trésoriers-Généraux, 35 million; the Société Générale, 60 million. The last should normally have been included with the other joint-stock banks. But it had been founded in 1864 with Rothschild sponsorship and had always enjoyed a privileged relationship to the private house.
47. Schwabach does make brief mention of the liquidation of the German group; the understanding was that no member would then turn around and try to share in the underwriting by getting admitted to either the French or English group. Apparently, however, the Berliner Handelsgesellschaft had violated the agreement and taken 25 million francs of the share alloted to André, Marcuard & Cie.; and it was now (26 June 1871) offering subscriptions, at the base price, to houses that would otherwise have subscribed with Bleichröders at the regular issue price. Schwabach to de Rothschild Frères, 26 June 1871, letter No. 2.
48. Letters of 27 and 28 June 1871, cited by Bouvier, *Le Crédit Lyonnais*, I, 409, n.2.

5 The Economic Development of Small Nations: the Experience of North West Europe in the Nineteenth Century

S. B. SAUL

I

The peculiar problems of small countries are the subject of much discussion in the literature on current developmental experience but have not been much analysed in a historical context. Yet the question of how such countries responded to the challenges offered by the industrial revolution in Europe raises many interesting issues. In this paper I have tried to put forward some general ideas that may form the basis of future research, looking at the development of a group of such countries in North West Europe – Belgium, Denmark, the Netherlands, Norway, Sweden, Switzerland. 'Small' is here defined in terms of population. In 1910/11 there were 7.4 m people in Belgium, 5.9 m in the Netherlands, 5.5 m in Sweden, 3.8 m in Switzerland, 2.8 m in Denmark and 2.4 m in Norway. The rate of growth of output per head (1870–1914) ranged from 2.3 per cent per annum for Sweden and 2.1 per cent for Denmark, the highest rates in western Europe, to 1.3 per cent for Switzerland and 1.4 per cent for Norway, among the lowest.[1] Growth in Belgium averaged 1.7 per cent but this kind of rate was experienced there for some three decades before 1870, considerably longer than in the other countries under discussion.

Though they were all relatively small in terms of population, that and physical proximity to Germany and Britain were all they had in common. There were important differences in the population/land ratio, in climate and natural resources as well as in important aspects of their recent historical developments. This heterogeneity is itself interesting, for I am not looking at these countries to try to find a common strand or model; the variety of solutions to the developmental problem is in itself fascinating. It may be argued that there is no point in writing about small countries as such, because their problems are no different from those of regions within bigger countries. There are clearly parallels but I do not have much sympathy with those who view western Europe as a single economic entity. Emphasis on the uniqueness of individual states is a vital part of European experience. Military considerations, social structures, commercial policies, the responsiveness of crown and government to unique internal influence all seem to justify the importance given to countries as opposed to regions. The most striking example of independent action made possible by sovereign control is to be seen in Luxembourg, where a grand-ducal decree of the 1860s laid down that licences for exploitation of local ore would be granted only to entrepreneurs who would smelt the ore into pig iron on the spot. The policy was maintained after 1878 when the Gilchrist–Thomas process gave the minette ore increased importance and in addition the steel companies were required to offer a proportion of their basic slag to local farmers at a low price.[2] The State, then, set the rules of the games. It represented the highest and most concentrated form of political organisation and in studying economic growth we have to look particularly at the political options adopted in each country, and this involves the decisions and values of the local ruling classes, their conflicts, the nature of the class struggle and so forth.

II

It has been argued by Kuznets that small nations, because of their greater social homogeneity and closer ties, may find it easier than others to make the social adjustments necessary to take advantage of the potentialities offered by new technology.[3] Kádár takes a similar view and also suggests that the national administrative institutions are more elastic and susceptible to change in small rather than large countries.[4] Fairly obviously this is not always the case. The misfortunes of history continue to pose immense internal problems for Belgium, and severe regional tensions are still to be found in Switzerland for example, but it could well be that the chances of such tensions existing are lower in smaller than in larger countries. However, one obvious feature of these countries is the ease with which the process of agrarian reform was carried through in the eighteenth and early nineteenth centuries. Certainly the nexus of feudal social arrangements in the agrarian sector was much less important in the Low Countries and in Switzerland and Norway than in most parts of the Continent, but it might be argued that it was easier to achieve the compromises and adjustments necessary for a smooth change in rural relationships in small rather than in large countries. In other words it may be that it is possible to achieve a more intelligent and rational economic policy in small countries where there are fewer interests to be reconciled. Taking tariffs as an example, in both Germany and France from the 1870s on there were long and bitter struggles between powerful conflicting forces. In neither was it possible to respond to the inflow of cheap grain after 1875 in the way Denmark did, because agricultural conditions varied so widely within each country and in any case in both the grain interests were too important. The solution of importing grain freely, using it as feed for livestock and developing the export of animal products, was well suited to the relative homogeneous farming pattern in Denmark. No doubt it would have benefited Schleswig Holstein and other north German states where co-operative creameries were started as early as in Denmark, but such an outcome was never remotely possible.

There was also the importance of being unimportant. Small countries could follow their own tariff policies without serious fear of retaliation. They could do the same over exchange rates, though this was not a matter of importance in the nineteenth century. Belgium could attract investment by operating the laxest company law of all the more developed countries in Europe. Of course the corollary of this was that they were unable to put much pressure on others either. Perhaps most interesting was their ability to go their own ways with patent law with little fear of retribution and in a manner that was important for the growth of a number of industries. Sometimes chaotic laws or the absence of any law helped the diffusion of technology. Before the unification of the German states began in 1833, ten states had no patent law and the other twenty-nine had different laws. The cost to an outsider of trying to patent was prohibitive and German manufacturers copied at will. Switzerland had no patent law to 1887 and it was partly for this reason that French dye makers crossed the border in the 1860s to manufacture fuchsine dye when they were being frustrated by patent holders in their own country. The Swiss Law of 1887 left all processes unprotected, covering only inventions that could be represented by a model. The ability of the Swiss chemical industry to concentrate successfully on the production of speciality dyes depended on the fact that German dye firms were unable to patent their own processes in Switzerland. The manufacture of aluminium in Germany made little progress before 1914 basically because of difficulties in sustaining the patents for the Héroult process. Consequently the A.E.G. group, holding the Héroult rights, set up their plant at the Rhine Falls in Switzerland where all the process patents for aluminium were ineffective. The Netherlands had no patent law at all from 1869 to 1910. This undoubtedly helped the Jurgens brothers to develop a French process for the manufacture of margarine after 1870. It was also very helpful to Gerard Philips who established an incandescent lamp factory at Eindhoven in 1891, making what was basically Edison's carbon filament lamp with only minor modifications. By 1913 he was one of the largest manufacturers in Europe and one element in his success was the fact that in the early years he was the only maker in western Europe not saddled with the burden of paying royalties to the Edison interests. Small countries may also have benefited from the inevitably limited range of their educational systems. Whereas German and British engineers and chemists normally received their training in local colleges and factories, the Swiss in particular moved all over western Europe for the purpose and went back home to pool their experiences.

III

It is sometimes argued that small countries find the cost of administering central government services unduly burdensome. The avoidance of some of these costs was certainly an attractive feature of unification to certain German states but a preliminary look at the general statistics of government expenditure per head for the small countries of the north west has proved to be inconclusive on this question. In 1912, for example, the administration of justice cost just under $1 per head in Norway, Denmark and Belgium compared with 25 cents in Russia and 30 cents in France. But apart from difficulties over standards and distribution of expenditure between central and local governments, we find the cost in Sweden also 30 cents. The per capita cost of diplomatic and commercial representation overseas was higher in small countries in 1912 than it was for Germany, for example, though again it is possible that smaller countries consciously aimed for service of a higher quality in some respects. Belgian consular reports in particular were re- markably detailed and the consuls themselves were frequently men of high commercial standing. Given the level of preparation for war going forward in the Central Powers in 1912, it is striking that with German war expenditure at round $5.30 per head it was as high as $4.46 in Sweden. In Denmark and Norway, however, expenditure was under $3 and in Belgium more like $2.[5] Small countries did not bother to try to emulate the Great Powers in that respect.

IV

However, basically it is the size of the home market which all writers have recognised as the main problem of small countries. The market is not large enough to enable their industries to reap scale economies deriving from indivisibility of plants, from bulk purchasing and from credit and marketing activities. Furthermore, they do not benefit as larger industrial countries do from the external economies derived from the simultaneous existence of a wide variety of industries. Limitations of natural resources almost inevitably make the small economy highly specialised and for this reason if for no other all these small nations of the north west were in the nineteenth century heavily dependent on foreign trade. This inevitably left their economies extremely vulnerable. Several of them suffered recession between 1815 and 1845 because of the stagnation or collapse of a major branch of their external trade at a time when population was expanding rapidly. In Belgium it was the linen trade, in Norway timber, in Sweden iron. As the nineteenth century wore on all, with the exception of Switzerland and the Netherlands, came to depend heavily on the British market where free trade, rising incomes and growing population offered unusually good opportunities. Later still Germany came to play a similar role. It might be thought that the export industries would continue to be peculiarly vulnerable in cyclical downturns. Certainly the Swedish timber trade reflected variations in British housebuilding but as this was only a small part of the total demand the overall effect was not serious. Belgian pig iron production seems to have been particularly sensitive to international fluctuations too; its share of world output rose from 4.39 per cent in 1868 to 4.86 per cent at the top of the boom in 1871 to fall back to 3.2 per cent in 1879.[6] There were similar falls in the early 90s and in 1901 and 1907, for example, but in general neither in the late nineteenth nor in the present centuries do the economies of the small countries as a whole seem to have suffered unduly during periods of slump. With world trade generally expanding, the small countries of the north west were growing in an unusually favoured environment not simply because demand was growing but also because they faced an enlarged variance of possible outcomes which reduced the likelihood of complete disaster during periods of trade depression.

The problem of access to markets was a particularly serious one for Belgium. The French revolutionary wars brought her within the French tariff walls, but after 1815 this advantage was lost and a joint monarchy was created out of the United Provinces to the north and the Austrian Netherlands and Liège to the south. Economically it was a failure. A country on the verge of an industrial revolution was joined to a declining colonial power. Access to that market could not compensate Belgium for the loss of access to the French. Independence in 1830 brought new problems because the cotton textile industry had geared itself to satisfying the Dutch home and colonial markets which were now largely lost. Belgian textile manufacturers began moving across the border into the Netherlands. The problems were intensified in 1839 when Belgium lost a further 400 000 of its population to the Netherlands. An attempt to establish a customs union with France failed because of opposition from French industry and a veto from the British Government on political grounds. The French in 1844 were to prevent Belgium from joining the Zollverein on similar grounds, though the formation of the Zollverein itself was vital to Belgian industry in the 1830s just as it was to Swiss, for it lowered tariffs over such a wide area – they were lower than those in Britain at that time for example. King Leopold sought to widen the market by development of promising overseas territories. There were many plans, most of them hopeless from the first: in the end the choice fell upon Guatemala. In 1843 a company to send emigrants there was sanctioned, and the next year 871 unfortunates made the journey. Within eighteen months 211 died and nearly all the others had returned. In the event the government's bold decision to build a railway network and its resolution in carrying it through completely drew the economy out of its stagnation. The concern for markets continued, however. Leopold II was unusual among monarchs and statesmen in Europe in taking a positive developmental view of colonies. He acted initially in the Congo as a private individual because he could not persuade the Belgian Government to go along with him, believing that his company could be profitable and at the same time extend Belgian trade. That he proved to be wrong on both counts in no way detracts from the view that concern for the market was a recurrent theme in Belgian public life.

Faced by problems created by the small size of the home market and the inevitable heavy dependence on foreign trade, how did the small countries develop their specialities? Those sectors that were purely resource based, such as Swedish timber and iron ore, offer little analytical difficulty, but more interesting questions arise out of the emergence of particular industrial sectors. Some writers have stressed the idea that small countries insert themselves into world trade by concentrating on 'niches' – forms of production where the returns to scale are not very marked or might even be negative. There is no reason why the countries with larger home markets should not compete too, but the niches are those areas where the smaller can and do compete. For example, Swiss textile machinery makers, facing the might of large firms in Lancashire, had no hope of competing in the general run of cotton spinning machinery. They won their markets by selling weaving machinery for which the demands were much more varied and the Lancashire machinery industry much less specialised, so that the two competed on more or less even terms, and by producing special embroidery machinery where a stream of innovations gave the Swiss makers a very real advantage. A dual form of specialisation appeared in Belgium in the 1840s. Local firms, working for the home market and concentrating on building small 20 H.P. steam engines could meet foreign competition easily enough but the Belgian textile manufacturers tended to buy their bigger engines overseas. This was a very specialised market dominated by the British and also in this instance by one great Belgian engineering firm of Cockerill which had always focussed its sights on the export market and built machines up to a capacity of 145 H.P. both for home and overseas.[7] The Cockerill 'niche' was based on locational advantages, an early start in European industrialisation, and a determination to achieve the size needed to compete on a continental scale.

There has been much discussion of a general kind in the literature about the significance of scale economies. There seems little doubt that by the end of the nineteenth century they were very important in certain process industries, chemicals above all but also in the manufacture of steel and glass for instance. It would require a very high concentration of industry in the small country and a very considerable export trade to achieve these economies, though as Cockerills showed, it was not impossible. The same was true for cheap cottons; for other fabrics and qualities of fabrics the difficulty was to compete with the already strongly entrenched position of the traditional leading exporters. In the metal manufacturing industries the problem was different. Here external economies were important, but scale economies were less significant than the learning factor. In a highly skill-intensive industry the operative steadily improves his work performance and the manager his control of the shop floor. In the aircraft industry today this is the chief economy achieved by a long production run and there is every reason to believe that these economies were at least as important in the yet more skill-intensive engineering trades of the last century. Where bulk orders for steam engines, machine tools, agricultural machines, locomotives, electric motors were available, the economies from learning were very large. In addition there would be normal scale economies to be obtained from buying-in parts in bulk – boilers and castings for example. Even so, it is not easy to substantiate the case for the existence of scale economies in wide areas of manufacturing industry much before 1870, say. One only has to look at the large number of firms active in many industries. For instance, in 1834 there were 1134 cotton mills in Britain, stabilising at around 2500 in the 1860s; in Ghent their number rose from 29 in 1817 to 78 in 1839. On the other hand, one can trace a dramatic concentration in the production of locomotives in Britain, France, Belgium and Germany, despite a great rise in output, for there the economics of buying in and of learning were outstandingly high.[8]

The Belgian economist Drèze has also modified the scale economy concept in a different manner. He makes a distinction between the total output of an enterprise and the output of individual homogeneous product lines.[9] A small industrial power like Belgium cannot hope to exert much influence on the tastes of its neighbours and so cannot export successfully goods characterised by style differences between different markets. She cannot change tastes nor can she effectively adapt to them but she can compete in goods manufactured to international standards for she can get long enough runs that way. It is noticeable that before 1914 Belgium concentrated on the export of intermediate goods in line with this pattern. Table 5.1. shows that the share of finished manufactures in her total trade in manufactured goods was very low by the standards of western industrial countries. The Swedish share was low too, largely because of exports of semi-manufactured timber but it is obvious from the table that this was only one form of specialisation open to small countries. Some were able to break down style differences to some degree at least and to persuade the world market to accept what they had to offer. Degrees of artistic sensitivity between one small country and another can hardly be ignored.

TABLE 5.1. *Finished manufactures as a proportion of total exports of manufactured goods, 1913 (%)*

Belgium	46	France	76
Sweden	57	UK	76
Germany	63	Switzerland	79

SOURCE A. Maizels, *Industrial Growth and World Trade* (Cambridge, 1963) p. 73.

Manufacturers in countries such as Sweden and Switzerland succeeded in world markets in circumstances where they were able to impose their styles on others largely as a result of technological innovation – power machinery is the obvious example. This usually took place in a limited range of linked industries and often where they were building to special orders: such circumstances allowed them to become industrial style-setters and often to manufacture in a scale economy fashion. Other small countries established skill-intensive niches, influencing taste through their specialised handicraft work. This was to be particularly true in Denmark where the share of handicrafts in industrial production was actually rising at the end of the nineteenth century, though to that date production was largely for the home market. On occasion a small country established an area of supremacy by changing the organisation of an industry in advance of competitors. The manufacture of shoes had always been carried on in Europe on a small scale despite the introduction of American machinery. The Swiss firm C. F. Bally changed the pattern by creating a series of small specialised units to service a large central factory. Its output in 1914 was much the largest in Europe. Timing was of the essence here as in several other instances.

We must be careful, however, not to attach too much importance to the argument that small countries *needed* to export because their home markets were too small and only opportunistic industries could survive. The challenge of market pressure is not enough, for it does not ensure a response; it merely offers the way out. Landes makes this point specifically about the Swiss watch industry and attributes its success to the influence of French refugee protestants – more specifically to the literacy and numeracy the protestants brought with them – and to the existence of a pool of cheap labour, for Swiss mountain wages were among the lowest in Europe.[10]

V

In turning now to examine more specifically the importance of size in determining the responses of small countries to the opportunities and problems of nineteenth century growth, one must not forget the role of more conventional factors. For a variety of reasons labour costs in industry in the Netherlands, Belgium and Switzerland seem to have been below those in Britain, Germany and France, for example. Such issues are not, however, the main concern of this paper. Belgium was unusual among the small countries because of her heavy emphasis on exports of capital goods. Her resources of coal and iron, and the spur to the iron and engineering industries given by the early burst of railway construction gave her a significant time advantage in European industrialisation. Belgian industrialists were therefore able to develop markets for iron and machinery in Europe before competition from Germany and France became significant, and indeed in the first instance their best markets were to be found in those countries. In some important respects, of course, the growth of the Belgian iron and steel industry was essentially part of the development of a whole region. As local supplies of raw materials dwindled, the industry began to import coal, coke, ore and pig iron from her neighbours. Some 17 per cent of the capital in the industry by 1914 was German. A highly concentrated industry, well to the fore in a technological sense, found no difficulty in operating plants near the optimum scale level. In 1905 the average output per blast furnace was 32 755 metric tons compared with 40 000 in Germany, 26 000 tons in the UK and 25 000 in France.[11]

To some extent the size of furnace was deliberately kept down because an industry so heavily dependent on exports needed a high level of flexibility in production and this was hard to achieve with a smaller number of giant furnaces. In fact in 1913 over a half of the iron and steel output was exported and this takes no account of the steel content of the almost equal value of exports of machinery and transport equipment. Such high proportions are typical of these small countries, as we shall see. The largest single market was the UK, but apart from that and considerable exports to the Netherlands, trade was in no way concentrated upon Europe.

An important element in the expansion of exports, however, was the role of the investment banks which were heavily involved in the industry itself and promoted its exports, not infrequently through the use of tied loans. The most important of these was the Société Générale which had been much to the fore in encouraging the growth of the coal and metal industries in the early years after independence and during the 1860s engaged heavily in international finance. With exports, direct and indirect, such a high proportion of total output, the role of these institutions that were actively promoting foreign trade was most significant. It is not surprising that the investment bank replaced the old captain of industry first in Belgium when one considers the economic and political problems the country faced in the 1830s. But in a small country an institution of this kind could have an influence on the industrial economy far greater than was possible in larger economies with their inevitably wider range of credit needs. The same could be said of the Tietgen enterprises in Denmark in the 1860s, and more strikingly of the Stockholms Enskilda Bank in Sweden, which was closely involved in the major engineering export industries around 1900.

Sandberg has written interestingly of Sweden as the 'impoverished sophisticate', a backward country with more than normal sophistication in some sectors and less than normal in others. Banking in particular was very advanced with an unparalleled ratio of bank assets to national income at any particular stage in the industrialisation process. Perhaps the explanation lay in a long commercial history and relatively high standards of education and also perhaps in the absence of any marked economies of scale in banking. It also gave her a disproportionate stock of human capital to set against poor availability of natural resources.[12]

Returning to Belgium, investment in railways by the Société

Générale and other banks much stimulated exports of rails and of equipment; in 1913 there were fourteen firms building locomotives in Belgium and a wagon industry employing 7000 men. A more unusual feature, however, was the financing and building of street railways, a speciality created out of the strength and interlinking of Belgian banking, engineering and steel making. Frankfurt, Cologne, Warsaw, Turin, Florence, Naples, Trieste, Munich, Barmen, Prague, were some of the cities involved in Europe alone, and in 1911 33 Belgian tramway companies were operating in Russia. The iron and steel industry in Belgium, built up initially on positive government (and crown) initiative to a degree that was not seen in other larger steel producing countries, maintained that role less because of the links with neighbouring steel industries, than because of its ability to create a world wide export business. In this it was helped, as were all the small countries of the north west, by the open British market, but also by the promotional activities of the banks. Given these conditions, scale economies provided no difficulty. Nevertheless the role of the banks in Belgian heavy industry had its unfortunate side for they showed a marked distaste for investment in final producer goods and consequently the forward linkage effects of heavy industry were less marked than they otherwise might have been.

Other Belgian specialities depended either on historic traditions – one such being the window glass industry which remained very labour intensive throughout the nineteenth century, so that the long built up skills remained important – or industries based on raw materials and fuel. She was the world's biggest exporter of cement in 1913. The monopoly of trade in zinc which Belgium and Germany held to 1880 was then lost but it was still an important industry in Belgium in 1914 even though the raw materials were now imported. A by-product of that industry was sulphuric acid, and she was the only country in the world exporting it in significant amounts. In all these industries the export proportion was very high – 70 per cent for zinc and zinc sheets, in the region of 90 per cent for glass. Even in the small motor car industry, the proportion was two-thirds.

The textile industries both in Belgium and elsewhere raise interesting issues. The bulk markets in cotton textiles were dominated by Britain and in wool textiles by Britain and France. But specialisation and particular market links gave the smaller countries possibilities here too. Belgium concentrated upon semi-manufactures – linen and silk yarn, and particularly carded wool from

Verviers of which some two-thirds was exported, mostly to Britain. Even in the less specialised cotton cloth industry growth could only be achieved through exports. Between 1880 and 1913 cloth output rose by 170 per cent, nine-tenths of the increase going to exports, and in the latter year 71 per cent of output was exported, the largest single market being Britain which took cheap white cloth for finishing and some cheap dyed fabric.[13] Although it was not a dominant industry as it was in Britain and even more so in Switzerland, textiles still accounted for some 15 per cent of industrial workers (including domestic workers) in 1911. The Dutch cotton industry on the other hand had a strong transformation base. In 1910 there were nearly four times as many employed in weaving as in spinning, so that although the Belgian cotton industry had three times the number of spindles, total employment in the two industries was very much the same. The Dutch had as many spindles as Sweden but total employment in cotton was nearly three times as great. It was a tiny industry in the world context but important in the Dutch situation. For example, in 1911 there were 19 factories in the Netherlands employing over 1000 workers and seven of these were cotton mills. Again two-thirds of the output was exported, the chief market being the Dutch East Indies.[14]

The differences between the Dutch and Belgian textile industries reflected differences to be found in their total trade patterns. Belgium specialised in semi-manufactures, metals as well as textiles. The Netherlands, deficient in raw materials, found its niche in processing – home and imported foodstuffs and imported steel as well as yarns. The Swiss managed the development of their textile industry differently. Based on eighteenth-century growth, it developed distinctive weaving techniques which provided a niche as well as having valuable engineering linkage effects. The Jacquard loom was adapted to cottons and specialised looms were developed for embroidery techniques. Theirs was the quality market and neither silks nor specialised cottons needed huge factories or coal resources but put a high premium on skill. Textiles became astonishingly important to Swiss industry, providing in 1892 44 per cent of employment and 57 per cent of the total value of exports.[15] In the classic manner the textile industry led the way to the manufacture of textile machinery, most of all special looms, and of power machinery with an emphasis on water turbines. From this base the major firms moved to other forms of high class machinery – locomotives, electric motors, diesels and steam turbines, all working almost entirely for export. In this context the much publicised watch industry was just one of a range of industries dependent on foreign markets.

It would appear that almost invariably the niches developed by the small countries originally had a home market base, or at least the major exporting firms began in that way. Swiss embroidered cottons, for example, must have had their origins in traditional peasant costumes; Denmark and the Netherlands had shipbuilding traditions geared to their colonial trades which Belgium did not, and this in part at least accounts for the late nineteenth-century distribution of shipbuilding among the small countries. Exceptions may be found in certain industries set up by refugees, such as the watch industry in Switzerland, diamond cutting in the Netherlands and glass making in Belgium. The home market influence can be seen in contrasting form between Belgium and Sweden. The agricultural machinery industry in Belgium was small and unimportant, largely because the mass of poor Belgian peasants working small farms demanded no more than the cheapest and simplest of machines. In Sweden on the other hand, the de Laval firm was most brilliantly successful in the export of cream separators. The base came from the powered machines which were required by cooperatives there. De Laval developed their own small high speed turbine for the machines and incorporated major technological improvements in the separator which had been rejected by their main competitor, Burmeister of Copenhagen, and the invasion of foreign markets began. In 1894 these separators provided 59 per cent of all Sweden's engineering exports and still 34 per cent twenty years later when 95 per cent of all those manufactured by de Laval were exported. They supplied 54 per cent of the whole Russian market, 80 per cent of the Dutch, 75 per cent of the North German and 90 per cent of the dairy separators in Denmark, the cradle of the creamery industry.[16]

There were, of course, special circumstances that helped the development of this group of small countries in particular. Their economies were not subject to the kind of institutional obstacles to adjustment that were present in the small countries of eastern Europe for example. Tariffs were relatively low and non-existent in Britain and world trade was rising rapidly. Technology helped; electric power made industries more footloose and hydro-electric power benefited Norway and Sweden even more directly. The rapid rate of innovation in engineering and food processing industries in particular gave opportunities to compete with the established industrialised countries. Skilled industries with a high labour content were becoming an important element in world trade. From these specialisations emerged great manufacturers in the small countries – Sulzer, Brown Boveri, Escher Wyss in Switzerland, de Laval in Sweden, Burmeister in Denmark, Carel in Belgium, Werkspoor and Philips in the Netherlands. The general growth of world trade gave a boost to service industries which typically have few scale economies. Here the Netherlands was particularly favoured by her historical traditions in insurance and banking, by geography in the development of the transit trade and by both in the emergence of Royal Dutch as a major force in the world oil trade before 1914. The same is true, as we have seen, of Sweden.

An exception to this pattern was the growing motor car industry. At first the industry spread rapidly because capital needs were low, demand active and the technology relatively conventional. But it soon became apparent that cars could not be made competitively outside the existing industrial complexes because the wide variety of bought-in parts could only with difficulty and great cost be brought together from distant suppliers. So Paris, Turin, Birmingham quickly became the focal points, and in Switzerland, Holland, Sweden and Denmark there was no motor car manufacture of any significance at all. Here the small countries faced one of their inevitable problems – real disadvantages in industries where external economies were important. Of course, as internal economies of scale grew more and more significant the smaller countries suffered from their small home base too. So the Belgian car industry had a good start before 1914 but one which proved very short lived. It was fortunate for the small countries that the motor car industry was by no means typical in its engineering economics.

Certain other factors helped the small countries too. Even the industry of a small country could get a significant boost from the coming of railways. Rails were usually imported (except for Belgium) but most countries built their own coaches and wagons – often importing the wheels. Some made a speciality of locomotive making; the widespread nature of the networks saw the beginning of locomotive construction in several German states by 1850, for example, especially as several of the railways were state-owned. Yet more of a spur came from railway repair and servicing establishments which by their nature were also very widespread. Servicing of agricultural machines and ship repairing had a similar impact. Most states took the precaution of providing at least part of their military requirements and their foundries provided a firm basis for private metallurgical development later. Bavaria owned mines and foundries in the Palatinate, for example; Württemberg owned eight such metallurgical establishments and Hanover six blast furnaces in the middle years of the nineteenth century.[17]

Shipbuilding was one of the most striking successes of small countries. The existence of such an industry initially was more a consequence of independence than of size but the question was one of maintaining it in the intensely competitive environment of the nineteenth century. At the end of the nineteenth century the leading Danish builders, Burmeisters, owed a great deal to the initiative of the East Asiatic Company in being willing to experiment with motor ships. The Dutch industry benefited from the requirement that shipping companies receiving government help must buy Dutch built ships where possible. The Norwegian shipbuilding industry, on the other hand, suffered from the slow transition of its shipping industry from sail to steam and by the tendency of those Norwegian shipping firms that turned to steam, to use secondhand vessels. Technical factors helped the small country producers. Labour costs formed a high proportion of total costs in an industry where the economies of scale in any one yard were not great and where individual, as opposed to batch building, remained the rule. Yards in Denmark and the Netherlands could buy their steel plates in Germany and Belgium frequently at prices below those maintained by the cartels in those countries. Forgings were imported in the rough state or made from scrap in open hearth furnaces. The labour intensive and costly process of machining these forgings was carried out locally with such effect that many Danish forgings were exported to British yards. The quality of engine building was high and both Danish and Dutch yards were to the fore in developing motor ships before 1914. Based on their hydraulic work at home, the Dutch built up a world reputation for dredgers and floating cranes for the building and improvement of ports throught the world. These huge works were transported by ocean-going tugs of Dutch construction, another area of specialisation which was thereby created. So demand, technology and innovation created another set of niches for the smaller countries.

Firms in the smaller countries were able to set up branches overseas and in that way achieve scale economies through exports of parts or basic materials and help cover research and sales overheads. Swiss dye firms had branches in France, Russia and Britain. Solvay's original soda works in Belgium remained small, for the market was limited and the raw material supply difficult, but other plants were established in most countries in Europe. Jurgens established a major role for themselves in the margarine industry in Germany. Cockerills set up a large steel complex in Russia and sold a great deal of steel-making plant in that country. But before 1914 most international investment of this kind was the work of American, British and German firms and on occasion such branch plants effectively prevented the emergence of a strong native industry in the smaller countries. This was true of electric engineering in Belgium, for example.

But one country, Norway, was not particularly successful in carving out niches in this way. We have already suggested why this was so in shipbuilding; what of other sectors of the economy? From 1850 to 1880 Norway re-established its eighteenth century role in the international carrying trade, jumping from eighth place to be the world's third largest carrier. The tonnage of the sailing fleet rose six times, the number of sailors from 19 000 to over 60 000 and Norway was no longer limited to carrying goods to and from her own ports. Her assets were the low wages and poor fare of her crews and the low capital cost of her sailing ships. But then came the squeeze of lower freights and competition from steam, and the growth of the industry, which had been the most expansionary force of the economy over the previous three decades, ceased and the number of sailors in Norwegian ships fell back to 50 000 by 1904.[18] The growth of the shipping and associated shipbuilding sectors had been of an enclave nature, giving relatively little boost to internal industrial growth, so that when these faltered the growing labour force in the coastal areas was pushed back into agriculture, remained unemployed or emigrated in growing numbers.

In addition to these difficulties the fishing industry remained largely coastal and failed to take advantage of the growing demand from the high income countries for fresh frozen cod caught on the Dogger Bank or off Newfoundland. Lack of capital prevented the Norwegians from building the much bigger vessels and the quick-freezing plants required for that trade. In a similar way the timber industry, its most accessible forests cut and such a large share of those remaining being in the hands of smallholders, failed to match the Swedish industry in sawmill technology and in the process trades such as pulp production and paper making. Only around the turn of the century did a considerable inflow of foreign capital lead to the tapping of Norwegian water power for hydro-electric purposes and the establishment of linked chemical and metallurgical plants, though again it was an enclave type of development, for very little of the output was destined for the home market.

The difference between Norway and other small economies in north west Europe brings out the point that although all of them were highly dependent upon foreign trade, success depended upon the development of the internal economy, providing the base from which the opportunities offered in the foreign trade sector could be grasped. As we saw earlier, in large measure the niches that the small countries created were based initially on home demand. In Norway, for reasons connected with the structure of rural society and also the physical make up of the country, internal development was slow and not much affected by the enclave type of activity in the sea ports. She was therefore not well placed to respond to the inevitable changes in the fortunes of the export staples. The contrast between the successful small economies of the north west and those of the Balkans can also be viewed at least partly in these terms. In the latter the survival long into the nineteenth century of a number of institutional obstacles to development such as serfdom, none of them fundamental but most of them no longer existing in the rest of the continent, created a gap that was hard to close. Railway systems created no indigenous engineering works. Alternative outlets if one staple faltered were hard to develop. By cutting costs and using second or third-hand vessels, Greek shipowners won their way into the Mediterranean tramp shipping trade, but as in Norway tonnage was stagnant for the last quarter of the nineteenth century and the conversion to steamships went forward very slowly. There was some increase in steam shipping after 1895 with the growth of the emigrant trade but this too provided no base for a native shipbuilding industry. For fifteen years after 1875 Greece rapidly expanded her exports of currants and in some years they constituted a half of all her exports, but then western grape growing began to recover and markets closed down. As a direct consequence the balance of payments so deteriorated that Greece defaulted on interest payments and the Great Powers took control of her finances.

On the other hand in western Europe, countries like Denmark by 1900 were finding the main impetus to growth arising in the urban centres expanding on their own momentum and not on the basis of exports. The agricultural niches helped resolve the balance of payments problems that might have been created by this autonomous urban growth but productivity was higher and rising most quickly outside the export sector. Inevitably small as well as large countries with rising incomes satisfied their own consumer markets to a considerable degree. Taste and fashion helped local firms obviously but there was also the impetus given to industries which were inevitably local such as brick-making, building itself, confectionery and drink and a whole range of service trades.

VI

My aim in this paper has been to try to illustrate the range of possibilities open to the small economies. In this they clearly had particular advantages as well as limitations. They were able to seize opportunities offered by the growth of incomes elsewhere which were small in themselves but sufficient markedly to transform sectors of their home economies. They could be influenced in this process by the work of single institutions or of government to an extent most unlikely in larger economies. The niches were very varied – standardised goods and semi-manufactures, specialised scale economy type goods, craft specialities, processing activities. The whole varied patterns of development raise some wider issues which are clearly very important but have only been lightly dealt with because so little is known about them. Above all there is the question of social cohesion and flexibility. There is no doubt that a striking feature of several of the small economies was the speed with which new opportunities were taken and old lines dropped. Possibly the argument could be that in small economies if the speciality ran into difficulties the opportunity cost of factors went near to zero, the possibilities for cross subsidy were few so something different simply had to be undertaken. Thinking in less purely economic terms it could be argued that the nobility were relatively weak. In many of these small countries, feudalism was less overpowering, partly at least because of poor land which did not produce a surplus to protect or to steal. Fishermen were typically freer spirits because of their mobility. Perhaps they were small because they were areas difficult to conquer and incorporate within an Empire or so readily conquered that they were difficult for any one vainglorious country to impose its fixed pattern of behaviour upon. Any of these may have contributed significantly to the attitudes that allowed the smaller countries of the north west to compete effectively in the new economic world of the nineteenth century – far more so than their counterparts in other areas of Europe.[19]

Of course, it is wrong to stress just the differences between large and small economies. In all countries the local industries which enjoyed the protection of immobility took a significant share of total employment. The small were able to make use of some of the devices of the large, especially where concentration of industry was concerned. Belgium's involvement in international as well as national cartels was relatively greater than that of any other country and surely reflected the fact that such protection was peculiarly important to capital goods industries so heavily dependent on foreign markets. But for all that the uniqueness of the situations facing small economies is important enough for future research to be directed specifically at elucidating the issues in a way that has not been the case to now. The greatness of Walt Rostow's work has always seemed to me to be less his definitive conclusions than the way in which he has forced upon generations of economic historians, time and again, new issues, new questions. This whole discussion of small countries is really simply a special feature of the nature, timing, degree of success of the pre-condition and take-off stages of growth. Without that initial inspiration we might well still not be groping towards an explanation.

NOTES AND REFERENCES

1. A. Maddison, *Economic Growth in the West* (New York, 1964) pp. 28–37.
2. A. S. Milward and S. B. Saul, *The Development of the Economies of Continental Europe, 1850–1914* (London, 1977) pp. 66–69.
3. E. A. G. Robinson (ed.), *The Economic Consequences of the Size of Nations* (London, 1960) p. 28.
4. See generally B. Kádár, *Small Countries in World Economy* (Budapest, 1970).
5. The statistics were taken from the House of Commons Command Paper *Statistical Abstract for Foreign Countries*.
6. A. Wibail, 'L'Evolution de la Siderurgie Belge de 1830 à 1913', *Bulletin de l'Institut des Sciences Economiques*, (1933) Appendix IV.
7. Joel Mokyr, 'Demand versus Supply in the Industrial Revolution', *Journal of Economic History*, xxxvii (1977) p. 998.
8. Ibid., 996. For locomotives see A. S. Milward and S. B. Saul, *The Economic Development of Continental Europe, 1780–1870* (London, 1973) p. 209 and S. B. Saul, 'The Engineering Industries' in D. Aldcroft, *The Rise of British Industry and Foreign Competition* (London, 1968) pp. 196–7.

9. See R. Vernon, *The Technology Factor in International Trade* (New York, 1970) pp. 179–181.

10. See D. S. Landes, 'Watchmaking: A Case Study in Enterprise and Change', *Business History Review.* LIII (1979) p. 34.

11. C. Reuss, E. Koutry and L. Tychan, *Le Progrès Economique en Siderurgie* (Louvain, 1960) p. 58.

12. L. Sandberg, 'The Case of the Impoverished Sophisticate. Human Capital and Swedish Economic Growth before World War I', *Journal of Economic History*, XXXIX (1979) pp. 225–241.

13. F. X. Van Houtte, *L'Evolution de l'Industrie Textile* (Louvain, 1949) p. 171.

14. J. A. de Jonge, *De Industrialisatie in Nederland tussen 1850 en 1914* (The Hague, 1968) Table 9.

15. Milward and Saul, *The Economic Development of Continental Europe, 1780–1870*, (1973) p. 156.

16. J. Kuuse, *Interaction between Agriculture and Industry* (Göteborg, 1974) pp. 180 and 191.

17. Milward and Saul, *The Economic Development of Continental Europe, 1780–1870*, (1973) p. 416.

18. See generally F. Hodne, 'Growth in a Dual Economy', *Economy and History*, XVI (1973) p. 99.

19. I am grateful to Charles P. Kindleberger for some of the ideas in the last paragraph and indeed for his kind help and encouragement in general both for the article and in many other respects over the years.

6 Income Differentials and Migrations

R. CORTÉS CONDE*

Those who distrust historical statistics are right in doing so, but they would be wrong in rejecting them. In fact, any understanding of statistical information is founded on distrust, and the classical problem of statistics is that of making valid inferences from observations that are known to be poor. To abandon the scraps of quantitative insight into the past merely on the grounds of general suspicion would be as foolish as to regard them as wholly accurate.[1]

In this paper I shall endeavour to examine the existence of certain factors which may influence the decision to emigrate. I shall deal with the case of the outward migration of Italians between 1880 to 1914 approximately, and in particular toward Argentina, covering the whole or part of this period according to available data. In the first place the purpose is to establish whether - there was a relationship between income (wages) differentials and the attraction of migrants (pull) as measured by the variations of migratory flows. The idea is that, besides other non-economic factors, the expectation of better wages must have been an important incentive to migrate. Hicks wrote that 'differences in net economic advantages, chiefly differences in wages are the main causes of migration'.[2] In Larry Sjaastad's words,

* I wish to express my thanks to Dr Manuel Cordomi (University of Tucumán, Argentina), to Dr Ana Maria Martirena-Mantel (Centro de Investigaciones Económicas, Instituto Torcuato di Tella, Buenos Aires, Argentina), and to Dr Philip Musgrove (The Brookings Institution) for their useful comments on a preliminary version of this paper. It goes without saying that they cannot be held responsible for its errors, which can only be attributed to the author.

The hypothesis is that there exists a specific functional relationship between the income received for an individual and his determination to search for superior opportunities in the countries to which he migrates.[3]

It is thus necessary to determine if such differences existed as far as Italian and Argentine wages were concerned, then, if there is a relationship between that differential and the migratory flows from Italy to Argentina. Furthermore, other substitute indicators are sought which may point to such a wage differential, as well as attempting to establish the existence of other factors that could explain the movements in migration. I worked with remittances sent by Italian emigrants to their country (of origin) – total remittances and remittances per emigrant. The focus is on all Italian emigrants abroad, and not just on those living in Argentina, since for this country the available data refer only to remittances made through 'postal giros' and the *Banco di Napoli*, and for a smaller number of years, starting in 1901 and 1902 respectively. It is assumed that the remittances not only indicate the existence of income differential between the country where the remittances were sent from and the country where the remittances were received, but that they had a more complex effect on migration. On the one hand they provided information on better economic opportunities, but on the other they also provided assistance in moving. Since *total* remittances were also the consequence of the volume of emigrants abroad, they reflected the level of individual wealth as well as the effect of the emigrant stock. Therefore the effect on the emigrant flow of the existence of an emigrant stock abroad, which would be reflected in the assistance to the new migrant provided by relatives and friends living abroad, has to be analysed. This assistance reduced the pecuniary and nonpecuniary expenses of moving and furthermore, it helped as an informal employment network in the labour market of the new country.

It is the aim of this paper to establish the existence of a relationship between migratory flows, income differentials and some of the other factors already mentioned.

MIGRATION – WAGE DIFFERENTIALS: ARGENTINA – ITALY, 1880–1903

There are various problems in comparing purchasing power to find out the wage differentials between workers in the country of emigration and in the country of immigration.[4] To compare the purchasing power of wages as expressed in the currency of both countries, the relative version of the doctrine of 'purchasing-power parity' shall be followed. Bela Balassa wrote in this respect,

> The purchasing-power parity doctrine means different things to different people. In the following, I shall deal with two versions of this theory that can be appropriately called the 'absolute' and the 'relative' interpretation of the doctrine. According to the first version, purchasing-power parities calculated as a ratio of consumer goods prices for any pair of countries would tend to approximate the equilibrium rates of exchange. In turn, the relative interpretation of the doctrine asserts that, in comparison to a period when equilibrium rates prevailed, changes in relative prices would indicate the necessary adjustments in exchange rates.
> . . . If we compare two equilibrium positions which differ only in regard to the absolute price levels prevailing in the two countries under consideration, the change in the equilibrium exchange rate will equal the change in the ratio of price levels between the two positions.[5]

Among other reasons, this version has been adopted in the present work because it was necessary to take into account strong monetary disturbances in Argentina – in 1885 it chose the inconvertibility of the *peso* – which had an effect on changes in relative prices. Instead, the *lira*/gold parity was maintained in Italy.

The year 1882 is taken as a base year. In that year there was also free convertibility, being a relatively normal year as far as the stability of prices was concerned. It is assumed that during that year the rate of exchange had reflected the price relationship between both countries. The composition of expenditure (*the family basket*) was similar because to a great extent it was affected by the weight of foodstuffs in consumption. The prices of agricultural goods, which accounted for nearly 50 per cent of the family basket, were set by the international markets and, in respect of other goods, both countries were price-takers. For the subsequent years the rate of exchange was adjusted in accordance with the relative variation in prices.

Thus

$$Kt_{(ia)} = Ko_{(ia)} \frac{P_{it}/P_{io}}{P_{at}/P_{ao}}$$

where

Ko = rate of exchange of the base year
$Kt_{(ia)}$ = rate of exchange of parity *lira/peso* in the year t
$Ko_{(ia)}$ = rate of exchange of parity *lira/peso* in the base year
P_{it}/P_{io} = Italian index prices in respect of base year
P_{at}/P_{ao} = Argentine index prices in respect of base year

The following are the results obtained by comparing the purchasing power of the Italian wages and Argentine wages, in *pesos*, and the proportion of the Argentine wages with respect of Italian wages.

The tables show that in the period of immigration there was, in the course of several years, an important differential between wages earned by workers in Italy and in Argentina, with the exception of the 1890s when there was also a substantial fall in migration toward Argentina. Finally, once the wage differentials were obtained, an attempt was made to learn whether there was a relationship between the variations in these wage differentials and the variations in Italian immigrant flows to Argentina. With this purpose a regression was carried out which did not yield satisfactory results.

Nevertheless, it seemed in principle quite clear that there were periods of high differentials – the 1880s and 1900s – associated with those of high immigration flows, and periods of low differentials associated with those of low flows – for instance, the 1890s. Then, as the failure to establish satisfactory statistical relationships could be due to a weakness in the data and not to the non-existence of such an association, an attempt was made to find another variable that could be used as an indicator of the existence of that differential, and for which there was continuous and reliable information.

TABLE 6.1.   *Wages: Argentina–Italy and differentials (in percentages)*

	Argentina (1)	Italy (2)	Percentage differentials $\left(\dfrac{1-2}{1}\right) \times 100$
1882	19.85	11.30	76
1883	23.14	11.22	106
1884	20.10	12.21	65
1885	23.37	10.44	114
1886	27.20	10.49	159
1887	19.40	14.89	30
1888	22.09	15.13	46
1889	21.63	15.25	12
1890	18.10	18.97	−5
1891	17.97	21.47	−16
1892	20.94	19.04	10
1893	20.57	17.66	16
1894	19.32	21.55	−10
1895	17.55	23.62	−26
1896	19.00	23.64	−20
1897	26.27	23.40	12
1898	36.07	19.55	85
1899	42.82	16.41	161
1900	37.38	18.34	104
1901	37.54	20.79	81
1902	38.45	20.82	85
1903	41.09	19.98	106

For Argentina, the wages considered are those of the industrial workers at the Bagley plant in Buenos Aires (see source for an explanation of the information included, methods used and representativity). They have been compared with other information on wages in the public and private sectors. The Bagley wages and those of unqualified workers in the public administration were similar throughout this period. The coefficient of correlation between both for the period 1880–1910 is:

$$R^2 = 0.91$$

SOURCE   R. Cortés Conde, *El Progreso Argentino* (Buenos Aires: Sudamericana, 1979)

TABLE 6.2. *Prices and nominal and parity rates of exchange*

	Prices Argentina (1)	Prices Italy (2)	(2) ÷ (1)	Parity rate of exchange (3)	Official rate of exchange (4)	Market rate of exchange lira/peso* (5)
1882	100.0	100	100	5.00	5.00	–
1883	95.2	97	102	5.10	5.00	–
1884	100.0	95	95	4.75	5.00	5
1885	85.7	97	113	5.65	5.00	3.64
1886	85.7	97	113	5.65	5.00	3.59
1887	122.2	97	80	4.00	5.00	3.20
1888	122.2	98	80	4.00	5.00	3.37
1889	122.2	99	81	4.05	5.00	2.77
1890	158.7	103	65	3.25	5.00	1.93
1891	181.0	103	57	2.85	5.00	1.33
1892	158.7	102	64	3.20	5.00	1.51
1893	144.4	100	64	3.45	5.00	1.54
1894	173.0	99	57	2.85	5.00	1.40
1895	190.5	99	52	2.60	5.00	1.45
1896	207.9	98	47	2.35	5.00	1.69
1897	185.7	98	52	2.60	5.00	1.72
1898	154.0	98	64	3.20	5.00	1.95
1899	127.0	97	76	3.80	2.20	2.22
1900	144.4	98	68	3.40	2.20	2.20
1901	163.5	98	60	3.00	2.20	2.20
1902	163.5	97	60	3.00	2.20	2.20
1903	158.73	100	63	3.15	2.20	2.20
1904	50.6	101	62	3.10	2.20	2.20
1905	51.74	101	59	2.95	2.20	2.20
1906	57.46	103	56	2.80	2.20	2.20
1907	56.07	108	58	2.90	2.20	2.20
1908	56.49	107	56	2.80	2.20	2.20
1909	58.76	104	54	2.95	2.20	2.20
1910	59.09	107	52	2.60	2.20	2.20
1911	–	109	53	2.65	2.20	2.20
1912	74.73	114	55	2.75	2.20	2.20

* The market rate of exchange for the period in which there was no convertibility for the *peso* was established *vis-à-vis* the price of gold in Argentine pesos. In Italy the *lira* was maintained united with gold to a fixed rate of exchange.

SOURCE 'Sommario de Statistiche Storiche Italiane 1861–1955', p. 172 (for Italy). R. Cortés Conde, *El Progreso Argentino* (Buenos Aires: Sudamericana, 1979) (for Argentina).

IMMIGRATION FLOWS AND INCOME DIFFERENTIALS

It was stated that the main interest of this work centred on finding out whether migrations were a result of the response of individuals seeking to improve their economic situation, a fact which would be reflected in the existence of income differentials between the country of emigration (Supply country) and that of immigration (Receiver country). It must be pointed out that such differentials should be greater than the pecuniary and nonpecuniary expenses of moving.

In a study carried out on British migration to Australia, Allen C. Kelly remarked,

> Income differentials can be obtained only at a cost. The latter includes, among other things, transportation expenses, foregone earnings during the transition from one job to another, and certain nonpecuniary elements, such as risks and discomfort of travel, severing friendships, and so forth. The rate of emigration is, therefore, supposed to be associated positively with the expected long-term economic benefits and negatively with the expense of moving, both as evaluated by the migrant.[6]

Among the pecuniary expenses the most outstanding were fares, the loss of wages during the period between the departure and the finding of a new job in the country of immigration and, among the nonpecuniary expenses, the risks and discomfort of travel and, above all else, the absence of known places, family and friends. Thus it was necessary not only to consider income differentials, but also the other elements that could considerably reduce those benefits, the pecuniary and nonpecuniary expense of moving.

Remittances sent by Italians abroad were chosen as an indicator of the variations in income differentials. Series of data were available, of an adequate continuity and reliability. The flow of remittances from one place to another was an indicator of higher wages (income) in the country where the remittances were originated. If it is assumed that income was made up of consumption plus savings, and that remittances were part of those savings, the existence of remittances indicates that it was possible to save. Furthermore, if it is assumed that consumption remained more or less constant in the short term, variations in remittances can be taken as an indication of variations in income. Therefore the remittances indicate the existence of a labour income differential, and their variations indicate variations in the latter. Also they had a wider effect, and as a result this indicator became more ambiguous. On the one hand, they supplied information on the existence of a savings capacity and on the other they allowed to pay for the immigrants' moving expenses, that is to say, they were an indicator of expected income, but they were moreover a definite factor in reducing the expense of moving.

This occurred with remittances *per emigrant*. *Total remittances* reflected as well the effect of the number of immigrants in the country of immigration, that is the effect of the assistance derived from the existence of that migrant stock. In their study on old and new migrations to the United States, Dunlevy and Gemery dealt with the effect of the migrant stock:

> Migrants stock is included as an explanatory variable to allow for the so-called 'family and friends' effect. It is believed that a larger number of persons born in a foreign nation and currently residing in a given state will result in a greater flow of information back to the home country about opportunities in that state. Further, the presence of family and friends is likely to ease the transition for the migrant who settles in their locale. For both of these reasons, the recent migrant is expected to be more attracted to those destinations in which a larger migrant stock of his countrymen currently resides.[7]

The 'family and friends' effect which arises from the existence of a migrant stock is revealed in the remittances, but it does not end here. The stock of fellow countrymen in a foreign country has other effects: very often on lodging but especially on the setting up of an employment information network making the labour market more fluid and effective, as a result of which it is possible to find quickly an occupation for the newcomers. This is a central issue in the formation of the labour market in the new countries. Other nonpecuniary effects should not be dismissed, since they help emigration when relatives and friends can be found in the new countries. In this respect, Philip Nelson found that

1. People prefer to live near present relatives and friends.
2. The distribution of information is important in determining the distribution of migration.[8]

It follows that:

1. Variations in remittances *per emigrant* are an indicator of variations in the savings capacity *per emigrant* in the new country and thus of income differentials – assuming that consumption is more or less constant in the short term and that savings in the country of residence do not replace remittances (something which will occur later on). They therefore have an information effect *vis-à-vis* the expectation of a larger income in the new world, as well as assisting in the reduction of the moving expenses. Philip Nelson has written in this respect:

> Relatives and friends are the most important source of job information at a distance only because they are the most important source of job information in the local labor market, for they are not very efficient carriers of information to distant places. We expect the distance elasticity of information distributed by relatives and friends to be greater than the average distance elasticity of information.[9]

2. In *total* remittances the effect of remittances per emigrant and the volume of emigrants abroad or in the receiver country – in this case, Argentina – are gathered. The stock effect is gathered here: this is the 'family and friends' effect, translated in the fact that help reaches a greater number of people who will be the eventual immigrants, help which is not limited only to information and remittances, but it also has a crucial effect since it sets up a resource-allocation network in the labour market.

The next step will be to find out whether there is any statistical relationship between flows of Italian emigrants

(a) to the rest of the world and
(b) to Argentina

and remittances per immigrant, total remittances and migrant stock as explanatory variables.

The analysis has been extended to include the case of Italian emigration to the rest of the world and emigrant remittances to Italy during the period 1880–1913, since this is the period for which the best information is available given that in the Argentine case the only data on remittances refer to those made through the *Banco di Napoli* and postal giros from 1902 onwards. The data always refers to Italian emigrants, since the aim is to learn which Italians left their country and which Italians received the remittances.

ITALIAN EMIGRATION ABROAD

Three regressions will be tried out, corresponding to emigrants from Italy and remittances made by them to Italy. The next one will refer exclusively to emigration from Italy to Argentina, and to the stock and remittances of Italians in Argentina.

Regression 1: Remittances per emigrant $(t-1)$ and emigration (flow)

It is assumed in the first one that variations in emigration flows abroad are dependent on variations in remittances during the previous period, in accordance with the following function:

$$m_t = B_o + B_1 r_{t-1}$$

$$\text{and } r = \frac{R_{t-1}}{M_{t-1}}$$

thus
$$m_t = B_o + B_1 \frac{R_t - 1}{M_t - 1}$$

where

R = total remittances
r = average remittance per emigrant
M = emigrant stock
m = emigrant flow

The result is such that:

$$m_t = -170.28 = 0.51\frac{R_t-1}{M_t-1}$$

(*) (-1.41) (4.61)

$$R^2 = 0.43$$
$$R^{-2} = 0.41$$
(**) $d_f = 28$
$$F = 21.30$$
$$DW = 0.095$$

(*)   the numbers in brackets correspond to Student's test (t)
(**) degrees of freedom

The independent variable explains the variation of 41 per cent in the dependent one, and test t of the parameter of the independent variable permits the rejection of the null hypothesis.

Thus, although the signs are correct, the explicit power of the average remittance variable is not too high, a fact that does not allow one to reach a more precise conclusion. Alternatively, it is possible to deal with variations in total remittances instead of average remittances, which include, totally or in part, past migration, that is the Emigrant stock (M).

In this regression the two variables have been separated, emigrant stock (M) and average remittance (r).

Regression 2

$$m_t = B_0 M_t - 1 + B_2 r_t - 1$$

where

$$\text{average remittance} = r_t - 1 = \frac{R_t-1}{M_t-1}$$

and the following results are obtained:

$$m_t = -115.08 + 0.05M_t - 1 + 3.04r_t - 1$$
$$(-1.29)\ (10.27)\qquad (2.31)$$
$$R^2 = 0.81$$
$$d_f = 27$$
$$F = 60.92$$
$$R^{-2} = 0.81$$
$$DW = 1.37$$

The results are satisfactory since the regression explains 81 per cent of the variations in migratory flows. The parameter signs are those expected, and t tests give values that result in the rejection of the null hypothesis, the value of t being much higher for the stock variable (M). There is no multicolinearity between the independent variables and the DW falls in the indeterminate area. It can be said then that variations in stocks and in average remittances explain to a very high percentage variations in flows of emigrants leaving Italy to settle abroad.

ITALIAN EMIGRATION TO ARGENTINA

Data are more scarce and for shorter periods regarding remittances sent by Italians living in Argentina to their country of origin. Taking into consideration that the present study ends in 1914 – since from this moment the circumstances impinging on migration were altered owing to the war – and that the series of data on remittances made by means of postal giros and the *Banco di Napoli* begin in 1901 and 1902, the observations that can be made are few and refer to incomplete data.

The tests carried out with Remittances did not yield satisfactory results. For this reason an exclusive relationship was postulated in its place between the flow of Italians who emigrated each year and the stock of Italians living in Argentina (included in the variable Total Remittances in the previous regressions). The purpose was to check the existence of the 'family and friends' effect partly revealed in the remittances. In this case, longer series (32 years) are available.

Regression 3

$$m_t = B_o + B_1 M$$

where

M = stock of Italians who travelled to Argentina and were not repatriated in the years 1876–1903 obtaining the following results:

$$m_t = 21.78 + 0.04\,M$$
$$(3.81) \quad (6.13)$$
$$R^2 = 0.54$$
$$F = 37.67$$
$$d_f = 32$$
$$R^{-2} = 0.53$$
$$DW = 1.36$$

In this instance the percentage explained rose to 53 per cent. t values permit the rejection of the null hypothesis that there is no association between the flows variable and the explanatory variable.

It would seem then that the variable that has a higher explanatory power over variations in flows of emigrants to Argentina, is the *stock* variable of Italians living in Argentina, a fact that reflects the 'family and friends' effect as well as the effect of 'remittances'.

CONCLUSION

1. The differential effect of *incomes*, measured by the changes in average remittances (assuming consumption remains constant) seems to explain a part, albeit not a very considerable one, of the response of Italian immigrants: 41 per cent in the case of emigration to the rest of the world.
2. Total remittances (a variable in which the immigrant stock is included) explain a very high percentage, 95 per cent of emigration to the rest of the world.
3. The immigrant stock, both in the rest of the world and in Argentina, is the variable explaining with a greater degree of satisfaction the response of emigrants from Italy.[10] As far as emigration to the rest of the world is concerned, remittances and stock explain 82 per cent; and to Argentina, the stock explains 53 per cent. It must be pointed out that the 'family and friends' effect is expressed in the stock, revealed in the existence of a volume of fellow countrymen in the receiver country. This in turn is translated in the remittances operating as an information factor as well as providing assistance toward the payment of

moving expenses: fares, period without employment, etc. Although there is no increase in the average remittance (r), the increase in total remittances (R) implies that a greater number of remittances reached a greater number of people – those who will subsequently emigrate.

It is important to point out that what apparently took place was the opposite of what was expected. The assumption is that the movement of the labour factor from low-wage situations to high-wage ones, should have tended towards their equalisation and therefore, to check the labour flow from one to the other.[11] If this had been so, the increase in the stock would be inversely correlated with the increase in immigration flows, instead the exact opposite occurs. Nonetheless this is explained by the fact that the existence of an emigrant stock (M) in the receiver country involves a reduction in the pecuniary expenses – owing to remittances, lodging, employment networks, etc. – besides other nonpecuniary expenses. Especially in employment the migrant stock has played the role of an efficient adjustment mechanism in the labour market. Consequently, even though the increase in migration could contribute towards lowering the price of wages, and thus reducing the benefits of migration, the existence of a greater volume of fellow countrymen (a greater stock) reduced the cost of moving. This was reflected in a chain-reaction resulting in the existence of greater flows, with the consequent greater stock, which in turn gave rise to greater flows, delaying the return to equlibrium positions. This could be maintained while there was a high marginal labour productivity in the new world.

NOTES AND REFERENCES

1. G. Ohlin, 'No safety in numbers – Some pitfalls of Historical Statistics', in R. Floud, *Essays in Quantitative Economic History* (Oxford: Clarendon Press, 1979) p. 60.
2. J. R. Hicks, *The Theory of Wages* (Gloucester, Mass.: Peter Smith, 1957) p. 56. In relation to the 'push and pull effect' see J. G. Williamson's more recent work, *Late Nineteenth Century American Development* (Cambridge University Press, 1974).
3. L. Sjaastad, 'The Relationship Between Migration and Income in the United States', in *Papers Proceedings*, Regional Science Association, vol. vi, 1960, pp. 37 *et seq.*
4. The problem of the international comparison of purchasing power has been

discussed in several works. See, for example, C. Clark, *The Conditions of Economic Progress* (London: Macmillan, 1940); the study undertaken by ECLA (Economic Commission for Latin America) in 1960–2, and those done for ECIEL (Joint Studies of Latinamerican Economic Integration) carried out by J. Grunwald and J. Carrillo in 'Integración Económica y Comparaciones de Precios y Valores en la América Latina' in *Estudios Eciel*, pp. 65–134, and M. Vega Centeno, 'Tipos de Cambio, Paridades y Poder Adquisitivo en el Grupo Andino', pp. 155–234.

5. B. Balassa, 'The Purchasing-Power Parity Doctrine: A Reappraisal', in *The Journal of Political Economy*, LXXII (Feb./Dec. 1964) 584 and 591.

6. A. C. Kelly, 'International Migration and Economic Growth: Australia, 1865–1935', *The Journal of Economic History*, 25 (1965) 333.

7. J. A. Dunlevy and H. A. Gemery, 'Economic Opportunity and the Responses of the "Old" and "New" Migrants to the United States', *The Journal of Economic History*, 38, no. 4 (December 1978) 907. Also M. Levy and W. Wadycki, 'The Influence of Family and Friends on Geographical Labour Mobility. An International Comparison', *Revue of Economics and Statistics*, 55 (1973) 198–203.

8. P. Nelson, 'Migration, Real Income and Information', *Journal of Regional Science*, 1, no. 2 (1959) 44.

9. P. Nelson, ibid.

10. P. Nelson, ibid., postulates a positive relationship between migratory flows and past migrations. He states that these are a function of the variables determining the settlement of migrants in the past. He attributes this to information provided by friends and relatives, information that increases the propensity to emigrate.

11. On this subject, see G. Laber, 'Lagged response in the decision to migrate – A comment' and M. Greenwood, 'Lagged response in the decision to migrate – A reply', *Journal of Regional Science*, 12, no. 2 (1972) 3, 7 *et seq.*

APPENDIX

TABLE 6.3. *Italian emigrant stock abroad–flows and remittances per emigrant*

	m (migratory flows) thousands ($M_t - 1$)	M (emigrant stock) thousands	r (Remittances per immigrant) $\dfrac{R_{t-1}}{S\,M_{t-1}} = r$
1881	135.8	1417	85.0
1882	161.6	1553	80.0
1883	169.1	1715	79.9
1884	147.0	1884	75.9
1885	157.2	2031	69.4
1886	167.8	2188	63.1
1887	215.7	2356	62.4
1888	290.7	2572	66.5
1889	218.4	2863	63.9
1890	215.8	3081	59.0
1891	293.6	3297	62.0
1892	223.7	3591	72.0
1893	246.7	3815	66.0
1894	225.3	4062	54.4
1895	293.2	4287	45.3
1896	307.5	4580	47.2
1897	299.8	4887	50.3
1898	283.7	5187	51.1
1899	308.3	5471	65.8
1900	352.8	5779	61.6
1901	533.2	6132	64.3
1902	531.5	6665	89.4
1903	508.0	7196	82.5
1904	471.2	7606	74.5
1905	726.3	7946	66.2
1906	788.0	8477	95.7
1907	704.7	9145	96.2
1908	486.7	9692	79.9
1909	625.6	9931	67.6
1910	651.5	10256	64.4

SOURCE *Instituto Centrale da Statistica, Sommario di Statistiche Storiche Italiane* (Rome, 1958.).

TABLE 6.4. *Italy: emigrants' re-mittances in the balance of payments*

Millions of lire	
1881	125
1882	137
1883	143
1884	141
1885	138
1886	147
1887	171
1888	183
1889	181
1890	203
1891	257
1892	251
1893	221
1894	194
1895	216
1896	246
1897	265
1898	300
1899	356
1900	394
1901	596
1902	594
1903	567
1904	526
1905	811
1906	880
1907	774
1908	671
1909	660
1910	805

SOURCE As Table 6.3.

TABLE 6.5. *Italian emigrants to Argentina*

Total to Argentina	
1881	15 899
1882	22 997
1883	24 127
1884	31 927
1885	37 710
1886	36 534
1887	52 383
1888	64 223
1889	69 008
1890	36 695
1891	24 125
1892	25 331
1893	32 541
1894	32 557
1895	41 029
1896	56 426
1897	36 712
1898	33 938
1899	44 168
1900	40 393
1901	59 881
1902	36 778
1903	43 915
1904	51 779
1905	86 158
1906	107 227
1907	78 493
1908	80 699
1909	84 949
1910	104 718

SOURCE As Table 6.3.

7 The Spread of Motor Vehicles Before 1914

T. C. BARKER

I

Some of the most productive works of history are those which stimulate controversy from which greater understanding emerges. *The Stages of Economic Growth* started not one, but a number, of such discussions. It was largely responsible, for instance, for goading others into making much clearer to us all the limited, if nevertheless vital and keynote, role of railways in nineteenth-century economic growth. That spectacular new form of mechanical transport, so dazzling and impressive to contemporaries, introduced big business to many parts of the world, speeded inter-urban transport in already settled areas and helped to open up much of the rest of the globe; but it made very little impact upon local transport, passenger or freight, either in rural areas or in the rapidly growing towns which were at the very heart of economic growth.[1] Throughout the world the number of horses grew enormously during the Railway Age. In Britain, the birthplace and natural home of steam railways, the number of transport horses, according to Professor Thompson's calculations,[2] rose from about half a million to a million and a half between 1851 and 1901, out of a total national horse population which grew from 1.29m. to 3.28m. during those years. (The comparable figure for the United States in the latter year was about 30 million.) As each horse consumed the produce of between four and five acres of farmland per year, all these animals were by then making very large demands upon the world's natural resources.[3] Here was a fuel crisis looming up which steam railway technology could not possibly solve. There were strong incentives to invent and develop other forms of mechanical traction. In the ensuing competition between vehicles powered by electric motors and others driven by the internal combustion engine, the former at first seemed to be a winner, at least for passenger traffic;[4] but as the internal combustion engine was developed, more efficient motor vehicles produced and better roads built, the newer and more manoeuvrable motors not only drove out most of the electrified street railways but also, as speeds and carrying capacity both increased, drew away an increasing amount of the railways' longer distance traffic, too, even though the railways themselves turned to the newer forms of traction in their own self defence. In the end the advantages of greater manoeuvrability and door-to-door service proved overwhelming: the more important railway networks could be preserved only by subsidy. And the motor vehicle could provide, for an increasing number of people, something the railway train could never manage to do: personal transport.

Many historians, from the antiquarian to the counterfactual, have written shelf upon shelf of books about nineteenth-century, and even twentieth-century, railways; but surprisingly few, apart from those who have addressed themselves to motor manufacturing as an industry[5] have taken much interest in these more recent and arguably far more important transport developments. Here again, however, the distinguished scholar in whose honour these essays have been written has given a lead. *The Stages of Economic Growth* took account of the dissemination of motor vehicles and included graphs, adapted and extended from Svennilson, indicating the pace at which car ownership per head rose in the United States, Canada, Great Britain, France, Germany, Italy and Japan between 1900 and 1957.[6] In *The World Economy* these statistics have been further extended to include other countries and additional information about the motor vehicle industry. Attention is drawn to the fact that in the United States by 1938 it had become the largest single consumer of the output of a dozen branches of manufacture, ranging from gasoline (90 per cent), rubber (80 per cent) and plate glass (69 per cent) to nickel (29 per cent) and steel in all its forms (17 per cent). By then the motor car had also brought widely-ranging social change: 'from courting habits to the get-away methods of bank robbers'.[7] The economic and social effects of all these notable developments, and others, still await further study: the literature, technical, commercial and anecdotal, is enormous. The purpose of this essay is merely to try to clear the ground a little by discussing further the earlier diffusion of motors down to 1914 not just in terms of grand totals which lump together motor cars and motor cycles, motor omnibuses, motor lorries and other commercial vehicles – vehicles of different type and purpose – nor in terms of the United States and the major European manufacturing countries alone, for the new technology made its presence felt all over the world far more rapidly than the railway had managed to do and soon penetrated even to its remotest inhabited extremities.

Motor vehicles are lethal and the authorities were quick to demand their registration. In any case, certain categories of wheeled vehicles often had to be registered for tax purposes already and governments were quick to seize the opportunity to tax them further when they became motorised. The details then collected, however, were rarely made readily available; and when they were, they could be misleading. So long as they were confined to what was referred to as 'pleasure motoring', cars were often registered for the summer months only, thus making totals from other times of the year (including year-end totals) inaccurate. Import/export figures could also be unhelpful. France and Germany published theirs for motor vehicles by weight and value not by numbers. Britain did publish numbers, but in and just before 1910, we are told, nearly half the cars imported were brought in by tourists for their own use.[8] Much guidance on these matters, however, including the last piece of advice, is to be derived from reports sent home at the time by consular officials who witnessed the arrival in their districts of these noisy, odorous and at first extremely unreliable new contraptions, and who did their best to quantify them and evaluate the market. It is upon the testimony contained in the published British and (especially) American consular reports that we shall depend for this account of the rapid early global spread of the various sorts of motor vehicle.[9] This source does not give a continuous account of the arrival of these new machines in all parts of the world, though it gives a fuller account than can be derived from anywhere else; nor are the statistics always very precise or reliable. But it does enable us to gain a better overall impression of the diffusion of the new technology than can be readily obtained from national statistical year books of the period which were usually rather slower to notice the importunate newcomers and, when they did waken up to their arrival, were reluctant to disaggregate the statistics in such a way as to encourage subsequent historians not to treat all of them as motor cars.

II

Unlike the electric tramcar, which replaced the horse-drawn omnibuses and trams with the intention of extending mass public transport in towns, the motor vehicle was at the outset small-scale, privileged and personal. It was sold first of all to the well-to-do: to people in that section of society known as 'carriage folk'. The younger and more active among them were also by the 1890s bicycle folk, and the early history of motorisation can be understood only when it is seen alongside that of the pedal cycle, the first personally owned mechanical vehicle. Before about 1900 these machines sold in England at about £20 each ($100 if, for convenience, we round the £1 up to $5) and were the property of the prospering and prosperous who, often forming themselves into cycling clubs with their own distinctive uniforms, rode for pleasure. (The position in the United States was rather different: 'The American youth', noted the US Consul in Nottingham in 1899, 'buys a wheel for from $35 to $50, uses it one or two seasons, and then buys a better one with intervening improvements, for about the same price. The English lad pays from $80 to $100 for substantially the same machine but he expects – and his family expects – it to last a lifetime'.[10] These cheaper and lighter American models, however, when exported to Europe about this time gave endless trouble and gained the Americans a reputation for unsubstantial and unreliable products which, as the consuls kept on reporting, survived well into the motor car period and, indeed, almost to the First World War.) When over-production brought the price of cycles in Britain down to £10 at the beginning of the present century, ownership spread down the social scale. Cycling ceased to be fashionable. By 1910, when the price of new push bikes had reached £6–£8, the US Consul in Birmingham reported that they were used 'chiefly for business, clerks, workmen and business men riding to their business on wheels, going home to lunch and riding back. There are cycling clubs which go forth in bodies on Sundays and holidays'.[11] The cycling clubs had become popular.

After the later 1890s the rich and fashionable switched their affections from cycles, now becoming cheaper and more vulgar, to the new motors, and a number of cycle makers, such as Singer, Humber, Enfield and BSA in Britain,[12] and others in France following the earlier example of Peugeot, diversified either into motor cycle or motor car manufacture (the former at that time little more than the fixing of a motor into the established diamond frame of a pedal cycle). For vehicles such as these the well-to-do were placing orders in such quantity that some firms could offer delivery only a year or more ahead.

The Germans, who had been so successful in developing the stationary gas engine from the 1860s, managed in the mid-1880s to put it on wheels and make it run, using petrol vapour instead of coal gas as the energy source which was exploded in the cylinders. In this important adaptation of a power source to transport they were emulating the British who had turned the stationary steam engine into a locomotive half a century and more earlier. But here the comparison stops, for the Germans failed to exploit the primitive motor vehicles of Daimler and Benz as the British had done the rudimentary locomotives of Stephenson and others. It was the French, not usually highly rated by economic historians of the pre-1914 period, who took advantage of the German patents and exploited the new technology commercially. 'Paris', wrote the US Consul General there in 1912, 'was the birthplace of the high-class gasoline motor vehicle, and the original makers who perfected the automobile have their factories in France, mainly in and near Paris'.[13] The good French roads and complete freedom to race a handful of these new-fangled vehicles upon them (at speeds which might average 15 m.p.h.) and the wide international publicity given to these surprisingly small-scale activities of the mid-1890s, brought to Paris from other parts of France and elsewhere (especially Britain) well-to-do customers who were prepared to pay cash down at the time of ordering their own particular motor car. Most inventions require much capital from their promoters before they can be developed to the point at which they can be profitably marketed. To a large extent the motor car's development costs were met by a relatively small number of wealthy customers without any financial stake in the motor business.

These swells were quick to form automobile clubs in their own regions in much the same way as they, and their predecessors, had formed cycling clubs. The most important motoring organisation of all, with which members elsewhere, often in other countries, were affiliated, was the Automobile Club de France which by 1901 already had a membership reported to number more than 79 000. It then published its own annual, 'giving all places of interest on the Continent, conditions and maps of all roads, distances, hotels, laws and regulations regarding tourists, depots of petroleum etc., and everything of advantage to the traveller'.[14] International touring in Europe was quick to develop, especially after the triptyque and international driving licence had been introduced. Nearly 8000 touring vehicles entered Germany in one year, September 1907/8, for instance,[15] and between 2000 and 3000 are said to have entered England every year between 1908 and 1910.[16]

Although these motor vehicles were substitutes for short-distance pedal cycles and horses – in Britain it was customary to refer to a stud of cars in their early days – some of the well-to-do motorists were prepared to travel considerable distances *on* – not in – their often underpowered and invariably unprotected vehicles. By 1903, for instance, Lord Edward Spencer-Churchill had 'travelled all over Britain in his 6 h.p., 2 cylinder Daimler'.[17] Alfred Harmsworth, the future Lord Northcliffe, 'perhaps the largest owner of motor cars in the world', who considered 120 miles 'a good average day's spin', had driven many thousands of miles in the United States and on the Continent as well as in Britain, J. W. E. Scott-Montagu, M.P., a leading motoring pioneer and soon to become the second Baron Montagu of Beaulieu, had already travelled not only in America but also in Japan, China, Egypt and South Africa. Women were also among the earlier motoring enthusiasts. The daughter of the Earl of Shrewsbury had 'piloted her 12 h.p. Panhard all over Great Britain and also through France and Spain'. Numbers of wives were extolled as enterprising *chauffeuses*: Mrs Cecil Powney, for instance, 'always most daintily dressed, whether steering a car in Piccadilly or Hyde Park, or taking a prolonged run through the New Forest, which is one of her favourite motoring haunts'. Others like Dorothy Levett, who took part in various competitions from 1903 onwards and claimed to drive 400 miles a week in all weathers, was much more practical when in 1909 she came to write *The Woman and the Car. A Chatty Little Handbook for all Women Who Motor or Who Want to Motor*.[18] ('Indispensable to the motoriste who is going to drive her own car is the overall . . . With the car illustrated, it is necessary to pump a charge of oil into the engine about every twenty miles. This is an easy matter and it is not necessary to stop the car to do it. Before starting out each day you should allow the 'used' oil to run out of the base chamber . . . Never drive the engine downhill'.) An increasing use began to be made of so-called pleasure cars for practical purposes. Doctors were quick to use them for their rounds. Marconi found a motor cycle useful for his wireless work in Cornwall at the beginning of the century. In 1903 Fred Karno was using a 10 h.p. car to carry his principals from one town to another. An increasing number of the wealthy used their new vehicles to drive (or be driven) between London and their country houses, and house agents, seeing that motor cars promised to raise the value of certain properties, took to advertising them in the motoring journals.[19] Very few heavier motor vehicles were as yet, however, coming into use as motor lorries or motor buses.

This is evident from information that was shortly to be collected in the United Kingdom as a result of the Motor Car Act, 1903. By September 1905, 37 665 motor cycles and 36 373 other vehicles were recorded. Of the latter, 30 296 were privately-owned cars. Only 4910 motor vehicles were registered for trade purposes, 2814 of which, with an unladen weight of under a ton each, must have been basically motor cars and were probably being used as delivery vans. 1167 vehicles were registered for public conveyance of passengers, and of these 516 were also under a ton in weight.[20] The motor car was undoubtedly important; but even more so was the motor cycle, which is often overlooked.

The picture in France was roughly similar in magnitude, and in proportion so far as motor car and motor cycle ownership was concerned: by 1903 France already possessed 19 886 motor cars and 19 816 motor bicycles – plus, it is interesting to note, 1.3m. pedal cycles.[21] Germany, however, lagged far behind. Even in January 1908 the German Empire still possessed only 14 671 passenger cars, 19 573 motor cycles and 1778 freight vehicles, 1160 of them motor tricycles or runabouts under 8 h.p.[22] It was in the ensuing pre-war boom that German car ownership increased more rapidly, to 43 000 at the beginning of 1912 and to 60 876 in January 1914. There were then 9639 freight vehicles (only 2019 under 8 h.p.) in Germany but only 22 457 motor cycles.[23] With a grand total of about 93 000 vehicles her motor ownership still fell far behind her two European rivals', however, and she was even farther behind in terms of vehicles per head. At the end of October 1913 the United Kingdom was reported to possess close on 426 000 vehicles, 227 907 of them cars and light commercial vans (201 469 in England and Wales, 17 087 in Scotland and 9351 in Ireland) and 18 005 heavy vehicles. It was in motor cycles, however, in which the British motor industry was excelling from about 1910, that vehicle penetration was particularly impressive. No fewer than 179 926 of these machines were registered (many of them by this time larger machines equipped with sidecars).[24] By 1913 the French owned 91 000 motor cars, 50 per cent more than Germany.[25] 'The motor cycle with side car', reported the American Vice-Consul in Paris later in 1913, 'already so popular in Great Britain, has invaded France and its vogue is increasing every day'. He went on to record that 28 641 motor cycles were already registered in France by the end of 1912, a modest 50 per cent increase over the decade.[26]

[Both London and Paris had introduced taxicabs after 1906 (there were 8400 of them in London in 1913 and 5000 in Paris even by 1910, including many, no doubt, soon to gain fâme by going to the Marne) and had brought in really efficient motor buses from 1909 (Paris had 500 of the famous rear-platform sort by the beginning of 1911 and were adding to them at the rate of seven a week; London had about 3500 by 1913, many of them soon to make the journey to the battlefront, too).[27]]

While goods traffic, apart from store delivery and post office work, some furniture removal and the like, continued to be horse-drawn, most passenger vehicles were becoming motor driven. A traffic census taken in London in 1911 showed that only 13 per cent of all passenger vehicles – buses, taxis, and private vehicles as well as tramcars – were then drawn by horse; and by 1913 this figure had fallen to a mere six per cent; but 88 per cent of goods vehicles were then still horse drawn.[28] Berlin, however, still had only 300 motor buses running even at the end of 1912 when 460 horse buses were still in service.[29]

After 1907 motor vehicle ownership in the United States had suddenly surged ahead of that of Europe. Information supplied to a British Royal Commission indicated that in 1905 there had been 63 373 cars registered in various parts of America from which returns could be obtained. These included 22 420 in New York State (pop. 8m), 14 050 in New Jersey (2m), 9977 in Massachusetts (3m), 4000 in California (1.9m), and 1099 in Maryland (190 000); but only 182 in Delaware (190 000), 171 in West Virginia (980 000) and 75 in Mississippi (1¾m).[30] If all these vehicles were indeed motor cars, not motor bicycles, then the more prosperous parts of America had already achieved a greater motor car density than the more prosperous parts of Europe. The subsequent registrations of cars in the United States (reported by the British Consul retrospectively as having been 270 000 in 1908, nearly 500 000 in 1910 and 1.26m. in 1913[31]) carried the United States into a league quite of its own and left Europe far behind. States like New York with 135 000 cars, and California with 115 000,[32] each had more motor cars than France or Germany where the new form of transport had started only about 20 years before. The British Consul was already reporting home in 1913 that 'one firm in Detroit, founded less than 10 years ago [Ford] is planning to produce 200 000 cars in 1913 [it nearly succeeded] . . . 90 000 tons of steel and 400 000 hides will be required'.[33]

The three European countries' differing and slower pace of motorisation is explained in the American consular reports. Germany witnessed a strict control of motor transport by the authorities and this did not encourage its development. So long as it remained 'more or less noisy, malodorous and subject to vibrations', the intending German purchaser held off.[33] Later, when more reliable machines were available, lack of purchasing power continued to restrict sales. 'The class of people financially able to own automobiles is much more limited in Germany than in the United States', the US Consul at Erfurt pointed out in 1910.

> . . . Business managers and others working in a subordinate capacity are not, as a general rule, nearly so well paid as in the United States where high-salaried employees constitute a fair proportion of those who can afford automobiles . . . Outside the great commercial centers there is absent that spirit of hustle so prevalent in most American cities, large and small. The people are conservative, and an automobile is ordinarily looked upon as a luxury which only the rich can afford.[34]

About the same time, somebody who had been engaged in selling American cars in England for some years made the same point:

> . . . The sale of cheap cars can never be as large in England as it is in the United States. The same class of people that find it easy to pay $650 dollars for a car in the United States, find it difficult to lay aside half that sum here . . .[35]

The English were, however, making an effort to become car owners, as the Consul in Birmingham testified. One of the leading house painters and decorators there had complained to him that people were starting to spend money on cars rather than on the upkeep of their homes. He had heard much the same from house furnishers, book sellers, clothiers and theatre managers. Some people even moved into smaller houses and spent the saving on motoring.[36] Given this narrower market base, even a Henry Ford (who did get the basic price of his Model T down to around $650 in 1912 in America) could hardly have suceeded, for there were not enough potential purchasers at that price even in England, then the richest country in Europe. The French realising this, had originally built up their businesses by supplying expensive cars to the rich.[37] When, in the years before 1914, Ford, enjoying profitable sales resulting from the depth of demand in his unique and protected home market, began to sell a few of his Model Ts in Europe, the European producers' strategy was to concentrate instead upon smaller and cheaper models; and, as has been seen, the British cultivated the even cheaper motor cycle. They were all gradually feeling their way forward in the direction of producing on a much larger scale and at much lower unit cost when rising purchasing power permitted this; but that time had not yet arrived.

Outside Britain, France, and Germany, national markets in Europe were surprisingly small. Italy, for instance, with a manufacturing capacity already estimated at over 7000 vehicles a year (4000 from Turin), in 1912 exported much of its product and could claim for itself in 1911 only about 10 000 cars, plus 302 trucks and 724 public motor vehicles of various sorts.[38] The latter already included buses and coaches, some of them running with state subsidies. In the following year 162 such subsidised motor bus services were already in operation in all the regions of Italy, covering a total of 3350 miles; a further 2000 route miles were then awaiting sanction.[39] In 1912 Austria-Hungary, which also possessed a significant manufacturing potential, ran only 7000 motor vehicles of all kinds, 680 of them being used as taxis in Vienna. There were 2000 in Hungary and 400 being used for goods transport.[40] Spain, home not only of the famous Hispano–Suisa works but also of a particularly evil collection of roads, seems at that time to have been less well served, if we are to judge from the 1500 vehicles registered in and around Madrid, 900 in Barcelona, 250 in Valencia, 130 in Seville and 50 or so in Malaga.[41] Belgium, an early pioneer – 300 motor vehicles were reported from Brussels alone so early as 1900[42] – which also had much motor-building capacity, was certainly better off than this but the consuls are silent on numbers. There may have been as many vehicles there by 1913 as was reported from Denmark: between 7000 and 8000, including many German three-wheelers much favoured by doctors and allowed to use the smaller roads banned to other cars.[43] The Netherlands, with 180 motors in 1900 and about 1600 in 1905,[44] was declared 'a poor field for the sale of motor cars' in the following year[45], but was probably in the same bracket as Belgium and Denmark by 1913. Switzerland then possessed 4065 motor cars (1132 registered in the canton of Geneva and 806 in that of Zurich), 4954 motor cycles and 751 trucks.[46] Elsewhere in Europe total registration can hardly have exceeded a very few thousand vehicles per country. Sweden had a reported 2600 in 1912,[47] Norway 1100 in 1914 – all commercial traffic there was still horse-drawn or went by water[48] – Romania 2000 (30 of them taxis and 50 commercial vehicles)[49] and Portugal fewer than that.[50]

Shortly before the First World War parts of the world remoter from the main manufacturing centres had caught up on these countries near the bottom of the European list and some had surpassed them by a considerable margin. By 1911 Toronto could already boast about 7000 motor vehicles, Montreal about 1250, the Province of Manitoba 3500 and British Columbia 2000.[51] (The latter total had grown to 6500 by August 1914.[52]) Australia's stock of motor vehicles had grown by the beginning of 1914 to the remarkable total of about 19 000 cars, 1000 lorries and 14 000 motor cycles.[53] The Consul General in New South Wales noted that in that State the motor car was extensively used 'not only in the cities but also in the smaller towns and country. Most of the big ranchmen own cars in which they travel the great distances to the residences of their neighbours or the nearest post office'.[54] Growth in parts of South America was also quite impressive. Despite the US Consul General in Rio's gloomy forecast, in 1903, that there was little future for automobiles in Brazil because 'in the Tropics, swift locomotion and the sense of comfort and pleasure are considered incompatible',[55] it was estimated that more than 3000 cars were running on the streets of Rio by 1912.[56] Argentina had already reached that total by 1910, and there were said to be 2000 cars in Uruguay (1300 of them in Montevideo) by 1913.[57] South Africa, with a much smaller population, had a considerably higher motor density. In 1911 there were over 1000 motor cars and 1000 motor cycles in Johannesburg and elsewhere on the Reef and 500 in and around Cape Town.[58] India, too, with good roads and cheap petrol available from Burma, also did well: by 1912 there were 1900 cars in and around Calcutta, 2000 in Bombay and its vicinity, about 850 in

Madras.[59] By 1913, perhaps so many as 3000 motor vehicles were running in Ceylon, one third of them motor cycles.[60] By the end of 1911 there were nearly 4000 motor cars reported in Java,[61] more than 300 in Singapore (which had been the home of two 'not much used and much abused' motors so early as 1902) and 15 motor cycles, and 336 in the Straits Settlements.[62] The new motors seemed to penetrate everywhere. There were even two of them in Dawson City in the Yukon[63] and four or five were sold every year in Siberia. ('All cars', would-be importers were advised, 'should be fitted, besides the ordinary brake, with an arrangement to prevent their sliding backwards on hills in winter'.)[64]

China was declared a complete desert so far as motor car ownership was concerned, apart from 'a very few machines owned as a novelty by wealthy Chinese'.[65] There were nevertheless some petrol-driven vehicles in the international settlement at Shanghai from 1902: in 1905, 22 of their owners banded together to form the grand-sounding Automobile Club of China to recognise the fact.[66] By 1913 their numbers had grown to 500.[67] Japan, too, was slow to take to mechanised transport. In 1911 there were only 150 motor cars reported in Tokyo, 40 in Yokohama and four in Kobe. Motor cycles were few and far between. Japan's one car maker had managed to produce only five vehicles during the previous four years and the US Commercial Agent in Japan, who passed on this information, complained that the local chauffeurs insisted on driving too fast and pulling up too quickly, 'thus knocking out the gear teeth' of the few vehicles the country possessed.[68]

The Turks and Russians were also very slow to take to motoring. Turkey had banned it altogether until 1908. By 1914 there were only 300 motors of all sorts in Constantinople and 500 more throughout the rest of the Turkish Empire.[69] A few makes of cars and motor cycles had reached the larger towns of Russia so early as 1902[70] and in the following year some were said to be used by the rich landowners on their estates,[71] but the numbers were small: only 1200–1500 motor cars and 1500 motor cycles in Russia, Poland and Finland by 1905. 'The warm weather', commented the US Consul, 'is practically the only time during which the automobiles may be run in Russia'.[72] A motor exhibition, held at St. Petersburg in 1908, was, we are told, 'the first time that the Russian public had the opportunity to examine closely every kind of automobile, for at this time St. Petersburg had not more than 200 automobiles all told, of which perhaps only five or six could be seen on the streets during the day, and then only during the summer months. Taxicabs were quite unknown'. A taxi service was started in the following year and by 1912 a fleet of 500 vehicles had been built up. The city then had about 1500 motor cars registered in all. The comparable figures for Moscow in 1912 were 79 and 826. There were then perhaps about 6000 motor vehicles of all kinds in the whole of the Russian Empire;[73] 3428 motor cars and 258 motor cycles were, however, imported into Russia that year and 5350 motor cars and 1825 motor cycles in 1913.[74] Several longer-distance motor coach services had been started and more motors were then being used by the wealthy on their estates and even by rich farmers. Cars were in use, too, in the Donetz mining region and in the Caucasus. 'The fact is,' the British Vice-Consul at Kharkov explained, 'the modern car has stood the bad roads far better than was expected, and has proved its value both in town and country as a means of rapid locomotion. Except in soft snow, loose sand or deep mud, the car can be used all the year round wherever a horse can pull a car.'[75] By withstanding the rigours of the Russian winter, not to mention the Russian roads, the new machine had indeed proved itself.

III

The pattern of motor car ownership in the different countries of the world, which had already been established, was to remain little changed for some time to come. By 1914 the United States had already moved far ahead of all other countries; probably half of all the world's motor vehicles were to be found there by October 1913 if the global stock of motor vehicles then totalled about 1.25m., as was estimated at the time.[76] This American pre-eminence increased during the next decade, as is well known. By the mid-1920s, when the League of Nations published motor statistics by country and by category of vehicle, over 20m. out of the world's stock of nearly 25m. *cars* were to be found in the United States.[77] European car ownership lagged far behind, but was still in the pre-1914 order: UK 706 000, France 670 000, and Germany 267 000; though by then Spain, 134 000, had moved ahead of Italy, 120 000; and Sweden 82 000 was ahead of Belgium and Denmark, 60 000 each, and the Netherlands, 50 000. The British still remained the motor cycle enthusiasts of the world with 693 000 of these vehicles. (Germany then owned 339 000 of them, France 252 000 and the United States 124 000.) Equally – perhaps more – interesting is the level of car ownership by this time in those other countries which had already developed an appetite for motoring before 1914; 840 000 of them (but a mere 7600 motor cycles) were registered in Canada, 348 000 (plus 84 700 motor bicycles) in Australia (and 111 000 motor cars and 35 000 motor cycles in New Zealand), 100 000 in India (14 000 motor cycles) and nearly 100 000 in South Africa (32 000 motor cycles). (Was it such a mistake for British industry to look especially to these markets before 1914?) In South America there were 206 000 cars registered in Argentina and 85 000 in Brazil, the leading importing countries in Latin America before 1914. Japan still owned only 35 000 motor cars (and 18 000 motor cycles). Russia had fallen back to a mere 8000 cars. Even the most underdeveloped parts of the inhabited world noted the existence of at least a few motor vehicles: 22 in the Yemen, for instance, and two motor lorries each in the Gilbert and Ellis and the British Solomon Islands.

The pattern of national car ownership was established before 1914 in a remarkably short space of time. It is already evident in Europe by 1905 and it may even be discerned in America by then, too. It was strongly confirmed in the years after 1907 when ownership increased quickly in the leading nations and spread more rapidly to almost every part of the globe as the rich man's (and, more often than is perhaps realised, rich woman's) motor vehicle took the place of the pedal cycle and the private horse-drawn carriage or two-wheeler. Some owners could afford chauffeurs: most of them drove themselves. All the early purchases helped to develop the vehicle from a light weight and low-powered adaptation of a horse-drawn vehicle to a higher powered and much more reliable product with a longer life.[78]

While the state of the roads was a deterrent, it was also a challenge to motor manufacturers and to earlier motorists alike, the triumph over bad roads being an essential part of the pleasures of motoring so far as the latter were concerned. 'A motor car can negotiate all parts of the country when the streams are not in flood', commented one observer rather revealingly from Uruguay.[79] 'The roads of Europe', noted an American consul in Germany who was greatly concerned about punctures which were to prove a major cause of mishaps and stoppages, 'are strewn with the hobnails which fall from the shoes of peasants.'[80] Lack of petrol supplies and repair facilities must also have added considerably to the early motorist's sense of adventure.

As motors became more numerous, however, so petrol supplies and repair facilities, not to mention car purchasing outlets, became more widespread, and pressures were exerted on governments, national and local, to improve the roads and build new ones. In the four leading countries there was considerable progress in all these directions, especially in the years just before 1914. Whole new industries, indeed, were created to keep the new vehicles on the road, industries which still await the attention of historians. But in most parts of the world, where cars remained few and far between, the challenge to motorists, despite improved vehicles, must have been almost as great as ever.

Cars soon came to be used for purposes other than mere pleasure. As has been seen, doctors began to use them for their rounds very early on. Postal authorities and stores adapted them as vans for delivery purposes, farmers used them to get to and from towns and owners of country properties took advantage of them for the same purpose. The continued use of the terms 'pleasure motors' or 'touring cars' becomes increasingly imprecise and misleading as time passes. Nor is it true to imagine that motor vehicles as a whole continued to benefit only the well-to-do. In America, of course, car ownership already penetrated much farther down the social scale than it did elsewhere. But in other countries non car-owners benefited from taxis or hire cars (which often seem to have formed a high proportion of the earlier national totals). More important, motor cycles, costing a quarter or less than a car, provided personal transport for those (especially the young) of more modest means. The larger motor bicycle of the immediately pre-war years, especially with sidecar, had particular attractions. The growing second-hand market for both cars and cycles must have helped to spread these vehicles down the social scale at this time, but about this virtually nothing is known.

For most people it was in the form of the motor bus or coach that motors were to bring direct advantages by providing faster and more extensive services at lower fares. As has been noticed, these vehicles had started to run not just in great cities like London, Paris and Berlin but also in other towns and in rural areas in remoter parts of the world. Their main impact, however, was to come in the inter-war years.[81] Heavier, motor-driven goods vehicles, which were also in due course to benefit all sections of society, were even less advanced by 1914. Indeed the improved steam-driven lorries often held their own in carrying the limited amount of goods traffic that went any distance by road in those days; and local goods traffic was still almost invariably horse drawn.

Yet by 1914 the million or more motor vehicles of all sorts were already exerting, either directly or indirectly, visually or odorously, dangerously or helpfully, a remarkable influence upon very many people scattered throughout the globe. Sometimes in very unexpected circumstances. A British consul noted just before 1914 that there were already 50 motor cars registered in Bosnia–Herzegovina, nearly all of German make. Sarajevo was the local motor supply centre.[82] People there were evidently already quite familiar with motor cars before 28 June 1914.

NOTES AND REFERENCES

1. Towns of up to a million inhabitants continued to depend upon road transport. Even the few great conurbations which began to develop urban railways in the later nineteenth century depended mainly on road transport for passenger traffic and wholly upon it for freight. In London, the largest nineteenth-century city and first to have both suburban and intraurban railways, passenger transport by rail was for a brief period about 1870 greater than that by public road transport, but thereafter the latter grew much more rapidly and by the middle 1890s was 50 per cent larger. In 1914 it was twice as large. See T. C. Barker and M. Robbins, *A History of London Transport. Passenger Travel and the Development of the Metropolis* (London, 1963), p. 271; 2nd ed. (1974), p. 191.

2. F. M. L. Thompson, 'Nineteenth-Century Horse Sense', *Economic History Review*, xxix, no. 1 (February 1976) 80.

3. F. M. L. Thompson, *Victorian England: The Horse-drawn Society* (Inaugural Lecture, Bedford College, London 1970), pp. 18–19.

4. See Barker and Robbins, op. cit. (1963) chapter X ('The Search for a New Form of Traction') and (1974) chapters 2–8.

5. See, for instance, A. Nevins, *Ford: The Times, The Man, The Company* (New York, 1954); A. Nevins and F. E. Hill, *Ford: Expansion and Challenge, 1916–1933* (New York, 1957) and *Ford: Decline and Rebirth, 1933–1962* (New York, 1963); A. P. Sloan, Jr, *My Years with General Motors* (London, 1963); P. Fridenson, *Histoire des Usines Renault*, I (Paris, 1972); J. M. Laux, *In First Gear. The French Automobile Industry to 1914* (Liverpool, 1976); S. B. Saul, 'The Motor Industry in Britain to 1914', *Business History*, vol. 1 (December 1962); P. W. S. Andrews and E. Brunner, *The Life of Lord Nuffield. A Study in Enterprise and Benevolence* (Oxford, 1955); R. J. Overy, *William Morris, Viscount Nuffield* (London, 1976); R. Church, *Herbert Austin. The British Motor Car Industry to 1941* (London, 1979); I. Lloyd, *Rolls-Royce*, 3 vols. (London, 1978).

6. W. W. Rostow, *The Stages of Economic Growth: A Non-Communist Manifesto* (Cambridge, 1960), pp. 84–6.

7. W. W. Rostow, *The World Economy. History and Prospect* (Austin and London, 1978), pp. 210–14.
8. *Foreign Markets for Motor Vehicles* (Special US Consular Report no. 53, Washington, 1913), p. 86.
9. The US Consular Reports published in Washington, are bound up in consecutive volumes. *Monthly Reports*, issued as miscellaneous documents of the House of Representatives, have been studied from volume 32 (January–April 1890) to volume 100 (June 1910). The *Daily Consular and Trade Reports*, issued by the Bureau of Manufactures, Department of Commerce and Labor and bound up quarterly, have been combed from vol. I beginning July 1910 until the end of 1914. The British Consular Reports are published in volumes of British Parliamentary Papers and are listed in the various B.P.P. indexes. I am grateful to the Social Science Research Council for the small grant which enabled me to employ Mr David Hebb and Mr Peter Lyth to extract much of this material during the long vacation of 1978. The American and British reports will be abbreviated as US and GB respectively.
10. US 232, January 1900.
11. US, July 1910, 303. See also A. E. Harrison, 'The Competitiveness of the British Cycle Industry, 1890–1914', *Economic History Review*, XXII no. 2 (August 1969) and that writer's more recent York Ph.D. thesis.
12. Saul, loc. cit., 26.
13. *Foreign Markets*, op. cit., 57.
14. US 250, July 1901, 449, citing *Le Journal de la Marine et des Locomotions Nouvelles*, Brussels, 28 March 1901.
15. US 346, July 1909.
16. *Foreign Markets*, op. cit., 86.
17. Unless otherwise stated this paragraph is based upon biographical information contained in the first edition of *Motoring Annual and Motorist's Year Book*, illustrated, (London, 1903).
18. Dorothy Lerett, *The Woman and the Car. A Chatty Little Handbook for All Women who Motor or who want to Motor*, (London, 1909) (reprinted London, 1970). Citations from pp. 27–8, 35, 72.
19. US 281, February 1904. I am grateful to Dr R. C. Richardson for this volume.
20. Report of the Royal Commission on Motor Cars, II (Minutes of Evidence), Appendix A. British Parliamentary Papers, 1906 (Cd 3081) XLVIII, 628–9.
21. US 293, February 1905.
22. GB 4282/1909. US 350, November 1909, gives somewhat higher figures, presumably for later that year: 'motor machines' 39 475, of which 20 928 were motor cycles, and 2252 commercial vehicles. 4641 vehicles were used by doctors.
23. US July 1914, 187.
24. US, January 1913, 195–6, quoting figures from *Car Illustrated*. These figures are rather higher than those published by the Motor Manufacturers and Traders during the 1930s and used by B. R. Mitchell and Phyllis Deane in their *Abstract of British Historical Statistics* (Cambridge 1962), 230. The grand total, however, is not far above the SMMT's estimate of 389 000 for 1914.
25. US July 1914, 186, which gives French motor car registrations since 1904 (17 107), 1905 (21 543), 1906 (26 262), 1907 (31 286), 1908 (37 586), 1909 (44 769), 1910 (53 669), 1911 (64 209), 1912 (76 771).

26. US, November 1913, 720–1.
27. For London, Barker and Robbins, op. cit., II, 170, 184–5, 329; for Paris, Laux, op. cit., 141, GB 4597/1910, US, June 1911, 144–5 and US *Foreign Markets* op. cit., 58.
28. Barker and Robbins, op. cit., II, 190.
29. US October 1913, 406.
30. Report of the Royal Commission on Motor Cars, I, British Parliamentary Papers, 1906 (Cd. 3080) XLVIII, 69.
31. GB 5332/1914, 31.
32. GB 5095/1913, 8.
33. US 263/August 1902, 650.
34. US 133/December 1910, 908.
35. US June 1911, 1268.
36. US August 1911, 919.
37. US 304, January 1906, 231.
38. US November 1913, 712; GB 5148/1913, 8–9.
39. US November 1912, 964.
40. *Foreign Markets*, op. cit., 52, 54.
41. Ibid., 102.
42. *Vehicle Industry in Europe* (Special US Consular Report, Washington 1900), 340.
43. US October 1913, 714–5.
44. *Vehicle Industry in Europe*, op. cit., 375; RC Motor Cars, op. cit., I, 69.
45. US 312, September 1906, 134.
46. US January 1914, which gives breakdown by canton.
47. *Foreign Markets*, op. cit., 105: US August 1914, 989.
48. US August 1914, 974.
49. *Foreign Markets*, op. cit., 106.
50. US November 1913, 711.
51. *Foreign Markets*, op. cit., 7 *seq.*
52. US September 1914, 1578.
53. US April 1914, 203.
54. *Foreign Markets*, op. cit., 130.
55. US 268, January 1903, 18.
56. GB 5049 1912/3, 7.
57. US April 1913, 99.
58. *Foreign Markets*, 121; US April 1912, 72 and November 1912, 999.
59. *Foreign Markets*, 111–3.
60. US November 1913, 771.
61. US November 1912, 997.
62. *Foreign Markets*, 116, 117, 140; US January 1903, 23.
63. *Foreign Markets*, 19.
64. Ibid., 115.
65. Ibid., 107.
66. US 303, December 1905, 251.
67. US October 1913, 135.
68. *Foreign Markets*, 113–14; GB 4511/1914, 20.
69. US August 1914, 1128.
70. GB 3062/1903, 36–7.
71. GB 3194/1904, 8

72. US December 1905, 246.
73. US 1912, 234; GB 5172/1913, 17.
74. US October 1914, 435–6.
75. GB 5114/1913, 19.
76. US January 1914, 196.
77. *International Statistical Year Book 1928* (Geneva, 1929). Table 90 gives motor vehicle statistics for 1927.
78. Fridenson, op. cit., 20, citing J. Morice, *La Demande d'automobiles* (Paris 1957), for the information that only 40 per cent of the cars made between 1898 and 1908 remained after seven years and none after fourteen, whereas of those made between 1908 and 1914, 78 per cent. survived seven years and not until after 21 years was none left.
79. US April 1913, 99.
80. UK 51/1896, 326.
81. For a useful sketch of what was happening in Britain, both before 1914 and between the wars, see John Hibbs, *The History of British Bus Services* (Newton Abbot, 1968) and a selection of reprinted articles edited by him in John Hibbs, *The Omnibus* (Newton Abbot, 1971).
82. GB 5067/1913, 7.

8 The Timing of the Climacteric and its Sectoral Incidence in the UK, 1873–1913

C. H. FEINSTEIN,
R. C. O. MATTHEWS and
J. C. ODLING-SMEE

The behaviour of the British economy in the forty years before the First World War has attracted the attention of an impressive array of British economists with an historical bent: Robertson, Cairncross, Phelps Brown, and Arthur Lewis, to name only the most eminent. However, it was not a British economist but an American one who was responsible for the renaissance of interest in the subject in the years immediately after the Second World War. Walt Rostow's *British Economy of the Nineteenth Century* was published in 1948, based largely on unpublished work done by its author before the war. (The oldest of the present writers vividly remembers how his interest in quantitative economic history was first aroused by an oral version of parts of the book given by Walt Rostow in lectures in front of a blazing open fire in the hall of Queen's College, Oxford, in 1946–7.) It raised new questions and offered new answers on the period 1873–1913. It also marked the first step in the post-war quantitative-theoretical movement in the writing of economic history.

One of Rostow's contentions in that book was that trends in output did not always match the impressionistic descriptions of the state of prosperity given by contemporary commentators and in contemporary controversies. When Rostow wrote, he did not have the benefit of the comprehensive data on national product that have since become available. These data have amply confirmed the contention just mentioned. They have, however, revealed new features and new problems.

It has become clear that production and productivity in the British economy underwent a slowing-down in their rates of growth some time in the period 1873–1913. Both the extent and the timing of this slowing-down have remained matters of controversy. The slowing-down was undoubtedly most rapid in the period after 1899, and one of the main issues is whether the slowing-down was chiefly confined to that phase or whether what happened in that phase represented merely a hastening of a process that started earlier.

In this paper we offer some new estimates bearing on these questions. The estimates relate to production and to productivity in the economy as a whole and by sector.[1]

GROWTH IN GDP

After Rostow's work modern discussion of the nature, timing and causes of the deceleration in British economic growth in the late nineteenth century was renewed with the article by Phelps Brown and Handfield Jones (1952) and the criticism of this by Coppock (1956). Since then there have been a number of important contributions, most recently by Lewis (1978)[2], and much has been done to improve the data. There are still two major obstacles in the way of a clear-cut resolution of the long debate on the extent and timing of retardation. The first arises from discrepancies between the three alternative measures of GDP, and might in principle be eliminated; the second is inherent and arises because the trend in the growth rate between successive peak-to-peak cycles was not a regular one. Both are apparent from Panel A of Table 8.1. While all three series for GDP are in very close agreement about the rate of growth over the whole period from 1873 to 1913 (Panel B), they show significantly different patterns between parts of the period. Inter-cyclical variance in growth rates is quite large in both the income and the expenditure series but is relatively insignificant in the output series.

The problem of the discrepancy between the three series is hard to deal with. In Feinstein (1972), pp. 16–20, it was suggested that the income data probably provide the best guide to *cyclical* movements. The underlying data on earnings (based on annual series for wage-rates and unemployment) and on profits and rents

TABLE 8.1. *Growth of GDP, alternative estimates and alternative sub-periods, 1856–1913* (annual percentage growth rates)

Period	Output data (1)	Income data (2)	Expenditure data (3)	Compromise estimate (4)
A Business cycles, peak-to-peak				
1856–1860	1.9	1.5	–	1.7
1860–1865	2.0	2.0	–	2.0
1865–1873	2.0	2.9	–	2.4
1873–1882	1.8	1.7	2.3	1.9
1882–1889	1.9	2.8	2.0	2.2
1889–1899	1.9	2.4	2.3	2.2
1899–1907	1.7	1.0	0.9	1.2
1907–1913	1.7	1.2	1.8	1.6
B. Division at 1873				
1856–1873	2.0	2.3	–	2.2
1873–1913	1.8	1.8	1.9	1.8
C. Divisions at 1873 and 1899				
1856–1873	2.0	2.3	–	2.2
1873–1899	1.9	2.2	2.2	2.1
1899–1913	1.7	1.1	1.3	1.4
D. Phases in 'long swings'				
1856–1873	2.0	2.3	–	2.2
1873–1882	1.8	1.7	2.3	1.9
1882–1899	1.9	2.5	2.2	2.2
1899–1913	1.7	1.1	1.3	1.4
E. Two complete 'long swings'				
1856–1882	1.9	2.1	–	2.0
1882–1913	1.8	1.9	1.8	1.8

(based on tax records) are defective in certain respects but it is likely that they do follow the actual movements in incomes quite closely. The output series, by contrast, almost certainly smooths out the short-term fluctuations. For services (accounting for about one third of total output in 1907) the volume of output is based on interpolation (for example between census data on population in the relevant occupations, modified in some cases by a constant annual increase in output per head).[3] For many of the components of the manufacturing index output is measured by the consumption of raw materials unadjusted for changes in stocks held by suppliers or manufacturers, and this too will tend to understate the fluctuations in actual production.[4] The expenditure series relies partly on indicators of consumption of manufactured goods and of services taken from, or similar to, the output series and thus subject to the same smoothing. It also includes an entirely arbitrary estimate for the annual changes in non-farm stocks which could significantly distort, and might exaggerate, the short-term fluctuations.

However, there is no reason to believe that any one of the GDP series is more reliable than the others as a measure of long-run growth rates,[5] and since the proposition about the merits of the income series is not proved, it seems best at the aggregate level to use the geometric mean of all three series (two before 1873), thus pooling all the available information. This is the series given in col. (4) of Table 8.1. It must be recognised, nevertheless, that the output series – which must be used as soon as we go behind GDP to examine individual sectors – almost certainly smooths out the differences in growth rates between the phases.

On any reckoning, the rate of growth of GDP was less in 1873–1913 than in 1856–73 (Table 8.1., Panel B). In the output series, the falling off was small and fairly steady and the period after 1899 was not significantly out of trend. According to the other series, however, the falling off after 1899 was of a different order from what had gone before (Table 8.1., Panel C). Hence arises the scope for two very different interpretations of the slow-down. According to one, it was a continuous process, associated, perhaps, with the beginning of the continuous decline in Britain's *relative* standing among industrial countries. According to the other, something special and unprecedented took place in the uneasy decade-and-a-half that preceded the First World War.[6]

There is no uniquely right way of arranging the figures or resolving their discrepancies. Both output and income series agree in showing a more than usually pronounced retardation in 1873–83, the first stage of 'the Great Depression', and a recovery in the 1880s and 1890s. This suggests a possible alternative arrangement of sub-periods, which is shown in Panels D and E of Table 8.1. This views the whole period 1856–1913 as made up of two 'long swings', with the 1880s representing the falling off from the peak of 1873 and the Edwardian period representing the falling off from the peak of 1899. This timing, incidentally, is roughly matched, with a lag, by that of domestic capital formation.

Focussing attention on the compromise estimate of GDP, we see that there was a retardation in the late 1870s and earlier 1880s

(Table 8.1. Panel D) and that the pre-1873 rate of growth was restored in the ensuing long-swing upswing of the late 1880s and the 1890s. The long-swing downswing after 1899 was much more severe. The severity of the falling-off in that phase was the reason why the rate of growth over the long-swing 1882–1913 as a whole was less than over the long-swing 1856–82.

On the same line of argument, if the period 1856–1913 is divided at the more familiar year 1873, some part of the reason why GDP grew less rapidly in 1873–1913 than in 1856–73 can be held to have been that 1873–1913 contained two low-growth phases of the long swing and 1856–73 none. However, the falling off in the first low-growth phase, 1873–82, was very moderate, and the main reason why growth was slower in 1873–1913 than in 1856–73 remains the poor performance after 1899.

The long swing is not, of course, a readily identifiable phenomenon. In particular, the two low-growth phases, 1873–82 and 1899–1913, were very different from each other: they would not have been recognised by contemporaries as belonging to the same

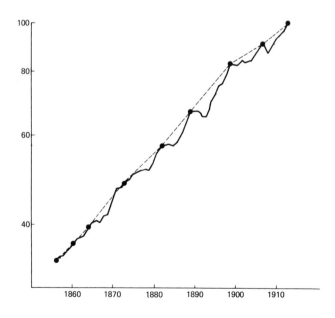

FIGURE 8.1   *GDP (compromise-index), 1856–1913, with trends between cyclical peaks*

species. Division into long-swing phases is one way of dividing up the period, and it does have some point (one clearly long-swing phenomenon affecting *productivity* after 1899 will be mentioned later, namely the building cycle). Both the 1873–82 low-growth phase and the 1899–1913 one had some of the characteristics of a cyclical reaction to phases of faster growth. However, both those periods, in their different ways, also involved trend features of a kind not previously observed. Discussion of these is outside the scope of this paper.

Attention has so far been confined to trends between peak years of business cycles, as being the best indicator of movements in productive potential. In certain cycles the exact identification of the peak year is debatable. The annual data for GDP in Figure 8.1. show that alternative definitions would make no significant difference.

Figure 8.1. does, however, bring out another point. The amplitude of fluctuations in GDP was smaller before about 1878 than after. Hence, in respect of average performance over the cycle, the later period (especially the 1890s) appears in a rather less favourable light than it does in respect of performance at cyclical peaks, and there was rather more retardation before 1899 than appears from the measures so far given. However, the difference is

TABLE 8.2.   *Growth in GDP (compromise estimate) between cyclical peaks and between notional mid-cycle points (annual percentage growth rates)*

1856–1860		1.7	
	'1858–1863'		1.7
1860–1865		2.0	
	'1863–1869'		2.1
1865–1873		2.4	
	'1869–1878'		2.2
1873–1882		1.9	
	'1878–1886'		1.8
1882–1889		2.2	
	'1886–1894'		2.1
1889–1899		2.2	
	'1894–1903'		2.0
1899–1907		1.2	
	'1903–1910'		1.3
1907–1913		1.6	

For explanation, see text

not at all large. A measure is given in Table 8.2. It compares actual peak-to-peak growth rates with growth rates between notional levels of GDP at mid-point of business cycles. The notional level for each mid-cycle year is defined as the peak-to-peak trend figure multiplied by the average ratio of actual figures to peak-to-peak trend figures over the cycle concerned. It thus allows for variations in the severity of recessions. The patterns in the two sets of growth rates are much the same.

GROWTH IN PRODUCTIVITY

Table 8.3. sets out data on rates of growth of output, inputs and productivity for the same time-periods as Table 8.1. GDP is the compromise estimate; employment (N) is the numbers in employment; capital (K) is gross fixed capital stock. The rate of growth of total factor input (TFI) is the weighted average of the rates of growth of N and K, the weights being derived from distributive shares. Two measures are given of the rate of growth of productivity. The rate of growth of labour productivity is the difference between the rates of growth of GDP and N. The rate of growth of total factor productivity (TFP) is the difference between the rates of growth of GDP and TFI. Labour productivity is the simpler concept; TFP is the more comprehensive measure and its growth rate consists, in principle, of that part of the rate of growth of GDP that is due to causes other than growth of N and K (the 'residual').[7]

The rate of growth of TFI was remarkably constant throughout the period from 1856 to 1913. Consequently, the rate of growth of TFP follows the same pattern as the rate of growth of GDP, discussed in the previous section. This stands out in the graphical representation of the data in Figure 8.2. (Since our present focus of interest is on the period after 1873, the years 1856–73 are treated here as a single period.) The time-pattern of the rate of growth of labour productivity is somewhat different, and the difference calls for further comment.

It comes about because there was a marked tendency for the rates of growth of N and K to move in opposite directions from each other between successive business cycles, as may be seen from Panel A of Table 8.3. It is this inverse movement that is responsible for the constancy in the rate of growth of TFI, which is the weighted average of the two. We cannot here consider at length the reasons

TABLE 8.3 *Growth of GDP, employment, capital, total factor input, labour productivity, and total factor productivity, 1856–1913* (annual percentage growth rates)

Period	GDP	N	K	TFI	Labour productivity	TFP
A. Business cycles, peak-to-peak						
1856–1860	1.7	1.2	1.4	1.2	0.5	0.4
1860–1865	2.0	0.7	2.5	1.4	1.3	0.6
1865–1873	2.4	0.8	2.1	1.3	1.6	1.1
1873–1882	1.9	0.6	2.4	1.3	1.3	0.6
1882–1889	2.2	1.1	1.6	1.3	1.2	0.9
1889–1899	2.2	1.1	1.8	1.4	1.1	0.8
1899–1907	1.2	0.7	2.4	1.5	0.5	−0.3
1907–1913	1.6	1.1	1.4	1.2	0.4	0.3
B. Division at 1873						
1856–1873	2.2	0.9	2.0	1.4	1.3	0.8
1873–1913	1.8	0.9	2.0	1.4	0.9	0.5
C. Divisions at 1873 and 1899						
1856–1873	2.2	0.9	2.0	1.4	1.3	0.8
1873–1899	2.1	0.9	2.0	1.4	1.2	0.7
1899–1913	1.4	0.9	2.0	1.4	0.5	0.0
D. Phases in 'long swings'						
1856–1873	2.2	0.9	2.0	1.4	1.3	0.8
1873–1882	1.9	0.6	2.4	1.3	1.3	0.6
1882–1899	2.2	1.1	1.7	1.4	1.1	0.8
1899–1913	1.4	0.9	2.0	1.4	0.5	0.0
E. Two complete 'long swings'						
1856–1882	2.0	0.8	2.2	1.3	1.2	0.7
1882–1913	1.8	1.0	1.8	1.4	0.8	0.5

NOTE: For definitions, see text. Rate of growth of TFI is weighted average of rates of growth of N and K (weights 0.59 and 0.41, 1856–1873, 0.57 and 0.43, 1873–1913). Rate of growth of TFP is rate of growth of GDP minus rate of growth of TFI. Components may not add to totals because of rounding.

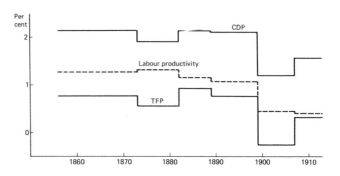

FIGURE 8.2   *Growth of GDP, labour productivity and TFP between cyclical peaks (annual percentage growth rates)*

for the time-patterns of N and K, but what happened, broadly speaking, was as follows.

Fluctuations in the rate of growth of N between successive business cycles after 1873 matched the timing of those in GDP – perhaps because the state of the economy, as measured by the rate of growth of GDP, affected the demand for labour and hence participation rates and net migration. Fluctuations in the rate of growth of K also roughly matched those of GDP but they did so with a lag of about one business cycle. This may be seen in the business cycles of 1873–82 and 1899–1907. In those cycles, as is well known, the peak rate of domestic capital formation occurred some years after the peak in the business cycle and as a result the cycles as a whole had a high rate of growth of K, notwithstanding that the rate of growth of GDP was poor.

The labour productivity measure and the TFP measure agree in their most important finding, that the deterioration before 1899 was small and that the main part of the falling off in productivity-growth came after that date. The most important difference between them concerns the 1870s and the 1880s. The rate of growth of TFP, like that of GDP, fell in 1873–82 and recovered in 1882–89. The rate of growth of labour productivity, on the other hand, was no lower in 1873–82 than it had been on average in 1856–73 but declined monotonically thereafter. There is a similar difference in regard to the relative standing of the cycles 1899–1907 and 1907–13.

Labour productivity and TFP measure different things. As an example, consider the cycle 1882–9. Labour productivity grew somewhat more slowly than before. However this increase in labour productivity was achieved with the aid of a much smaller increase in K than in the preceding cycles. Hence there must have been an improvement in other sources of productivity growth; and this is what is measured by the increase shown in the rate of growth of TFP. Note also the difference between what is shown by the two measures in regard to the phase-division adopted in Panel E of Table 8.3., where the whole period 1856–1913 is divided into two phases, before and after 1882. The decline in the rate of growth between the two phases was greater in labour productivity than in TFP. This is because the rate of growth of K declined between the two phases. The labour productivity measure, as an indicator of economic performance, embraces all influences on the productivity of labour. The TFP measure concerns itself more narrowly with the efficiency of the use made of productive resources. It therefore seeks to abstract from the effects on productive potential of changes in the rate of growth of K, treating these as a matter for separate study.

OUTPUT AND PRODUCTIVITY IN THE MAIN SECTORS

Estimates of the growth-rates of output, inputs and productivity between cyclical peaks are given in Table 8.4. for each of the main sectors of the economy.

These estimates are subject to a number of problems arising from the deficiencies of the available data. The sectoral output data are, of course, those making up the output-side estimate of GDP and therefore they cannot be summed to yield a total consistent with our preferred indicator of GDP, the compromise estimate. As noted above, the output-side data probably understate the extent of the variations between periods and the extent of the deceleration after 1899. Other difficulties are indicated in the notes to Table 8.4. For the sake of completeness, we have given estimates for all sectors, but measurement of productivity is not meaningful in the case of two of them (public and professional services and occupation of dwellings) and in the case of a third, commerce, the estimates of output are partly dependent on employment indicators and are therefore doubtful.

Not surprisingly, a considerable variety of experience appears between the sectors, alike in average rates of growth of output and

TABLE 8.4. *Growth of output, employment, capital, total factor input, labour productivity and total factor productivity by sector, 1856–1913* (annual percentage growth rates)

	Output[a]	N[b]	K[c]	TFI[d]	Labour productivity	TFP[e]
AGRICULTURE, FORESTRY AND FISHING						
1856–1860	0.4	−0.7	0.2	−0.5	1.1	0.9
1860–1865	0.4	−1.2	0.4	−0.8	1.6	1.2
1865–1873	−0.1	−1.1	0.4	−0.8	1.0	0.7
1873–1882	−0.8	−0.9	0.2	−0.6	0.1	−0.2
1882–1889	1.1	−0.8	0.2	−0.5	1.9	1.6
1889–1899	−0.4	−0.8	−0.4	−0.7	0.4	0.3
1899–1907	0.3	−0.5	−0.4	−0.5	0.8	0.7
1907–1913	0.0	0.2	−0.2	0.1	−0.2	−0.1
MINING AND QUARRYING						
1856–1860	4.2	2.1	1.2	1.8	2.1	2.4
1860–1865	4.4	1.6	4.2	2.5	2.8	1.9
1865–1873	3.2	1.6	3.8	2.4	1.6	0.8
1873–1882	2.2	1.7	2.4	2.0	0.5	0.2
1882–1889	1.6	2.2	1.4	1.9	−0.6	−0.3
1889–1899	2.0	2.0	2.0	2.0	0.0	0.0
1899–1907	2.5	2.1	2.6	2.3	0.4	0.2
1907–1913	1.2	2.7	1.2	2.2	−1.5	−1.0
MANUFACTURING						
1856–1860	2.5	1.5	0.9	1.3	1.0	1.2
1860–1865	1.7	0.9	3.9	1.8	0.8	−0.1
1865–1873	3.2	1.0	4.0	1.9	2.3	1.3
1873–1882	2.3	0.3	3.4	1.2	2.0	1.1
1882–1889	1.9	1.2	2.0	1.4	0.7	0.4
1889–1899	2.3	0.9	1.8	1.2	1.4	1.1
1899–1907	1.6	0.7	3.5	1.5	0.9	0.1
1907–1913	2.0	1.2	2.8	1.6	0.8	0.3
CONSTRUCTION[f]						
1856–1860	5.2	2.3	−	3.1	2.9	2.1
1860–1865	10.7	1.9	−	3.9	8.8	6.8
1865–1873	−2.5	1.9	−	0.8	−4.4	−3.3
1873–1882	2.6	2.0	−	2.2	0.6	0.4
1882–1889	−0.4	0.1	−	0.0	−0.5	−0.4
1889–1899	4.8	2.2	−	2.8	2.6	2.0
1899–1907	−0.7	−0.1	−	−0.2	−0.6	−0.5
1907–1913	−3.0	−0.2	−	−1.0	−2.8	−2.0

TABLE 8.4 (*Contd.*)

	Output[a]	$N^{(b)}$	$K^{(c)}$	$TFI^{(d)}$	Labour productivity	$TFP^{(e)}$
GAS, ELECTRICITY, WATER						
1856–1860	6.2	10.0	6.9	8.2	−3.8	−2.0
1860–1865	5.8	3.4	4.0	3.7	2.4	2.1
1865–1873	4.9	3.0	4.5	3.9	1.8	1.0
1873–1882	5.2	2.4	3.6	3.1	2.8	2.1
1882–1889	4.5	4.6	2.9	3.6	−0.1	0.9
1889–1899	4.7	4.9	4.0	4.3	−0.2	0.3
1899–1907	5.0	2.5	4.9	4.0	2.5	1.0
1907–1913	6.5	1.6	2.1	1.9	4.9	4.6
TRANSPORT AND COMMUNICATION						
1856–1860	2.9	3.2	2.9	3.0	−0.3	−0.1
1860–1865	2.5	2.8	4.7	3.6	−0.3	−1.1
1865–1873	3.2	0.8	2.4	1.5	2.4	1.7
1873–1882	2.8	2.5	2.5	2.5	0.3	0.3
1882–1889	2.8	2.6	1.9	2.3	0.2	0.5
1889–1899	2.6	2.7	1.8	2.3	−0.1	0.3
1899–1907	2.5	1.1	2.3	1.6	1.4	0.9
1907–1913	2.6	1.1	1.1	1.1	1.5	1.5
COMMERCE[g]						
1856–1860	2.4	2.0	1.2	1.7	0.5	0.8
1860–1865	1.9	1.8	1.4	1.6	0.1	0.3
1865–1873	2.7	2.3	1.8	2.1	0.4	0.6
1873–1882	1.9	0.8	2.4	2.0	1.1	−0.1
1882–1889	2.5	1.5	1.0	1.3	1.0	1.2
1889–1899	1.7	1.2	1.8	1.4	0.5	0.3
1899–1907	1.7	1.1	1.9	1.5	0.6	−0.2
1907–1913	2.1	1.7	0.6	1.2	0.4	0.9
PUBLIC AND PROFESSIONAL SERVICES[h]						
1856–1860	1.8	3.6	1.4	2.9	−1.8	−1.0
1860–1865	1.2	0.9	2.0	1.3	0.3	−0.1
1865–1873	1.4	0.4	2.4	1.1	1.0	0.3
1873–1882	2.8	2.2	4.6	3.0	0.6	−0.3
1882–1889	2.3	1.5	2.5	1.9	0.8	0.4
1889–1899	2.5	3.0	2.9	3.0	−0.5	−0.5
1899–1907	2.5	1.0	3.0	1.7	1.5	0.8
1907–1913	2.5	0.7	1.8	1.1	1.8	1.4

TABLE 8.4 (*Contd.*)

	Output[a]	N[b]	K[c]	TFI[d]	Labour productivity	TFP[e]
OWNERSHIP OF DWELLINGS						
1856–1860	0.8	–	0.9	0.9	–	–0.1
1860–1865	1.0	–	1.4	1.4	–	–0.4
1865–1873	1.0	–	1.9	1.9	–	–0.9
1873–1882	1.2	–	2.2	2.2	–	–1.0
1882–1889	0.9	–	1.5	1.5	–	–0.6
1889–1899	1.2	–	2.0	2.0	–	–0.8
1899–1907	1.0	–	2.3	2.3	–	–1.3
1907–1913	1.2	–	1.2	1.2	–	0.0

Notes to Table 8.4
(a) Measured from output data.
(b) Man years. The underlying figures are very uncertain: they were obtained by interpolating between the decennial census estimates (Feinstein (1972) Table 60) and adjusting for unemployment on the assumption that unemployment rates in each sector were the same as for the economy as a whole.
(c) Gross fixed capital only.
(d) Average of rates of growth of N and K, weighted by very rough estimates of distributive shares in the sector in 1856 for 1856–73 and in 1873 for 1873–1913.
(e) Rate of growth of TFP is rate of growth of Output minus rate of growth of TFI. Components may not add to totals because of rounding.
(f) No direct data available for K; rate of growth assumed to be the same as for output in construction.
(g) Includes distributive trades, finance, catering and miscellaneous services.
(h) Includes public administration, defence and professional services.

productivity, in the direction of change of these in the course of the period, and in the timing of change.

Our comments will be confined to movements in productivity, as measured by TFP.

An attempt to summarise the contributions of the main sectors to trends in TFP in the economy as a whole is made in Table 8.5. The figures here are first differences between weighted sectoral growth-rates of TFP, where the weights are the sectors' shares in GDP in the opening year. Figures are shown for only those sectors where the measurement of TFP is reasonably satisfactory conceptually and statistically. The sum of these weighted sectoral figures differs from the corresponding figure for the economy as a whole (measuring GDP from the output side) by the amount of the contributions of the three sectors not shown, plus a small residual item which reflects the effects of shifts of factors between sectors with differing levels of

TABLE 8.5. *Differences between periods in weighted sectoral annual percentage rates of growth of TFP*

	1856–73 to 1873–1913	1856–73 to 1873–82	1873–82 to 1882–99	1882–99 to 1899–1913
Agriculture, forestry, fishing	−0.10	−0.19	+0.11	−0.05
Mining, quarrying	−0.07	−0.05	−0.01	−0.02
Manufacturing	−0.04	+0.06	−0.05	−0.14
Construction	−0.03	−0.02	+0.03	−0.09
Gas, electricity, water	+0.01	+0.01	−0.01	+0.03
Transport, communications	+0.02	−0.01	+0.02	+0.07
Total of above	−0.21	−0.20	+0.09	−0.20
GDP (output-side)	−0.2	−0.1	0.0	−0.2
GDP (compromise)	−0.3	−0.2	+0.2	−0.8

productivity, and also the effects of certain rounding errors.[8] The rate of growth of TFP in the economy as a whole, based on the compromise-index of GDP, is given in the bottom row as a memorandum item. The first column divides the period 1856–1913 at 1873; the remaining columns divide it at 1873, 1882, and 1899, thus corresponding to the phase-division in Panel D of Tables 8.1. and 8.3.

It is obvious from Table 8.5. that the discrepancy between the output-side and compromise estimates of GDP makes it impossible to identify satisfactorily the sectoral sources of the falling-off in the rate of growth of TFP after 1899. Assuming that the compromise index is the one nearest the truth, there must have been a substantially greater decline in the rate of growth of TFP after 1899 in some or all sectors than we are able to trace.[9] This is a major qualification. However, as far as concerns the comparison of other periods with one another (including the comparison of 1856–73 with 1873–1913), the movements in the sectors identified in Table 8.5. account reasonably well for the movements in the economy as a whole.

Attention may be called to the following features.

(i) Agriculture made a major contribution to movements in the total. It was the largest source of decline between 1856–73 and

1873–1913 as a whole, and also between 1856–73 and 1873–82. Part of the trend is attributable to the decline in agriculture's share in the economy, and part to the decline in TFP growth within agriculture. It was also the largest source of recovery between 1873–82 and 1882–99.

(ii) Mining was the second largest source of decline between 1856–73 and 1873–1913.

(iii) Manufacturing was no more than a minor source of the overall decline between 1856–73 and 1873–1913. The rate of growth of TFP in manufacturing between 1873 and 1899 was on average no lower than it had been between 1856 and 1873;[10] its movements, incidentally, in 1873–82–99 were in opposite directions from those in the economy as a whole. However, manufacturing *was* the largest identified source of the deterioration in 1899–1913 compared with earlier periods. These findings, it may be noted, run rather counter to the oft-stated hypothesis that foreign competition with British manufactures (in both export and home markets) was the source of the country's economic problems in the forty years before the First World War: manufacturing's contribution to the overall decline in the rate of growth of TFP from 1873 on was relatively small and it was concentrated in the period after 1899 when net exports of manufactures were growing rapidly.

(iv) Construction made a significant contribution to the deterioration after 1899. The violence of the long-swing in output in construction stands out prominently in Table 8.4. The decline in the volume of construction in the Edwardian period was no doubt largely responsible for the behaviour of TFP, but one cannot entirely rule out the possibility that there was also some element of causation in the opposite direction – adverse trends in productivity contributing to the severity of the downward phase of the long-swing in output on this occasion.

(v) Utilities and transport did not share the general tendency to declining rates of growth of TFP.

CONCLUSIONS

The main purpose of this paper has been statistical, not interpretative. Its chief conclusions are as follows.

1. While divergences between alternative indicators of GDP prevent any entirely satisfactory resolution in the timing and

sectoral incidence of retardation in the British economy after 1873, the compromise-index is probably the most reliable, and it indicates that the falling-off in the rate of growth of GDP in 1873–1913 compared with 1856–73 took place chiefly after 1899. However, there was also a falling-off in 1873–82. This was largely made good in the 1880s and 1890s.

2. The rate of growth of total factor input varied remarkably little between phases of the period. This was partly because of a systematic tendency to non-synchronisation between movements in the rates of growth of labour input and capital input. Consequently, the rate of growth of total factor productivity followed essentially the same path as that of GDP. The timing of the path of labour growth of productivity was somewhat different. In particular, the rate of growth of labour productivity did not turn down in 1873–82 (by comparison with 1856–73) but did turn down in 1882–89 – the opposite of GDP and total factor productivity.

3. The falling-off in the rate of growth of total factor productivity in 1873–1913 compared with 1856–73 was common to most sectors, but the largest contributions to the trend in the total came from agriculture and mining. The falling-off in the rate of growth of total factor productivity in manufacturing was virtually confined to the period after 1899. The generally poor performance of productivity in the period after 1899 owed a certain amount to the sharp long-swing contraction in building, but this was not, apparently, the dominant item.

NOTES

1. The present paper is an offshoot of Matthews, Feinstein and Odling-Smee (1982), to which reference may be made for an account of sources and methods.
2. See also Aldcroft (1968); Crafts (1979), Kennedy (1973–74); Landes (1965); Levine (1967); McCloskey (1970), (1974) and (1979).
3. See Lewis (1978), p. 264.
4. This would apply, for example, to the output series for cotton and woollen yarn and cloth, flour and bread, tobacco, soap and vegetable oils, paper, leather, rubber, furniture and other timber products; see W. G. Hoffmann, *British Industry, 1700–1950* (1955), pp. 250–88. Some of the additional series calculated by Lewis (1978), pp. 251–7, are based on interpolation between benchmarks (chemicals, food manufacture) or given a rather arbitrary pattern of cyclical fluctuations.

5. The deflated income series used by Phelps Brown (1952) was rightly criticised by Coppock (1956) on the grounds that it made insufficient allowance for the price of services and of manufactured goods, and gave too large a weight to imported food and raw materials. However, the price index used to deflate the present income estimates is the deflator implicit in the expenditure based GDP series at current and constant prices. It should thus be a broadly reliable and appropriately weighted indication of the changes in the prices of domestic expenditure on final products, exports and imports.

6. 'The case for a late Victorian failure in productivity, then, appears weak. Indeed, the failure, to be precise, was Edwardian.' (McCloskey (1970), p. 458). Most authors have inclined to the alternative view.

7. For discussion of concepts and methods see Matthews, Feinstein and Odling-Smee (1982). The measures given in Table 8.3. for TFI and TFP correspond to those designated in the book TF_yI and TF_yP, with capital defined as gross fixed assets. Thus labour is measured in man-years without regard to quality. For the sake of consistency with the figures given in the book, the distributive shares of 1856 are used in Table 8.3. for the whole of the period 1856–73 and those of 1873 for the whole of the period 1873–1913. The theoretically preferable procedure of using as weights the distributive shares in the opening year of each sub-period within those periods would not alter the results significantly.

8. See Matthews, Feinstein and Odling-Smee (1982), Chapter 9.

9. The error could lie either in an overestimate of sectoral TFP-growth after 1899 or in an underestimate of it before 1899 or (most likely) in both.

10. The rate of growth of *output* of manufactures did decline after 1873, but there was also a decline in the rate of growth of inputs (first labour, then capital).

REFERENCES

Aldcroft, D. H. (ed.), *The Development of British Industry and Foreign Competition* (London: Allen and Unwin, 1968).

Coppock, D. J., 'The Climacteric of the 1890s: a Critical Note', Manchester School, 24, (January 1956) pp.1–31.

Crafts, N. F. R., 'Victorian Britain did Fail', *Economic History Review*, XXXII, 4, (November 1979) pp. 533–7.

Feinstein, C. H., *National Income, Expenditure and Output of the United Kingdom, 1855–1964* (Cambridge University Press, 1972).

Hoffmann, W. G., *British Industry, 1700–1950* (Oxford: Basil Blackwell, 1955).

Kennedy, W. P., 'Foreign Investment, Trade, and Growth in the United Kingdom 1870–1913', *Explorations in Economic History*, II, 11, 4, (1973–4) pp. 415–44.

Landes, D. S., 'Technological Change and Development in Western Europe, 1750–1914', in *The Cambridge Economic History of Europe*, vol. v, Part II, Chapter v (1965).

Levine, A. L., *Industrial Retardation in Britain, 1870–1914* (London: Weidenfeld and Nicolson, 1967).

Lewis, W. A., *Growth and Fluctuations 1870–1913* (London: Allen and Unwin, 1978).

McCloskey, D. N., 'Did Victorian Britain Fail?', *Economic History Review*, XXIII, 3 (1970) pp. 446–59.

'Victorian Growth: a Rejoinder', *Economic History Review*, XXVII, 2 (1974) pp. 275–7.

'No it did not: a reply to Crafts', *Economic History Review*, XXXII, 4 (November 1979) pp. 538–41.

Matthews, R. C. O., Feinstein, C. H. and Odling-Smee, J. C., *British Economic Growth* (Stanford University Press, 1982).

Phelps Brown, E. H. and Handfield Jones, S. J., 'The Climacteric of the 1890s', *Oxford Economic Papers*, 4, 3 (October 1952) pp. 266–307.

Rostow, W. W., *The British Economy of the Nineteenth Century* (Oxford University Press, 1948).

Index